AUTHORITY AND THE CHURCH

Gregory G. Bolich
Christian Studies Institute

UNIVERSITY
PRESS OF
AMERICA

82102522
Copyright © 1982 by

University Press of America, Inc.

P.O. Box 19101, Washington, D.C. 20036

ISBN (Perfect): 0-8191-2323-4
ISBN   (Cloth): 0-8191-2322-6

Library of Congress Catalog Card Number: **81-40935**

Dedicated to

J. Byron Evans,

who has struggled with these same matters and made the local churches he has served the beneficiaries of his labors.

ACKNOWLEDGEMENTS

"No man is an island." I could not have completed this book without the steady and enriching services of Margo Dalager, who both typed and edited the manuscript from the day of its birth. I am exceedingly grateful.

I wish also to thank various publishers for their special and kind permission to make particular use of some sources. All quotations from *The Creative Theology of P. T. Forsyth*, copyright 1969 by the Wm. B. Eerdmans Publishing Co., *The Pattern of Religious Authority*, copyright 1957, 1959 by the Wm. B. Eerdmans Publishing Co., *A Handbook of Contemporary Theology*, copyright 1966 by the William B. Eerdmans Publishing Co., *The Witness of the Spirit*, copyright 1959 by the William B. Eerdmans Publishing Co., *The Ministry in Historical Perspective*, copyright 1956 by Harper & Row Publishers, Inc., and "Who Is Our President?", copyright 1967 by Interpretation: A Journal of Bible and Theology, are used by permission.

All quoted material in this text is carefully cited with reference to its author, date, and publisher, and follows accepted scholarly guidelines established by current practice and style manuals, and in conjunction with current copyright statutes. I am indebted to all of the authors who are cited within these pages, and I wish to thank all of them for their service to mankind, and to myself in particular.

TABLE OF CONTENTS

INTRODUCTION: THE CRISIS OF AUTHORITY

Somewhere we seem to have lost the *good* meaning of authority. The term is filled with a multitude of meanings by those who wield authority and discussed pejoratively by many who resist it. For most of us our ideas of authority are ones colored by dark images. We think that authority is *against* us.

Perhaps experiences are to blame for this state of mind. Probably all of us have followed some leader who has directed us into such a poor situation that we felt compelled to rebel. Or perhaps education has misled us. An authoritarian God has become, after all, the conceptual symbol for the ultimate arbitrary, capricious, and malicious despot. Authority has come to mean *this* versus *that*, an endless and uneasy struggle for supremacy. We have determined finally that authority is at best, a *necessary* evil, and at worst, a necessary *evil*. We are trapped by authority.

There should be little surprise, then, that crises occasioned by authority have always abounded. Rome had Julius Caesar—and Brutus. Jesus fought with Pharisees and Sadducees. Martin Luther was constrained to take a stand against the Pope. At the root of innumerable conflicts has been controversy over the nature, the extent, and the legitimacy of one or more "authorities". Thus, no one can state accurately that our situation today is "unprecedented". Credibility problems in the Watergate period, leadership clashes in the Third World countries, and continuing unrest in the Middle East all marked the 1970s as part of the desperate drama of coming to terms with authority. This drama shows no signs of weakening in the 1980s.

In the relatively closed confines of the Church we have been embarrassed often by problems about different issues of authority. Christian teaching has often confirmed the spectre of an authoritarian God sitting over against us in cruel judgment, waiting to condemn us all in the name of holiness! But even where theology gives us a God of love and mercy, we still often find that we

1

are brought up short by authoritarian codes of morality, prefects overdressed in robes of ecclesiastical power, or the tyranny of strictly orthodox doctrine. In short, the Church, like the world, has continually stumbled on the hard rock of authority.

Daniel Day Williams' observation more than twenty years ago that the issue of authority commanded both the most attention and the deepest interest among theological students is once again accurate.[1] Across the broad spectrum of theological opinion varied authority issues have surfaced as today's most vital concerns. Everyone is affected by one or more of such issues as ecclesiastical politics and policies, controversy over biblical authority, and scholarly debate over the legitimate influence that different systems of interpretation carry. Church attenders are often unwittingly ensnared in the finer points of disputation. To them the theological merits often appear as contrivances for expedient pragmatic action. Many people are distressed by the power struggles, doubtful about the sense of trusting a Bible they are assured they do not understand.

The brunt of the whole problem, for most believers, comes to rest at the vague expectations impressed upon them for moral behavior. Here authority again displays awful, dark colors in stone tablets of prohibitions, or in slates wiped clean of any clear ethical direction at all. More than a decade ago Clyde Holbrook pinpointed the difficulty when he noted that "Christian ethics has difficulty clarifying to itself and the outside world the nature of the authority to which it appeals for jurisdiction over moral experience and ethical discourse. The difficulty is enhanced by talk of revelation, faith, and commitment, which suggest that a hopelessly inarticulate arbitrariness lies at the heart of the whole enterprise."[2]

The result of this ambiguity in the Church has been predictable: confusion and controversy. Very few of us should find it difficult to concur with Bernard Ramm's statement that, "the concept of authority has become one of the most controversial notions of modern times."[3] That this concept has stood behind a variety of issues called by other names, must not obscure the *fact* that it is, finally, with *authority*—its nature, extent, function and legitimacy—that we must come to terms. At the same time, the wrestling with authority must be understood as a requisite key to rightly answering the questions which so prominently engage us today.

Within the Roman Catholic world, for centuries the most notable example of authoritarian stability, there

2

has often been confusion over the function or extent of leadership. This is sparked usually by changes in the papacy, or new liturgical, ecclesiastical, or theological shifts. With the deaths of Popes Paul VI and John Paul I, and the papacy of the Polish John Paul II, there have occurred the predictable authority crises attributable to transition. These, combined with the continuing unsettledness after the Vatican II Council, have created tensions that are variously regarded as insignificant, minor, expected, or critical. But as Rome has addressed itself to the controversial issues of doctrine and practice these tensions have heightened. Raoul Dederen, professor of Roman Catholic theology at Andrews University, offers a succinct analysis of the situation:

> First of all, there is a crisis regarding the proper exercise of authority and the appropriate response to it. Catholic education, from elementary catechetics to the education of seminarians, is in disarray. Catholics in vast numbers ignore the moral and disciplinary decrees.
>
> These and other problems have either not been dealt with by those in authority or have certainly not been *perceived* as having been dealt with by the Catholic episcopate. As a consequence, the faithful at every level—and this includes clergy and religious—are increasingly demoralized and discouraged. At times some of them have even been reprimanded by authority figures for demanding action or clarification.[4]

The situation in mainline Protestantism does not appear much differently. In many denominations the key authority issue is centered in the debate over the ordination of women. The subject strongly challenges long established patterns of male dominance in ecclesiastical functions. The debate encompasses arguments about the male-female places in creation and whether or not the data of Scripture reflects the Christian liberation of women to works and offices of ministry previously occupied exclusively by men.

Within the Charismatic Renewal, the movement that blossomed in the sixties and seventies, there remain many unsettled authority issues. With less dependence on ecclesiastical structure and more on the immediate work of the Holy Spirit a host of unanswered questions has arisen. A continuing major problem has been establishing and measuring the legitimacy of competing charismatic claims to authority. Ambiguity at this point has allowed scandal to appear again and again.

The evangelical community, unseen in the 1960s but

very visible in the last decade, has received widespread attention concerning its hot controversy about biblical authority. Several major books and a large number of articles have made their way into print. Evangelicals have left no doubt that they consider the problem fundamentally significant. In simple point of fact, of the varied Christian communities it is the evangelical camp that is most vigorously and decisively wrestling with the question of authority in the Church.

As a member of a wider conservative community that embraces evangelicalism without being identical to it, the evangelical struggles are both of critical personal interest and also of valuable community interest for the whole Church. An evangelical coming to terms with biblical authority has tremendous potential to enrich the whole of conservative Christianity. So, too, do those struggles in evidence in Charismatic, Catholic, and liberal Protestant circles. But at this time the evangelical tensions are particularly significant. They are so because they most consciously concern themselves with the central points of the issue of authority itself.

It is my intention, as a conservative Christian, to address the idea of authority and the Church with reference to several issues, but with particular regard to the evangelical community and its discussions on biblical authority. This does not mean mine is but one more voice expressing a vote for or against biblical inerrancy. I am not concerned to focus only on biblical authority but rather to place that facet in its place in a more general and foundational approach to the topic of authority and the Church.

My approach is not without its hazards. Writing about authority can always be unintentionally provocative and in today's evangelicalism the subject is particularly dangerous. I cannot help but concur with the assessment by Richard Mouw that, "evangelicalism is in many respects an immature movement. There are many crucial items on its agenda, matters with which it can deal effectively only if it rids itself of some of its worst collective traits. Unfortunately, some of these traits seem only to have been reinforced in the atmosphere created by its recent successes. " [5] First among these bad traits specified by Mouw is what he calls, "the highly politicized manner in which evangelicals conduct basic theological debate. " [6] Far too often the actual importance of the theological subject matter is obscured by ecclesiastical politics or personal slander. Whether this tendency is viewed as either a cause or an effect, it is clearly related to what Mouw has called " one of

4

the most regrettable facts of evangelical life: . . . evangelical theological scholarship in this century has been, for the most part, a wasteland."[7]

This does not need to continue to be true. Evangelical theology can, and must, turn to positive and constructive dialog. It can begin to do so now as it is confronted by the vexing, critical importance of biblical authority and, by natural connection, the necessity of a more general treatment of authority and the Church. Certainly, the fundamental importance of authority can now be seen most clearly among conservatives and upon us has been placed the responsibility of providing the Church with profitable studies on authority.

Yet even without the specific issues that in these days have demanded our attention the continuing ultimacy of authority in its relation to the Church should call forth new dogmatic statements within the Church in every new generation. The problem of authority is its startlingly familiar penchant for precipitating precarious situations in both the world and the Church. This problem exists precisely because authority occupies its own proper place of importance. Authority is absolutely essential for order. In every part of our society some manifestation of authority is a necessary element. The fact is, authority is a primary sociological concern.

Scarcely a year passes without some publication restating this basic fact. But very few studies have attempted to construct positive statements on authority designed to aid the human race to more effectively come to grips with the place——and thereby the problem too—— of authority. The studies are principally analytical in nature and with a decidedly areligious character. The gamut runs from Camus' The Rebel to Weber's The Theory of Social and Economic Organization. Varying widely in perspective and purpose all of these studies have made a contribution.

Of course, those works that have emerged from the context of the Church are especially important. Both the biblical witness and the thoughts of learned men across the years of the Church's history are vital to the Church today. Bernard Ramm, in his own informative book on authority, has presented a compelling argument for giving close attention to these labors of the past:

> There are three reasons why the interpreter of reve-
> lation must pay due regard to the history of theology:
> (1) The Holy Spirit is the Teacher of the Church, and
> surely in some manner the history of theology reflects
> this teaching ministry. (2) The present Church is the

inheritor of all the great scholarship of the past. Some of the finest minds of western civilization have devoted their energies to Biblical and theological studies. Their products are worthy of much esteem and much consideration. The scholarship of one generation rests upon the achievements of previous generations of scholars, and so the scholarship devoted to the interpretation of the Word of revelation is dependent upon the previous scholarship devoted to the interpretation of the same Word of revelation. (3) Theological and ecclesiastical crises drive men to think deeper and clearer than they do in ordinary circumstances. Out of such past crises have come great formulations of Christian truth.[8]

In agreeing with Ramm, I find myself committed to the listening and speaking that constitutes meaningful dialog. Accordingly, the pages of this study hopefully reflect both my speaking *and my listening.* I have tried to let others have their say and yet avoid too tedious a conversation. Admittedly, I have listened with most attention to those whose convictions I share and they speak the more loudly in my own words and in the words I let them voice in these pages. But I have not ignored or disdained those who depart from me. Their role has simply become less because I am promoting a constructive statement on the subject and not presenting a forum for disputation.

To state the matter as briefly and as clearly as I can, my goal is twofold: first, to address the Church, with regard to both the current and the permanent issues of authority, by means of a few concrete propositions. Second, I intend to apply these theses to specific contemporary issues. My theses are themselves simple and fundamental. I have given some room to elucidation of them apart from their application to issues in order to show their general as well as their specific character.

It should become clear that while I address the whole Church my own theses emerge from a conservative community. I trust my more liberal brothers and sisters to show their open-mindedness by listening to me before they correct me. At any rate, we can all agree that it is a decidedly Christian task to once again affirm to our people and the world the genuinely *good* meaning of a rightly apprehended authority. No matter our more or less orthodox bearing we can all agree that this good meaning is only recovered by meeting the God disclosed by Jesus Christ.

References Cited—Introduction

[1] Daniel Day Williams, "Authority and Ministry." Union Seminary Quarterly Review, Vol. XIV, No. 1 (Nov., 1958), p. 17.

[2] Clyde A. Holbrook, "The Problem of Authority in Christian Ethics," Journal of the American Academy of Religion, Vol. XXXVII, No. 1 (Mar., 1969), p. 26.

[3] Bernard Ramm, The Pattern of Religious Authority (Grand Rapids: Wm. B. Eerdmans, 1957, 1959), p. 9.

[4] J. R. Spangler, "The Papal Visit: The Religious Issues" (Interview with Raoul Dederen), Ministry, Vol. 52, No. 11 (Nov., 1979), p. 12.

[5] Richard J. Mouw, "Evangelicals In Search of Maturity," Theology Today, Vol. XXXV, No. 1 (April, 1978), p. 42.

[6] Ibid., p. 43-44.

[7] Ibid., p. 44.

[8] Bernard Ramm, The Pattern of Religious Authority, p. 59.

ONE

PRELIMINARY CONSIDERATIONS

The Church in centering herself upon God-in Christ
delimits considerably the subject of authority. Within
the Church, however, the parameters fixed by this center
are by no means certain. Accordingly, Schubert Ogden,
a prominent liberal theologian and exponent of process
philosophy, believes he can argue very reasonably that,
"whether by way of a metaphysical justification of religious claims or by way of a merely phenomenological
account of their meaning and truth, Protestant theologians today generally concede the earlier liberal point
that specifically Christian religious claims must somehow be shown to be warranted by universally human experience and reason."[1]

But this does not exclude the importance of Christ.
Ogden lists two sources for authority: "the experience
of God as decisively revealed in Jesus the Christ," and
"universally human experience of ultimate reality as
originally revealed in our existence as such."[2] Experience, along with reason, validates claims to authority.
The role of reason consists, at least in part, of providing a more complete context in which to comprehend
experience. Therefore, talk of authority and the Church
still requires for Ogden, "that we make use of the conclusions, even if we do not develop the arguments, of a
philosophy of authority in general."[3]

Ogden is right that a "philosophy of authority in
general" is essential to the Church. He is correct also
in arguing on behalf of the importance of both human
experience and reason. I cannot go so far as to credit
these with the weight Ogden bestows on them, but they
cannot be passed by in favor of some abstract notion of
authority. I like, too, the desire to solidly connect
the uniquely Christian claims for authority to the needs
and experience of the non-Christian world. However, I
believe that such a connection is effected only by the
proclamation of the Gospel in a fashion that preserves

8

a distinction between Christian and non-Christian experiences, reasoning, and authorities. This distinction still permits a correct identification with humanity alienated from God, but insists that this identification stems from the central and definitive relationship that the Church maintains to the Word of God.

The Christian Church, liberal and conservative, embraces as its first presupposition the centrality of the person of Jesus, called the Christ. Liberal and conservative differ not in the place they accord Jesus but in their understanding of him. Both liberals and conservatives have been found guilty at times of creating a false center. That is, Jesus is named but is not central. When this occurs the Church endangers its own name and minimizes its own importance.

If I part company with Ogden it is where conservatives always begin parting with liberals (and, to be fair, where liberals part from conservatives). I think Ogden makes less of the centrality of Christ than he should, and, at the same time, moves toward a false center where experience determines God, man, and the universe. Christ himself, the existing God-in-Jesus figure of history past, present, and future, can only be the definitive Christian center to talk about authority.

This means that, in a certain sense, talk about a Christological focus is incorrect. The Christian center is properly *Christ,* not Christology. I believe that Diogenes Allen is right: "At the core of the Christian life is the fact that Christians have a Lord, someone to whom they belong and to whom they are obedient."[4] This *someone* is identified by the confession, "Jesus is Lord!" The person, Jesus Christ, gives rise to that perspective in theology termed Christological. But it is important to retain the understanding that Christology properly developed is simply making the thoughts, actions, and behaviors of the Church concretely related to this actual person, Jesus of Nazareth. Christology, where it lapses into abstractions, betrays the Church by creating the most deceptive of all false centers. Where so-called Christology has replaced the living, Incarnate God the Church has become sterile and "otherworldly", not positively and practically related to the world.

The relation between Christ and his Church defines both in many respects. With regard to authority this relation forms the foundational presupposition for the Church. Every person related to God-in-Christ is united by the basic confession "Jesus is Lord!" This witness, whatever else it may mean, must mean that all authority begins for the Church with this person and nowhere else. This confession of this central relation thus forms the nucleus of the Church's perspective, its own definitive distinction from any other entity. This Christological perspective makes the Church an entity committed to a positive and practical relation to the world. Thus the Church exists to promote the centrality and preeminence of Jesus Christ in the lives of those around her (the world) and in her own life as well. But this promotion of Christ must be concrete.

For the Church to address the world as Christ has done she must in actuality display his Lordship as it exists *for all of us.* This alone is the recovery of the positive meaning of authority. Like Christ, the Church must incarnate herself in the age and culture in which she finds herself. Any notion of authority vis-á-vis the Church must be communicated in a Word given carefully to those who *would* hear it so that they *can* hear it. Robert C. Johnson is right in insisting that, "it is a matter of first importance that we recognize that the recurrent decision that Protestantism makes on the matter of theological authority is never one made *in vacuo,* but it is always made at a particular time and place, and within a given historical setting." [5] This decision, and its effects, is the province of each and every generation.

The concrete or *actual,* character of both Christ and the Church's relation to the world stems, of course, from the condition of both as *living.* The most dynamic expression of this theologically is in the concept of *the Word of God.* The Reformers' three-fold distinction of this one Word is the one particular shaping of our Christological perspective that best benefits the Church in her thinking on authority. Therefore, the carrying out of a concrete notion of authority from this presupposed perspective follows the three-fold form of the one Word of God.

The Word of God in each of its forms is characterized in every time by contemporaneity and in every culture by relevance. The nature of God's Word is always potentially concrete. It is abstracted when, for instance, the twentieth century Church addresses American culture with a sixteenth century European word. On the other hand, the concreteness of God's Word is sustained when and where the Church is itself contemporaneous and relevant. It is evident, then, that the role of God's Church is acutely important.

The Church's role is to provide a context for God in introducing authority into the world. The context for authority is, in one sense, all creation, but the more immediate context, that place from which a right conception of authority must emerge, is the Church. I think Richard Coleman is right then, in insisting that, "it is inevitable that any crucial theological issue becomes an ecclesiastical one."[6] This is so for two reasons: first, theology exists properly only to serve the Church. Specifically, theology serves the Church in her proclamation of the Gospel. Second, theology is only sensible when it becomes an actual, physical manifestation of itself both in and through the Church. The Church provides not only a context for theological reflection concerning the relationship of authority to the Lord of the Church, and the expression of authority to the world, but also for the physical manifestation of that same authority as actualized in the behavior by which the Church conducts herself in the world, and the behavior which she advocates before the world as right and fitting. Both the behavior that the Church enacts and which she advocates, is bounded by the authority found in God-in-Christ. Therefore, Richard Drummond is right in insisting that, "consideration of the authority of the church's faith and life is an inquiry into its basic *raison d' etre*, and should open before every interested person the inner life of faith and reveal something of its primary or motivating springs of action."[7]

The context of the Church, in regard not only to authority but to all issues, is one that calls for careful attention to the faith and life of her constituent members as they are found in Christ. For the idea of authority and the Church necessarily involves the faith which is itself essential to the existence of the Church as the Church. Faith is the instrument by which Jesus Christ's authority is received and confessed. Or, as P. T. Forsyth has argued, "our authority is what takes the initiative with our faith."[8] In bringing faith into the discussion, it becomes clear that because of the divine interaction of God with the Church on behalf of man, authority is something that originates from outside of man and his institutions. Authority is *not* a facet of creation as such, not, at any rate, in the way in which it now comes to the Church and world in Christ. As Forsyth noted, authority now appears " . . . in the nature of a miracle."[9]

The conservative church has always assigned some measure of credibility to miracles. In fact, it has always recognized that faith is among the greatest of miracles. Nevertheless, within the conservative church, particularly the evangelical wing, a neglect of the importance of the Church has at times greatly endangered whatever credibility there is to the notion of miracles, and rendered the incredible nature of authority simply obscene. Richard Mouw has complained that, "many evangelicals . . . operate with an extremely weak ecclesiology. This is not merely a weakness which shows up in one area of their theology; it tends to pervade the evangelical theological enterprise."[10] In seeking to determine the reason why this is the case, Mouw found that the evangelical church has all too often neglected that "it is an important function of the *church* to help Christians distinguish between trivial and non-trivial issues, and to decide what is and what is not central to the redemptive message. Christians are called to participate in the believing community to whom the gifts of the Spirit are offered, including the gift of discernment."[11] This work of the Church is generally invisible in the evangelical community.

While the evangelical church has, in this day and age, seemed to recognize the critical importance of the issue of authority, it has still steadfastly neglected the importance of the context of the Church in regard to the whole discussion of the issue of authority. Instead, by focusing strictly on the idea of biblical authority, the evangelical church has cut itself off from its own proper context, and thus spoiled many possible insights about even biblical authority by abstracting the issue of authority rather than relating it concretely to its proper context. Yet there *is* hope. The evangelical community still has at the heart of its faith an important concern for the recognition of the necessity of an evangelical experience of regeneration and, as P. T. Forsyth has noted, "authority at the last has no meaning except as it is understood by the evangelical experience of regeneration in some form, which is the soul's re-creation, surrender, and obedience once and for all in a new creation and direct communion with the God of the moral universe."[12]

It should be clearly understood that authority must indeed be considered in its relationship to the high place that Holy Scripture occupies. Scripture, too, is the Word of God. Nevertheless, it is the Church, in her proclamation of that Word found in Holy Scripture, that is the first and proper concrete context for authority in the world. Martin Luther once remarked that, "the entire life and substance of the Church is in the Word of God."[13] Church and Word are inextricably bound together. But this Word, as it encompasses both Christ and Scripture, also embraces the preaching of the Church as God's direct and immediate concrete authority in his

12

world.

In all considerations of the relationship of the Church to the Word of God, it is important to first see the Church as the Church has attempted to see herself. From the very beginning this self conception has stemmed from Holy Scripture. From that Word has emerged three important pictures of the Church. These are first, the Church as the Incarnate Christ; that is, his body. The second picture is the Church as a new covenant fellowship; that is, Christ's bride. Finally, third, is the picture of the Church as the liberated bondsmen giving their allegiance to Christ their Lord. In each of these pictures can be seen a point of union between Christ and the Church, and a point of distinction. Seen together, this union and this distinction develop a point of immediate significance to a Christian view of authority.

The first picture, the picture of the Church as the Incarnate Christ, has already been alluded to. If the Church is to communicate effectively the Gospel of Jesus Christ, she must assume, as he did, a form relevant and contemporaneous to the time and culture in which she finds herself. The Church in her image as Christ's body finds her point of union with Christ in the fact that he and the Church together constitute only *one* body. This is the central thrust of Paul's message in 1 Corinthians 12. Yet in the midst of this union, there cannot be blurred an important distinction. This distinction is the fact that in his relationship to the Church, Christ occupies the first place, as the *head*, which gives direction to the body. The significance of this headship of Jesus Christ is in its representation of his *natural* claim on the Church. That is, the idea of headship implies that the claim of authority which Christ places on the Church which bears his name is not a foreign claim, but a *natural* claim, a claim altogether fitting by virtue of their existence together as body and head in one living entity.

The second picture of the Church is that of a new covenant fellowship, or the bride of Christ. Here the point of union is seen in the picture that Paul presents in Ephesians 5. This picture is drawn, in turn, from the first two chapters of the book of Genesis, the creation story. Here is the union of an intimacy in the *mutuality* of one flesh: two made one. The notion of covenant which dominates the Old Testament here rises to prominence. Yet, in the mutuality of this covenant, there remains an important distinction. Christ is the *husband*; the Church the wife. Although these two exist in fellowship, Christ as the husband is again placed in

authority, now over his bride, the Church. The significance of this is seen in Christ's *relational* claim to
the Church. Christ's authority over the Church is established by the relationship both parties enter into
by mutual consent. The covenant between Christ and the
Church, initiated by Christ, is thankfully received by
the Church.

The third picture is of the Church as liberated
bondsmen. The point of union here is that of both Christ
and the Church bound together in a freedom both for and
toward each other. That is, the Church and Christ have
a point of intersection, the desire of each simply to
please and to serve the other. Yet here too emerges a
distinction. The desire of the Church to serve and to
please her Lord stems from her existence as men and
women who are *free servants* of one they acknowledge as
their Master. Jesus Christ also serves, but he serves
as Lord. His service is defined continually by his Lordship, even as his Lordship bears the complete and total
character of a sacrificial servant. At no point in time
does the Church, exalted as she is by her Lord, dare
exalt herself as Lord. The significance of this picture
lies in its presentation of the authority of Christ as
his rightful, *legal* claim upon us; this claim is a legal
one that is first stated, and then validated, in the
crucifixion and resurrection.

Each of these images uses the language of analogy.
This means they can easily be pressed too far. Nevertheless, in all three of these biblical pictures, there
emerge certain common elements expressing the relationship of the Word of God, Jesus Christ, to the Church.
The first element is that each picture is conceived in
terms of both *union* and *distinction*. In other words,
while the Church and Christ enjoy the closest possible
mutuality, there remains important distinctions and a
definite order between them. This, then, is the second
element: order. Christ, the living Word of God, is
placed over the Church. Certainly it is true that his
authority in this order exists for the benefit of the
Church. Nevertheless, it is *over* the Church. But, the
third and decisive element is, in fact, the purpose to
be glimpsed in all of these images. Christ, the living
Word, exists, not for himself, but for the Church, and
the Word of God in its authority *over* the Church is a
Word given by God *for* the Church. The good meaning of
authority is visible in each of these biblical pictures.

Admittedly, a definite methodology is required to
use these images in any relation to the subject of authority and the Church. Certainly, if the Christian

begins with a perspective of Christ and the context of the Church, there must accompany these a Christological methodology and a dogmatic manner of inquiry and expression. The name, "Christological method," is likely to elicit immediate suspicion and disapproval. By it I do not mean an artificial allegorizing of data to present Christ where he is not. I take the name from the work at Chalcedon (c. 451 A. D.), and would be happy to call it a trinitarian method if this latter designation is less misleading.

Christological (or trinitarian) methodology is a practice of limited use and value designed specifically to evaluate disparate materials in order to see interrelationships existing along both the lines of union and distinction. In confessing its beliefs about Christ, Chalcedon adopted the formula (paraphrased), "union without fusion, distinction without separation."[14] By applying this brief formula to theological subjects some highly enlightening insights may result. Appreciating the interrelationship, for instance, between justification and sanctification is enhanced by this method. Apart from this manner of thinking there would be no "orthodox" doctrine of Christ as it has existed. The Trinity would be completely incomprehensible. So, utilizing this method together with other means encompassed by dogmatics is valuable in more completely apprehending the interrelationships between the Word of God and the Church, and, as well, between authority and the Church.

Any "philosophy", or "theology", or "theory", of authority formulated in the Church must proceed not only outward from its center in Christ but directionally toward two specific and distinguishable audiences. The first of these is the Church herself. Beyond the Church is the world with which the Church is united but from which she is now distinct by the election of God-in-Christ. In proceeding directionally toward these audiences the Church must engage in the task of dogmatics.

That the term dogmatics has fallen into wide disrepute in the Church is less distressing than that the practice of dogmatics has been so poorly conducted in the Church—that is, where it is practiced at all today. Of course, there are notable exceptions. Karl Barth's Church Dogmatics is a monument to the greatest dogmatic effort of recent times. But Barth did not intend that his work become a monument. His work purposed to promote others in his own and succeeding generations to take up the same labor and push beyond his own conclusions. Dogmatics is a continuing task.

Barth's working definition of dogmatics is of

practical value: "As a theological discipline, dogmatics is the scientific test to which the Christian Church puts herself regarding the language about God which is peculiar to her."[15]   To perform this task the Church implements all of those tools of science, theological and otherwise, which can assist her in evaluating her confession.   The language of the Church is put to the test and measured not only by its faithful accord with the language of Scripture but also, under the guidance of the Church's confessions, its faithful accord with the thought and purpose of Scripture.   The language of the Church must be both accurate and relevant.   This does not mean an accommodation of the Church to the world by capitulation of the Gospel to contemporary culture. It does mean that the Church's proclamation, as the Word of God, must translate first century thought into terms more readily accessible to twentieth century men and women. Dogmatics is the testing of the Church's success in accomplishing this.

[1]Schubert M. Ogden, "Sources of Religious Authority in Liberal Protestantism," Journal of the American Academy of Religion, Vol. XLIV, No. 3 (Sept., 1976), pp. 403-416.

[2]Ibid., p. 411.

[3]Ibid., p. 405.

[4]Diogenes Allen, "The Paradox of Freedom and Authority," Theology Today, Vol. XXXVI, No. 2 (July, 1979), p. 167.

[5]Robert Clyde Johnson, Authority in Protestant Theology (Philadelphia: Westminster Press, 1959), p. 189.

[6]Richard J. Coleman, "Biblical Inerrancy: Are We Going Anywhere?", Theology Today, Vol. XXXI, No. 4 (Jan., 1974), p. 302.

[7]Richard H. Drummond, "Authority in the Church: An Ecumenical Inquiry," The Journal of Bible and Religion, Vol. XXXIV, No. 4 (Oct., 1976). p. 329.

[8]P. T. Forsyth, The Principle of Authority (London: Independent Press, Ltd., 1913), p. 20.

[9]Ibid., p. 58.

[10]Richard J. Mouw, "Evangelicals In Search of Maturity," Theology Today, Vol. XXXV, No. 1 (Apr., 1978), p. 45.

[11]Ibid., pp. 44-45.

[12]Forsyth, The Principle of Authority, p. 59.

[13]Werner Elert, The Structure of Lutheranism, trans. W. A. Hansen (St. Louis: Concordia, 1962), p. 259.

[14]The actual language of Chalcedon is, in part, "one and the same Christ, Son, Lord, Only-begotten, to be acknowledged in two natures, inconfusedly, unchangeably, indivisibly, inseparably; the distinction of natures by no means taken away by the union . . . " (Philip Schaff, The Creeds of Christendom, III, (Grand Rapids: Baker Book House, 1977), p. 62).

[15]Karl Barth, Church Dogmatics, I/1, trans. G. T. Thomson (Edinburgh: T. & T. Clark, 1936), p. 1. Read Barth's first fifty pages. Cf. this phrasing: "Dogmatics is the science in which the Church, in accordance with the state of its knowledge at

different times, takes account of the content of its proclamation critically, that is, by the standard of Holy Scripture
and under the guidance of its Confessions." Barth, <u>Dogmatics
in Outline</u>, trans. G. T. Thomson (New York: Harper & Row,
1959), p. 9.

TWO

PERTINENT DEFINITIONS

There remains yet one critical process to undertake
in these preliminary considerations. Any understanding
of authority and the Church along the Christological
lines already indicated must include some initial definitions. Principally, this means establishing a more
complete idea of what is entailed by "Church" and "authority". The "Word of God" also needs elucidation.

The "Church" originated in the New Testament era.
This does not, of course, exclude any theological belief
that the Church existed beforehand in the true Israel
of God. It is simply the recognition that God's people
were first called the Church only after the advent of
Christ. Then, too, it needs to be recognized from the
first that the more specific Greek term for "Church",
kuriakon, meaning "the Lord's house," is *not* the term
represented in the English Bible. Instead, the New Testament calls God's people an *ecclesia*, "an assembly."
It is this concept embodied rather generally in the use
of the term "Church". Thus, the word "Church", more
formally drawn from *kuriakon*, takes its material sense
from *ecclesia*.

In the course of her history the Church has filled
her name with a vast richness of meaning. Many descrip-
tive phrases have been coined to describe her. Perhaps
the best known one is "communion of saints" (*communio
sanctorum*). Luther used this description and in our
own day Bonhoeffer popularized it with his book by that
title. But there are many others. The Church has been
called "the congregation of the saints" (*congregatio
sanctorum*, M. Luther), "the congregation of the faithful" (*congregatio fidelium*, K. Barth), "the confedera-
tion of witnesses" (*coniurato testium*, Barth), "the
Church militant" (*ecclesia militans*, Luther and Barth),
"the whole body of the elect" (*praedestinatorum univer-
sitas*, Wycliffe and Huss), "the holy congregation of the
believers" (*sancta fidelium congregatio*, early Luther),
and also, "the visible assembly" (*ecclesia visibilis*,
Melancthon). Luther affirmed "the Church triumphant"

19

(*ecclesia triumphans*), and called her a "spiritual communion" (*geistliche Gemeine*). By this latter designation Luther meant that, in an important sense, "the Church is hidden, the saints are concealed" (*abscondita est Ecclesia, latent sancti*).

All of these phrases are valuable in glimpsing the nature of the Church, or catching a small part of her character and mission. The Reformation Confessions used these concepts, and others, to express together a carefully articulated concept of the Church. On the Lutheran side, the Ansbach Council of 1524 said the Church "is the number of those whom God chose in eternity for redemption through Christ." The Hungarian *Confessio montana* added the thought that the Church is "the visible assembly of those who hear, believe, and embrace the pure and uncorrupted doctrine of the Gospel and use the sacraments." The Copenhagen Articles affirmed that the Church is the congregation "of all men who are justified."

From the side of the Reformation associated with Calvin, Zwingli, and others, also came contributions to the idea of the Church. Calvin himself set the tone by opening his remarks on the Church in Book Four of the Institutes by writing: "When in the Creed we profess to believe the Church, reference is made not only to the visible Church . . . but also to all the elect of God, including in the number even those who have departed this life."[1]   In his Catechism on the Apostle's Creed, Calvin answered the question, "What is the Church?" by writing that it is, "the body and society of believers whom God has predestined to eternal life."[2]   Under his preparation, the French Confession of 1559 stated:

> . . . we believe that it is important to discern with
> care and prudence which is the true Church, for this ti-
> tle has been much abused. We say, then, according to
> the Word of God, that it is the company of the faithful
> who agree to follow his Word, and the pure religion
> which it teaches; who advance in it all their lives,
> growing and becoming more confirmed in the fear of God
> according as they feel the want of growing and pressing
> onward. Even although they strive continually, they
> can have no hope save in the remission of their sins.
> Nevertheless we do not deny that among the faithful there
> may be hypocrites and reprobates, but their wickedness
> can not destroy the title of the Church.[3]

Other Reformed Confessions, notably the Westminster Confession and Catechisms, and documents from the Anabaptist tradition helped develop the concept of Church as Protestants embrace it. Naturally, particular groups claim special distinctives. Lutheran and Reformed are not completely in agreement. Protestants differ from Catholics. But the whole Church has viewed herself as unique, set apart, an assembled people brought together by God. The Church is believers, confessors, or supplicants. She is marked by God-in-Christ and claims for herself a high calling and a noble purpose. Yet the Church also remembers her frailty in her grandeur. She is, despite her power, often very feeble. Nor is she in her holiness unsoiled. The Church knows her own, yet continually is beset by division. There are, among the faithful, "hypocrites and reprobates." But Calvin was right: their wickedness cannot destroy the title of Church.

However she would understand herself, the Church, where divine and human intermix in union without fusion, and distinction without separation, is still, in simple terms, a sociological reality. The Church is an institution in the World. In the midst of her self-identification, the Church, the living organism, has never been permitted to forget that she is also an "it", an institution more or less personal at any given time or place.

In his refinement of Reformation thinking on the Church, Melanchthon, in his Apology, uses his conception of association to describe the Church in sociological terms. Melanchthon wrote that the Church is not, "an association of external things and rites as are other states, but it is principally an association of faith and the Holy Spirit in the hearts, which nevertheless has external marks."[4] Werner Elert has noted:

> Even though a parallelism to political structures is rejected, the concept "association" (*societas*) makes the church analagous to them. And if here only the "association in spirit" (*Verbundenheit im Geiste*) seems to be thought of, yet shortly after this the same thing is expressed as follows: "the association of the same Gospel or doctrine and the same Holy Spirit" (*societas cuisdem evangelii seu doctrinae et eiusdem Spiritus Sancti*) . . . . Accordingly, even at that time Melanchthon looked upon "doctrine" and the sacraments not only . . . as "marks" (*notae*) of the church and its unity but also as means of binding together the members of the church in a sociological respect.[5]

More recently the eminent sociologist, Max Weber, has provided concepts valuable for continuing this kind of understanding of the Church.[6] Although perhaps more indirectly than Melanchthon, Weber also established the

basis for a sociological distinction, as well as simi-
larity between the Church and other institutions. The
Church is an *organization.* "An 'organization' (*Betreib*),"
wrote Weber, "is a system of continuous purposive activity of a specified kind."[7] this is, of course, easier
to discern about the Church as she is visibly manifested
in a multitude of localized and distinctive institutional forms. The Southern Baptists as a group display this
character more clearly than the Church universal, and
any local Southern Baptist church may show this organi-
zational nature even clearer still. Yet, the Church is,
in her fulness, susceptible to sociological determination, if only very generally.

Although an organization, the Church is more particularly a *voluntary association* (*Verein*, is Weber's
term). This, according to Weber, is "a corporate group
originating in a voluntary agreement and in which the
established order claims authority over the members only
by virtue of a personal act of adherence."[8] This has
never been truer than it is today. Church leaders live
with the awareness that it is all too easy to "offend"
an attender who is quite ready to move his membership to
another congregation. The authority of the leaders is
measured by the degree of loyalty of the people to them
or to the group. This seriously affects *power* (*Macht*)
in the Church. "'Power'," said Weber, is "the chance of
a man or of a number of men to realize their own will in
a communal action even against the resistance of others
who are participating in the action."[9] There exists, in
many of today's churches, a potent instability of power.

While this sociological character of the contemporary Church may be jarring, it is an indisputable reality. It cannot be dismissed by even the most clever
theological formulations. But, the sociological Church
can be changed. This change is a real possibility for
two reasons: first, because the Church is also a living
organism, and then second, because as an institution the
Church is a *charismatic* organization.

As a charismatic institution, the Church is the
product of a zealous commitment to the historical person
Jesus of Nazareth. The Church originated as a charismatic institution from this first charismatic leader, and
through his gifts (*charisma*), his charismatic bestow-
ments. Although charismatic institutions are always
endangered and may lose their uniquely original charismatic character, that quality can be recaptured or re-
produced. Weber observed that "it is the fate of charisma, whenever it comes into the permanent institutions
of a community, to give way to powers of tradition or

22

of rational socialization."[10]   Nevertheless, at least
some of the crucial elements of the charismatic organization can, and must, be renewed in order to reform and
strengthen the sociological condition of the Church.

While traditional descriptions of the Church are
theological, for the most part contemporary descriptions
view the Church from wider angles.   Common today is the
two-fold analysis of the Church as an *organism*,   and as
an *organization*.   I think a three-fold picture is more
complete. In addition to being an organism and an organization, the Church is also an *occasion*.   It bears the
character of an event.

Certainly, the Creeds speak of those who are the
Church.   But these persons are the Church not just in
who they are but in what they do in bearing out their
distinctive relationship to God and to one another. The
Bible also permits this second idea, principally in the
description of the Church as she is manifested.   If the
Church sees herself as a living organism, and the world
sees her as an organization, the one manifestation that
gives a legitimate base to both views arises from the
occasion of the Church assembled. This peculiar happen-
ing defines the Church, but defines her precisely by the
consituent events of this assembly.

Accordingly, the Church as an occasion is defined
by her acts centered in and around the ministry of the
Word of God.   This occasion,   the assembled Church, is
characterized by gladness.   The need of this occasion
to rightly be the Church is met in the ministry of the
Word, and particularly in preaching and sacraments.   As
an organism, the Church is characterized by growing life.
For this she needs the sustenance supplied especially in
her assembly.   As an organization, the Church is characterized by governmental order. But this order demands
the unique substance of the Word to have meaning.

In the light of such incomplete glimpses at the
Church it may not yet be clear why she demands the authority she has for her existence.   But these glimpses
are helpful in terminologically determining the general
outline of what is meant by the Church.   Before she can
be related most profitably to authority, the concept of
authority must also bear scrutiny.

More than one biblical term can be translated "authority". In the Old Testament the Hebrew *toqeph* (Esth.
9:29) is used of Mordecai's "full, written authority"
(AV and RSV).   The Hebrew *rabah* (Proverbs 29:2) is rendered as the "authority" that the righteous will one day
exercise (AV, RSV).   This latter term suggests a kind of

'fleshing out' or *increase*. *Toqueph*, on the other hand, hints more at a strong, *firm* authority, an authority that it is not inconceivable to believe could show its power in oppression. Individuals can exercise might, but it is to the righteous one (or ones) that the true "authority" is given. Authority belongs principally to the Word of God, his creative, inspiring Spirit, and to the Law. The authority of man derives from these.

In the New Testament, terms rendered "authority" by the AV include: *exousia*, *katexousiazo*, *dunastes*, *huperoche*, *authenteo*, and *epitage*. Of these, *exousia* is the most prevalent and important. It is translated often as "power". The distinction is a fine one and the term chosen by one translator may be by-passed in favor of the other by a different translator. *Exousia* can be applied to miraculous power (Mk. 6:7; Lu. 5:24), and to individuals placed in authority (Tit. 3:1; Jn. 19:10). All *exousia* comes from God (cf. Rom. 13:1), though some is in rebellion to God (Col. 2:15). Jesus is recorded by Matthew as establishing a unique privilege for himself in saying, "All *exousia* in heaven and on earth has been given to me" (28:18). Yet this *exousia* which belongs to Christ serves the beneficial foundation to his Great Commissioning of the Church. Thus both Old and New Testaments agree in an orderly progression of authority from God for man to be exercised by mankind to the benefit of all people.

In the early Church, critical decisions were made, if somewhat tentatively, about the extent, nature, and expression of authority both *by* the Church and *in* the Church. Her originally charismatic nature, however, gradually gave way to tradition, to formal rational concepts, and to the pressures of political expediency. New ways of understanding authority were introduced and older concepts modified. As authority issues multiplied, new terms were formulated to make fine distinctions and carefully legitimate exercises of power.

Thus the Church eventually had to distinguish between *de facto* and *de jure* authority. That is, simply because authority may exist and be recognized (*de facto*), it may not yet possess the *right* to be that authority (*de jure*). This is similar to the distinction between *ontic* and *noetic* authority. The former term means an authority which is, *in fact*, authority. The latter term signifies an authority conceived by the mind. Again, the distinction between *formal* and *material* authority is brought to mind. Formal authority bears an external resemblance to the substantial, or material, authority to which it is related. Finally, an *actual* authority

24

differs from *representational* authority. The former is authority resting in itself while the latter is authority resting in someone or something else.

Other distinctions were made. Authority might be *absolute*, that is, both final and self-enclosed, or *relative*, subordinate in extent and function. Some authority is *direct*, or unmediated, while other is *indirect*. Virtually synonymous to this idea is the distinction between *immediate* and *mediated* authority. These terms recognize that authority may be obvious, or it may only appear by means of someone or something quite apart from any special claim to authority of its own.

A constant concern is the rightness of authority. Some authority is *legitimate*, and has a right to exist as it does, while some authority is *illegitimate*. This distinction, quite necessary, recognizes that any claim to authority may be backed by every appearance of authority and with a demonstration of power and yet not be a *genuine* authority. Power disguised as authority often gains its strength from the lust for authority.

Because deception is a real possibility, certain legitimate *forms* of authority have been suggested. All of these stem from the various *sources* recognized for authority. These sources include *law*, *respect* (i.e., the power of esteem or of influence), *testimony* (i.e., first-hand, trustworthy observation), and *freedom* (i.e., the permission or warrant to do something). Religious sources of *God*, *revelation*, or *inspiration* are frequently appealed to. The question of the legitimacy of this or that source is a constant problem since any source determined legitimate must be respected and placed in its proper order while a rejected source must be combatted.

The different sources have given rise to several theories of legitimate *forms* of authority. The legitimacy of the form is completely dependent on the acceptability of the source. Although there are a substantial number of schemes that have been devised to distinguish kinds of authority, it is enough to examine only two.[11]

Bernard Ramm, in his book, <u>The Pattern of Religious Authority</u>, lists six kinds of authority. They are:

Imperial authority: the right to rule and prescribe because of the superior position of the ruling person or group.

Delegated authority: the authority to act, to compel, to have access to, in virtue of right granted by imperial authority.

Stipulative authority: the authority determined by

stipulation, that is, by convention.

Veracious authority (the authority of veracity or truth): that authority possessed by men, books, or principles which either possess truth or aid in the determination of truth.

Functional authority: a sub-class of veracious authority. Functional authority may refer to those materials which a scholar may use in place of originals, such as photographs, copies, or impressions. (Also termed *substitutional authority*).

Authority of custom: the power to determine social decorum by virtue of social veneration acquired through the prestige of time and repetition.[12]

For Ramm, *"revelation is the key to religious authority."*[13] Unlike other kinds of authority, revelation establishes a *pattern* of authority. This helps explain Ramm's central thesis which is that *"in Christianity the authority-principle is the Triune God in self-revelation."*[14] But authority itself means, *"that right or power to command action or compliance, or to determine belief or custom, expecting obedience from those under authority, and in turn giving responsible account for the claim to right or power."*[15]

While Ramm relates his understanding of authority specifically to the Trinity and advocates revelation as the key to apprehending this authority, he is aware that this answer is not representative of all theologians of the Church. In another book, Ramm summarizes the present theological options as follows:

Religious liberalism centered its doctrine of authority in the religious experiences of men in contrast to fundamentalism which centered it in the sheer inspiredness of sacred Scripture. Contemporary theology has moved away from both positions. To put it in a most general way, supreme authority is located in God Himself and the Scriptures are made a relative authority. However, the authority which Scripture carries is given a more precise interpretation.[16]

Ramm has tried to distinguish himself from many of the representatives of the modern movement by resisting any monistic principle of authority. Ramm believes, "the principle of authority in Christianity is really a pattern of authority. That pattern is the intersection of the authority of Jesus Christ, of the Scriptures as the revealed word of God, and the Holy Spirit in his internal witness to Jesus Christ and the Holy Scriptures."[17] Into this framework must the varied kinds of authority be fitted and explained.

Max Weber takes a different approach. Where Ramm can order all other authorities by assigning to them a place under God, Weber simply breaks all authorities into what he terms "three pure types." These are named *Rational—legal* authority, *Traditional* authority, and *Charismatic* authority. Each of these has a basis by which to demonstrate the validity of its claim to legitimacy. Likewise, each makes clear to what or to whom obedience is owed.[18]

Rational-legal authority, Weber explains, has its claim based on "rational grounds—resting on a belief in the 'legality' of patterns of normative rules and the right of those elevated to authority under such rules to issue commands (legal authority)."[19] Obedience to this authority is owed "to the legally established impersonal order."[20]

Traditional authority, according to Weber, bases its claims on "traditional grounds—resting on an established belief in the sanctity of immemorial traditions and the legitimacy of the status of those exercising authority under them."[21] Obedience is owed "to the *person* of the chief who occupies the traditionally sanctioned position of authority and who is (within its sphere) bound by tradition."[22]

Finally, charismatic authority, Weber maintains, is based on "charismatic grounds—resting on devotion to the specific and exceptional sanctity, heroism or exemplary character of an individual person, and of the normative patterns or order revealed or ordained by him."[23] In regard to the function of obedience, Weber claims that "in the case of charismatic authority, it is the charismatically qualified leader as such who is obeyed by virtue of personal trust in him and his revelation, his heroism or his exemplary qualities so far as they fall within the scope of the individual's belief in his charisma."[24]

With a baffling array of theories and schemes confronting her, it is little wonder that the Church has at times appeared confused. Subtle distinctions of seemingly little importance could, at any moment, create major debates or undermine political positions. Yet in every time, and through every duress, the Church has hearkened back to God-in-Christ. This has not been true for only a few contemporary theologians but for liberals and fundamentalists as well. On the liberal side, as noted earlier, religious experience was centered at the experience of God-in-Christ—however either diluted or misunderstood that might be. On the other hand, those who place their trust in inspired Scripture remember

that God is the final author of the Bible and that it is
to God-in-Christ that Holy Writ points.

In view of this situation it is accurate to state,
as Richard Drummond has, that "authority, as the word is
used in the Christian community, derives from the com-
pulsive or demanding nature of the claim made upon its
people by the Object of its worship."[25] However little
or incomplete is the state of the Church's knowledge at
a given time of this Object or claim, it is still here,
and nowhere else, that authority resides. P. T. Forsyth
was right: "the great question is not really as to the
seat of authority, but as to its nature."[26]

The nature of God as the Object which is the source
of authority for the Church is a primary concern. It
demands attention to the Word of God as God's claim upon
the Church. The Word of God is *one* Word in a *three-fold*
form. The one Word is made known through each and all
of its forms. That this Word is one Word in three-fold
form can be adduced from Scripture.

The Bible speaks of Jesus Christ as the Word of
God preeminent (John 1). Jesus called the Old Testament
writings the Word of God (Mk. 7:13), and to them were
added the New Testament writings by the Church (cf. 2
Pet. 3:15, 16). Most frequently, it is the preaching of
the Gospel that is called the Word of God (1 Thess. 2:13;
1 Pet. 1:25). But each of these is named in the same
fashion. The three forms remain distinct, yet in unity.

The Reformers refined and accentuated the doctrine
of the Word of God. By it they were able both to accord
Christ his real and absolute authority and maintain a
potent Church gathered to hear and proclaim the witness
to Christ preached most forcefully by God's Spirit in
Holy Scripture. Without having to bow first this way
and then that, now to Christ, now to the Bible, and now
to the Church, the Reformers found freedom under the
Word of God. And the Word of God manifested *its* freedom.

This dynamic resurfaced in Barth's treatment of
the Word of God. In following, extending, and refining
the Reformation thought, Barth formulated an understanding too important not to consider. For, as Barth developed it, the Word of God becomes the prolegomena, the
first and foundational word, of dogmatics. The Word of
God visibly reinforces the positive authority of God,
but as G. W. Bromiley notes:

> An odd thing happens here, for as Barth develops au-
> thority and freedom in this way the two finally amount
> to very much the same thing. In its authority the Word

28

is free—in its freedom it exercises authority. So, too, the church achieves its freedom when it is subject to the authority of the Word, and in this freedom of obedience it can speak and act with genuine authority. Today, as always, the church and the Christian are hard pressed by the questions of authority and freedom in both thought and life. Under current pressures the two tend to fall apart, and with authoritarianism on the one side and self-will on the other, there is in the last resort neither freedom nor authority. Forgotten in this dilemma and conflict are the authority and freedom of the Word under which the church's freedom and authority can be reconciled. Perhaps the best aspect of Barth's total doctrine of holy scripture as the written Word is that it drives us back beyond the interminable squabbles about inspiration and inerrancy to this concrete issue of the authority and freedom of the Word. When this is recognized, the authority and freedom of the church can be restored, and the confusion of much of its teaching and practice can be healed.[27]

Freedom with and under the Word of God has created, defined, and sustained the Church. God's Word has demonstrated its power in the Church. That power in freedom is not diminished by dogmatic effort as if man by dogmatics could control the Word of God. Rather, dogmatic reformulations aim at paralleling the freedom and contemporaneity of the Word.

Within conservative circles where the authority of God's Word has been unchallenged, the freedom of that Word has often been unrecognized. Orthodox dogmatics have fallen to a state of static disrepair. The genuine authority of the Word in the here-and-now has been bypassed for the past authority of that Word. Thus orthodox formulae have hindered as much as helped the evangelical community by being allowed to stifle the creative reformation and renewal of the Church in our own time. Where creeds and catechisms should guide a developing evangelical tradition there exists instead the dead weight of a misapprehended orthodoxy.

[1] John Calvin, <u>Institutes of the Christian Religion</u>, II, trans. H. Beveridge (Grand Rapids: Wm. B. Eerdmans, 1970), p. 281.

[2] Karl Barth, <u>The Faith of the Church</u> (A Commentary on the Apostle's Creed according to Calvin's Catechism), ed. Jean-Louis Leuba, trans. G. Vahanian (N. Y.: Meridian Books, 1958), p. 133.

[3] Philip Schaff, <u>Creeds of Christendom</u>, III (Grand Rapids: Baker Book House, 1977), p. 375.

[4] Quoted in Werner Elert's <u>The Structure of Lutheranism</u>, trans. W. A. Hansen (St. Louis: Concordia, 1962), p. 268.

[5] Ibid., p. 268.

[6] Other sociologists might also be used profitably. But Weber's ideas about authority, and charisma, have aided me greatly.

[7] Max Weber, <u>On Charisma and Institution Building</u>, ed. and intro. S. N. Eisenstadt (Chicago: Univ. of Chicago Press, 1968), p. 15. Hereafter cited by <u>On Charisma</u>.

[8] Ibid.

[9] H. H. Gerth and C. Wright Mills, <u>From Max Weber: Essays in Sociology</u> (N. Y.: Oxford University Press, 1958), p. 180.

[10] Weber, <u>On Charisma</u>, p. 28.

[11] Two are sufficient because the two selected enumerate the major authority sources, albeit the names and certain features may vary widely among authors.

[12] Bernard Ramm, <u>The Pattern of Religious Authority</u> (Grand Rapids: Wm. B. Eerdmans, 1957, 1959), pp. 10-12.

[13] Ibid., p. 20.

[14] Ibid., p. 21.

[15] Ibid., p. 10.

[16] Bernard Ramm, A Handbook of Contemporary Theology (Grand Rapids: Wm. B. Eerdmans, 1966), p. 19.

[17] Ibid., p. 20.

[18] Weber, On Charisma, pp. 46-47.

[19] Ibid.

[20] Ibid.

[21] Ibid.

[22] Ibid.

[23] Ibid.

[24] Ibid.

[25] Richard H. Drummond, "Authority in the Church: An Ecumenical Inquiry" The Journal of Bible and Religion, Vol. XXXIV, No. 4 (Oct., 1966), p. 333.

[26] P. T. Forsyth, The Principle of Authority (London: Independent Press, Ltd., 1913), p. 10.

[27] G. W. Bromiley, Introduction to the Theology of Karl Barth (Grand Rapids: Wm. B. Eerdmans, 1979), p. 44.

THREE

PROPOSITIONS ON AUTHORITY

At the time of Jesus' transfiguration the disciples
Peter, James, and John received a remarkable affirmation
from God about their Master. Mark's Gospel reads: "And
the cloud overshadowed them and a voice came out of the
cloud, 'This is my beloved son, listen to him!' And
suddenly, looking around they no longer saw anyone with
them but Jesus only" (Mk. 9:7-8; cf. Mt. 17:1-8, Lk.
9:23-36). The disciples had been caught in the splendor
of this majestic event. Excited and frightened, Peter
had voiced thoughts that likely could be found in the
minds of the other disciples as well. "Rabbi," Peter
had said, "It is well we are here, let us make three
booths" (9:5). But the voice from above commanded a
different action: "Pay attention not to yourselves or
these others, but see my Beloved Son, my Chosen, and
listen to him." Immediately the scene cleared and the
disciples saw no one else with them but Jesus.

The impression on the disciples showed itself more
in its long-term effects than in the rest of Jesus' brief
earthly ministry. Shortly after the experience, about
which they kept quiet for a long time, the disciples
again exhibited their pre-Pentecost lack of understanding. While faithfully following Jesus, they remained
confused about the purpose and direction of the authority which his power so clearly indicated. Enticed and
misled by other voices the disciples were usually unable
to focus on the one Word which God alone was saying.

The disciples' difficulty in centering their attention on God's revelation has remained. God-in-Jesus is
veiled even in his unveiling. But by God's Spirit the
Church can hear God's Word. Yet, the fact remains that
the Church sometimes does not hear that Word or does not
hear it rightly. The problem is often not in the hearing, but in hearing it *alone*, with no competition. All
too frequently the One Word is found among many. The

one Word of God becomes swallowed up in all too human babble.

This is not to suggest that the Church has no good words of its own. However, the Church is subordinated to the Word of God. The function, the duty, and the obedience of the Church is first to listen, and then to speak. First comes the Word of God which the Church must hear, and only then may the Church speak and speak rightly and properly. When the Church does speak, the Church's word is to say "God-in-Christ". The duty of the Church is not to originate some other revelation. Such attempts, no matter how noble, must always fail. Nor is it the principal domain of the Church to "defend" the faith through apologetics. Evangelical preoccupation at this point has endangered the preaching of the Gospel in some sectors. The obedience of the Church is to preach Christ. Thus, the Church's words are often exercised in the form of dogmatics, and one of those duties of dogmatics includes the formulating of contemporary confessions.

The formulation of a confession is not a light matter. It is, in fact, one of the most serious responsibilities the Church can undertake. The creeds of the Church must demonstrate themselves first to be faithful to Holy Scripture, and the testimony of Scripture to Jesus Christ. Second, they must be a valid expression of the faith in that time, so that they speak to the people to whom they are addressed, and direct those people to God and him in Christ alone. Third, they must remain valuable guides to the Church in succeeding generations.

Of the Church's outstanding and accepted creeds, the Barmen Declaration of 1934 speaks directly to the issue of the authority of God's Word in a world where many words confuse the Church. The Barmen Declaration was framed in Nazi Germany immediately prior to the beginning of the Second World War. It was a product of the so-called Confessing churches.

But to understand Barmen, one must go back before the Nazi era. After World War I there occurred a rather general collapse of the evangelical church in Germany. Those churches, conservative and liberal alike, which had supported the Kaiser's cause as God's cause were totally shattered by the defeat that Germany suffered in the First World War. Nationalist and racist traditions already latent in Germany became expressed in several movements both within and outside the Church. The rise to power of Hitler encouraged these trends within the Church. This was due in no small measure to the close ties of Church and state which have always been a part of German life. Eventually, the so-called German Christian Church gained state supported momentum. But this movement, though supported by the state, did not gain ascendency without opposition.

When the Nazis supported the election of Ludwig Müller as Reichbishop on 27 September, 1933, a young movement began to undertake earnest opposition. This counter movement was a coalition, principally Reformed and Lutheran traditions, united in what became known as the Confessing Church. Martin Niemöller, leader of the Pastors' Emergency League, emerged as the principal ecclesiastical figure in the Confessing Church. The theological architects, both of Barmen's Declaration in 1934, as well as the other theological documents of the Confessing Church, were Dietrich Bonhoeffer, and the Swiss Karl Barth.

Barth, in particular, played a prominent role in the early struggles in the Church in Germany. These culminated with the deportation of Barth. After Barth's departure, Dietrich Bonhoeffer, who had gone to England, returned to Germany and again took an active role which lead to his eventual arrest for complicity in the plot to assassinate Hitler and his execution in the last days of the war. Niemöller, imprisoned perhaps longer than any other Church figure, did not suffer the same fate, but emerged after the war to be a principal figure in the reconstruction of the German Church.

The theological foundation of the Confessing Church movement was set forth at the Barmen Synod held 29 — 30 May, 1934. The chief author of the document was Barth. Although the Confessing Church had an uneven history, being generally weak and ineffective, it did serve to largely discredit the German Christian Church, and to serve notice to the world that not all German Christians had capitulated their faith to the State. Nevertheless, the declaration itself was a rallying point and served as a confession of true faith in a time of great duress. It also served another function. It was part of the battle for recognition of the Confessing Church as the legal entity of the evangelical church in Germany.

The declaration, in each of six main paragraphs, exposed New Testament texts and expounded them. Each of these points was accompanied by a repudiation of errors perceived by the Confessing Church in contemporary Germany. The declaration was not a long explanation of orthodox doctrine. It was, indeed, short and to the point. As John Leith has commented, "it said with clarity the one thing that needed to be said, 'The

Christian must listen to Jesus Christ and to Him alone.'"[1]

The theology of the Barmen Declaration is perhaps best summed up in its principal statement contained in Article II Point 1:

> Jesus Christ as he is testified to us in the Holy Scripture, is the one Word of God, whom we are to hear, whom we are to trust and obey in life and in death.
> We repudiate the false teaching that the Church can and must recognize yet other happenings and powers, images and truths as divine revelation alongside this one Word of God, as a source of her preaching.

Today's Church may profitably start from this heritage of confession given in a time of great confusion and stress. A contemporary statement on authority and the Church must be guided by this declaration's appeal to Scripture. Barmen cannot simply be repeated, but it still speaks eloquently as a guide to our own words. To try to speak in the tradition of Barmen and yet be true to the right hearing of Scripture as addressed and expressed to the current Church situation is a laudable goal. I intend Barmen to stand behind my own hearing of the Word.

Yet Barmen cannot be heard alone, as if it were the only voice of the Church's tradition appropriate to address the Church today. If Barmen is peculiarly appropriate, it is not uniquely so. Barmen is my starting point. As such, it is not merely reiterated, although it is retained. It guides a developing tradition without solidifying it once for all. Barmen speaks today, but with a voice best suited to its own time and place. Today's voices must be added to say afresh, and personally, that Jesus Christ alone is Lord.

Thus, the following foundational theses present statements or propositions on authority arising from the Word of God as dogmatically expressed today. I agree with Richard Drummond when he states, "it is our contention . . . that the authority of the God of Christian faith may be effectually known through the reciprocal working of what we may call three coefficient factors . . . . These coefficient factors are: (1) the specifically Christian faith—experience of personal redemption and reception of revelation; (2) the discipline of the corporate life of the Christian community; and (3) the Holy Scriptures."[2] But I believe these coefficient factors must not, as such, form the base of our understanding of authority. They are misleading, ambiguous, and subject to a wide variety of misunderstandings. Yet, they must be preserved. I think they are in the theses which follow:[3]

    I.   Jesus Christ is the one Word of God who reveals the trinitarian God as the first and final authority.

    II.   The witness of the Holy Spirit to the one Word of God is, as the inscripturated Word of God, the mediating authority established for man by God.

    III.   The proclamation of the Church, in its adherence to the Spirit's testimony, is, as the translated Word of God, the functional authority among God's people.

About these theses only a few preliminary remarks are necessary. We have already noted Ramm's conviction on the theme of the first thesis.[4] I agree with it. Drummond, too, writes, "the historic claim of the Christian faith is that the source and the norm of authority for the church lie in the Triune God, who is the Object of the church's faith."[5] Drummond is also right when he argues, "authority in the church ought to reflect the kind of authority which is exercised, as Christian faith believes, by God himself, as an authority of love."[6] But this love is the concrete Word of God, God-in-Christ.

As we have seen, this idea is not new. The Church is always being called back by God to himself. Luther ably put it: "in the end, all authority comes from God whose alone it is; for he is emperor, prince, count, noble, judge, and all else, and he assigns these offices to his subjects as he wills and takes them back again for himself."[7] The authority that originates with God, proceeds from him, and returns to him, is the work of the Holy Spirit. Ramm has said that, "the witness of the Spirit focuses at the center of the divine revelation—the person and work of Jesus Christ."[8]

The Spirit keeps authority centered upon Christ. He does this in no small measure by Holy Scripture. The Bible is truly what Luther called it, the Spirit's own sermon. Biblical authority resides in this work of the Spirit. But even where this is denied, the de-facto authority of Scripture is easily seen. As John Leith has noted, "the historical fact is that Christian theology without Scripture is practically unthinkable."[9]

The vehicle by which Scripture's message is translated immediately and personally by the Church is also the Holy Spirit's work. His own preaching comes in the proclamation of God's people. Again the goal is Christ himself. Luther knew that the "preaching of the gospel is nothing else than Christ coming to us, or we being brought to him."[10] Together, Scripture and preaching demonstrate the proper and vital place accorded to man

36

by God's Word. Thus, authority is revealed as originating outside of man, but which graciously incorporates man into its scope and function.

The Word of God, however, does not belong to man. It is not his creation, nor does he control it. The relative authority of, for instance, creation and conscience, is markedly different from that of the Word of God. The Word is free, creation and conscience are in bondage. But even more importantly, the Word of God shows itself as an authority for us, on our side. Both creation and conscience serve mankind as well, but their authority is directed only against us. Only God's Word can save us, even while judging us; but creation and conscience only consign us to bondage and condemnation.

These theses, simple in form and unpretentious in content are the gospel of authority. That is, they are a recovery of the good news that God's power and authority are intended for salvation. The Church must recover this truth, and accord to it its proper place and work. But there remains some necessary explanation of these propositions, and some application, if these theses are to best serve the Church.

References Cited--Chapter Three

[1] John Leith, <u>Creeds of the Churches</u> (Richmond: John Knox Press, 1963, 1973) pp. 517, 518.

[2] Richard H. Drummond, "Authority in the Church: An Ecumenical Inquiry" <u>The Journal of Bible and Religion</u> Vol. XXXIV, No. 4 (Oct., 1966), p. 330.

[3] These factors are truly reciprocal in their working and, while I do not specifically point them out in succeeding chapters, they are certainly at work.

[4] See page 26.

[5] Drummond, "Authority in the Church: An Ecumenical Inquiry", p. 329.

[6] Ibid., p. 334.

[7] Martin Luther, "The Church in Society" III, <u>Luther's Works</u>, Vol. 46, ed. R. C. Schultz (Phila: Fortress, 1961) p. 126.

[8] Bernard Ramm, <u>The Pattern of Religious Authority</u> (Grand Rapids: Wm. B. Eerdmans, 1957, 1959), p. 36.

[9] John Leith, "The Bible and Theology," <u>Interpretation</u>, XXX, 3 (July 1976), p. 227.

[10] Martin Luther, "Word and Sacrament" I, <u>Luther's Works</u> Vol. 35, ed. E. T. Bachman (Phila: Muhlenberg Press, 1960), p. 121.

FOUR

JESUS CHRIST IS THE ONE WORD OF GOD WHO REVEALS

Jesus Christ is the one Word of God who reveals the trinitarian God as the first and final authority. The first, and last, word about authority and the Church is also a name: Jesus. He is not only the one named by the Church, but he is preeminently the name above all names, the one named by God as his own Son. Jesus' name is "the Word of God" as well. He is the one whose name means all that God has disclosed about himself. Thus, Jesus alone is all God says revealing himself.

Knowing just this much answers already the question as to who Jesus is. He is who God is, he is what God says. He is the revelation of the Triune God, he is the *one* Word of God. But he is this yesterday, today, and forever. Jesus, the real person, the actual revelation, the concrete Word, has past, present, and future.

The historicity of Jesus means many things. It means, first of all, the birth of a charismatic institution called the Church. This explains, secondly, the rationale for the call by the Church to the world for an immediate and personal, existential decision for God. The history of Jesus means that God is in our midst; that God, in assuming flesh, has come and dwelt among us. This also brings with it a substantial and imminent judgment. Thus, the call by the Church is a continuation of the Word of God as first spoken in Jesus Christ. This Word, calling for a decision for God, is a call issued as a reflection of the true, genuine, imminent presence of judgment. Third, the historicity of Jesus means the origin of an irrefutable and direct authority. It is God himself who is revealed in Jesus. This irrefutable and direct authority is conferred by Jesus on others, yet it originates only in Jesus and in him solely by the presence of God. This direct authority also carries with it in the person of Jesus, as shown even in his earthly ministry, the promise of the coming Holy Spirit.

39

The Spirit, when he comes, continues this authority without it being in any way lessened.

The charismatic leader, as Jesus certainly was, has
been profiled by Weber.   Such an individual is one who
readily surfaces in troubled times. As Weber noted, "the
natural leaders in distress have been holders of specific
gifts of the body and spirit; and these gifts have been
believed to be supernatural,   not accessible to every-
body."[1] The context in which such a leader appears makes
the belief that this person possesses unusual abilities
quite popular and acceptable.   The "gift" becomes increasingly prominent. Weber observed, "all of them have
practiced their arts and ruled by virtue of this gift
(charisma) and, where the idea of God has already been
clearly conceived, by virtue of the divine mission lying
therein."[2]   This sense of mission moves the leader and
his followers to "transcend" the context in which they
surface. In fact, Weber commented, "in order to do justice to their mission, the holders of charisma, the master as well as his disciples and followers, must stand
outside the ties of this world, outside of routine occu-
pations, as well as outside the routine obligations of
family life."[3]   Charisma accentuates the unusual. In a
penetrating analysis of charisma's operation Weber wrote,

> Charisma knows only inner determination and inner re-
> straint. The holder of charisma siezes the task that is
> adequate for him, and demands obedience and a following
> by virtue of his mission. His success determines whether
> he finds them. His charismatic claim breaks down if his
> mission is not recognized by those to whom he feels he
> has been sent. If they recognize him, he is their mas-
> ter—so long as he knows how to maintain recognition
> through 'proving' himself. But he does not derive his
> 'right' from their will in the manner of an election.
> Rather, the reverse holds: it is the *duty* of those to
> whom he addresses his mission to recognize him as their
> charismatically qualified leader.[4]

Of course this means, as Weber saw it, that "by
its very nature, the existence of charismatic authority
is specifically unstable."[5] This is only natural because
"the charismatic leader gains and maintains authority
solely by proving his strength in life."[6]   Thus, time
works against charismatic authority. To repeat what was
noted earlier, "it is the fate of charisma, whenever it
comes into the permanent institutions of a community, to
give way to powers of tradition or rational socialization."[7]

However, Jesus, though definitely a charismatic
leader, solved the inherent problems of such leadership

40

in a unique manner. His death was, as expected, a final, crushing blow to his disillusioned disciples. But his resurrection from the dead proposed a permanent triumph of the living over the dead and showed a leader of such unusual charisma that his authority was not only permanent, but also absolute. Peter's sermon in Acts 2 argues from these events in space and time that Jesus, first of all, lives after having died; second, that this proves not only his extraordinary charisma, but also his election by God, his divine mission, and his present Lordship. Moreover, third, in all of this Jesus reveals a Triune God.

Jesus' charisma, in light of his resurrection, made his constant claim to be the Son of Man give way to the Church's confession of him as the Son of God. Jesus *is* God. But his being God in space and time is also a controversial scandal. The revealed God is hidden in *this* flesh? The power of God resides in *this* weakness? Even the miracles are suspect when the miracle worker cries, bleeds, and dies. Yet the disciples, by the grace of God, knew he was the Christ.

Why is Jesus called the Christ? Peter's sermon argued for the legitimacy of such a claim from the events in time and space. But beyond this lies the basis in the existence of the Church. This should not be minimized as it often is. That the Church has called Jesus the Christ in no wise minimizes the actual, historical objectivity to which Peter appealed for a right basis in calling Jesus "Christ". What it does, instead, is substantiate Peter's claim. The fact of the Church in time and space is, in itself, the reality of a continuing existence that has drawn its source and strength from this very objectivity in history.

But the Church was formulated in the New Testament period as a charismatic organization. Its charismatic origin can be traced directly to Christ, and despite the long passage of time, the Church has retained charismatic elements in its developing tradition. Nevertheless, as was to be expected, these charismatic elements gradually gave way under the weight of tradition. Thus, with every passing generation, the need re-establishes itself that those original charismatic elements not only be retained but refined in order that the nature and vitality of the Church, as it originally existed, be maintained. This explains, in part, both the importance and work of the promised Holy Spirit. The Holy Spirit is the immediate and personal presence of Jesus Christ in his Church. It is through the Spirit and his gifts that those charismatic elements original in the Church are retained.

The Holy Spirit reaffirms the actuality of Jesus Christ and his continuing presence. Understanding this accounts for the characterizing of the Spirit's work in the New Testament as bearing witness to Christ and continuing Christ's work in the work of his followers. Thus, it is the Spirit who is imparted and becomes part and parcel of the life of the Church in each individual disciple, as well as in the community as a whole. All of this keeps the *necessity* as well as the *reality* of Jesus' Lordship, and inspires the continuing confession that has characterized the Church from the beginning, that is, "Jesus is Lord!"

This confession opposed the scandal of the Incarnation. The Resurrection is, as it were, a causal event. It gave rise to the early confessions of the Church. Yet even the resurrection was veiled to some degree, as seen first in the unbelief of the disciples, and the continued unbelief in the temple authorities, and second, in the need for the Ascension and Pentecost. The Spirit's coming in power proved to the disciples what Luther would discover sixteen centuries later: " . . . hold fast to this: no Christian authority can do anything against Christ."[8]

The opposition to the world and its judgment posed by the Christian confession demanded decision. The authority of Jesus as Christ does not mean compromise with the World but the capitulation of all other authorities to his own. Other authorities must be ordered under his. This decision, like the confession that sets it forward, is concrete, individual, and definitive on the person's own history. It is at root a decision for freedom and obedience, or for rebellion. A decision for freedom means a new voice added to the confession of the Church. It means an active testimony to the irrefutable authority and irresistible graciousness of God-in-Christ.

The resultant new life under the authority of God means freedom. But it is particularly freedom for three things: first, to hear, second, to trust, and finally, to obey. Unheard news of liberty leaves men and women in their bondage even when the objective basis of that bondage has been shattered. Without hearing of the demise of former authorities and the simultaneous, decisive justification of God's authority, men and women remain as effectively imprisoned by the illusion as they were by the fact. So all must hear of this glad authority revealed in Jesus if they are to become free.

Hearing takes place by speaking. Thus, the act of God in Christ announcing the vindication of his eternal authority is the most fundamental form of the Word of

God. Luther saw the matter clearly when he declared, "For the preaching of the gospel is nothing else than Christ coming to us, or we being brought to him."[9] This encounter can only take place in the Church—an outsider who hears the Word proclaimed is convicted by the Church (1 Co. 14:24), by the Spirit of God within the Church (Jn. 16:8). If the Church really is the Body of Christ, it is so by its preaching, wherein man and God meet one another in and through the person of Jesus Christ. So Luther also saw the primitive Church and its preaching when he commented, "And what is the New Testament but a public preaching and proclamation of Chirst, set forth through the sayings of the Old Testament and fulfilled through Christ?"[10]

This proclamation of God is sacramental in character. God in Jesus speaks in this human flesh. The Word become flesh is concrete grace. This Word is such that the Church has rightly said, "That which was from the beginning, which we have heard, which we have seen with our eyes, which we have looked upon and touched with our hands concerning the Word of Life, the life was made manifest and we saw it and testified to it, and proclaimed to you the eternal life, which was with the Father and was made manifest to us, that which we have seen and heard, we proclaim also to you so that you may have fellowship with us and our fellowship is with the Father and with the Son Jesus Christ and we are writing this that our joy may be complete. (1 Jn. 1:1—4) .

But there is but *one* Word. It is *this* God-man, Jesus, who reveals the ultimate establishment of God's good authority for man. The Church is to put her trust in Christ alone, and him only is she to obey. This personal Word saves and liberates as it is heard, trusted, and obeyed. In this one Word is the Gospel, and even as there is only one Word, there is but one Gospel (cf. 2 Co. 1:18-20, Gal. 1:6—9).

The Word of God, found in Jesus Christ saves as it is heard, trusted, and obeyed. The thought put forward by P. T. Forsyth that, "the revelation of the holy can only come through redemption by the holy,"[11] is brought to mind. Jesus reveals God, and he does so by his saving acts. He thus reveals God as the God who saves. Yet this same God is revealed by these same acts as the holy God, since it is from sin that he saves mankind.

The salvation of God is the principal act of his authority. It cannot be separated from his revelation nor from his power. God's self-disclosure in his Word shows its authoritative power in this redemption. The Word is completed in its being heard, trusted, and obeyed, but even quite apart from these, it is still spoken, albeit spoken with every intention of being fulfilled (Is. 55:10, 11, cf. Is. 45:22, 23; Phil. 2: 1—11). Thus, the *objectivity* of God's redemption is not diminished by the need of a personal response by men and women to the Word of God.

The unity of revelation in salvation is in the activity of the self-disclosing God. This activity is fundamentally personal encounter: God meets man. There are three facets to this encounter which must be particularly noted: first of all, this encounter is personal. Any instrument that God may use in disclosing himself is nevertheless aimed at a personal, face-to-face meeting between God and the individual. Yet secondly, this encounter, despite its personal character, is in a very important sense always indirect. This must mean that the God fully made known by Jesus, still has chosen in his freedom to remain hidden in such a fashion that it is only through the ongoing activity of the role of the Spirit in revelation that he makes himself known in a manner sufficient for salvation. Thus, this third and crucial element: only by means of the Holy Spirit does revelation take place. The Holy Spirit uses both Scripture and the proclamation of the Church as God's Word to witness to *the* Word, Jesus Christ, and to bring about the personal encounter which is the goal of the whole activity of revelation.

But this encounter bears the character of the Word in that it is a command-demanding decision. Thus, the announcement of the Gospel also bears in it the requirement laid on those that hear it to "repent and be baptized in the name of Jesus" (Acts 2:38). Then comes forgiveness of sins and the promised Holy Spirit. Apart from the Word of God, salvation is unknown, unknowable, and impossible. Yet, apart from salvation, the Word is empty, powerless, and meaningless. Both need the other. Although distinct, they are in complete union. The Word speaking and effecting salvation is the self-establishment of the authority of the righteous God making his claim upon us in Christ.

The revelation of God is also united with salvation in the representational character that revelation bears in those forms of the Word of God known as Scripture and preaching. These are sacramental in character. The Church also bears a sacramental nature. She is the body of Christ, the community of the faithful, and true humanity as humanity in Christ. She is also the conveyer and translator of the Word of God as God freely elects her words to be his own.

44

In this relation to the Word and salvation of God, the specific sacraments of the Church "save" too. The authority of baptism and communion, created by the command of the Lord, is an authority and power identified with God's redemptive work. Their authority is as "saving" acts of God's grace, that is, as true *sacraments*. They neither diminish any other constituent part of God's work nor effect by themselves the regeneration of souls.[12]

The sacraments of the Church, and those things that bear a sacramental nature, unite salvation to revelation. The revelation of God-in-Christ, in union with God's salvation, is a self-verifying epistemology whose God is shown as Savior and proved Savior by his saving act. That *God* makes himself known means God makes himself *known*. This also takes place through the sacraments and sacramental things, but it would be incorrect to say that by these it is shown that God in either his revelation or salvation needs or requires assistance.

The specific avenue by which God makes himself known through the work of the Spirit is in the Spirit-inspired faith that wells up within an individual believer. This explains both of those familiar Latin phrases, *Credo ut intelligam*, I believe in order to understand," and *fides quaerens intellectum*, "Faith in search of understanding." This is the proper order: faith, that which is given as a gift of the Spirit, reaches out for that knowledge that comes by God's revelation. The knowledge of God discloses the trinitarian God. Conversely, it is the disclosure of the trinitarian God that alone constitutes true knowledge of God. Knowledge of God in his triune character is at the same time, the revelation of authority, for it is in this triune character that the revelation of authority reaches its fullest measure, and this is expressed concretely in Christ, and through Christ in the Church.

Finally, revelation must be understood as an observed phenomena. That is, there is a science to the observation of revelation by the Church. This is true because revelation is objective. That is, it takes place apart from its being engendered by the Church, even by the Church in faith. Because revelation presents God as an object of inquiry, it is God himself who controls the methods and scope of inquiry. This, then, explains the *necessity* of faith. It is faith that God, by his Spirit, makes the necessary requirement for an understanding of himself, and, in fact, for any approach to himself. Faith then, under the guidance of the Spirit, applies this knowledge that it receives from the object. This ultimately compels decision and confession.

It is the Church's distinctive nature that her confession, in light of the fact that Jesus Christ is the
Word of God, is that the revelation of God has always
been summarized by testifying that "Jesus is Lord!" As
we shall see, this confession is itself a confession of
God's authority.

[1] H. H. Gerth and C. Wright Mills, <u>From Max Weber: Essays in Sociology</u> (New York: Oxford University Press, 1958), p. 245.

[2] Ibid., p. 246.

[3] Ibid., p. 248.

[4] Ibid., p. 246.

[5] Ibid., p. 248.

[6] Ibid., p. 249.

[7] M. Weber, <u>On Charisma and Institution Building</u>, ed. and intro. S. N. Eisenstadt (Chicago: Univ. of Chicago Press, 1968), p. 28.

[8] Martin Luther, "Christian in Society" I, <u>Luther's Works,</u> Vol. 44, ed. James Atkinson (Phila: Fortress Press, 1966), p. 138.

[9] Martin Luther, "Word and Sacrament" I, <u>Luther's Works</u>, Vol. 35, ed. E. T. Bachman (Phila: Muhlenberg Press, 1960), p. 121.

[10] Ibid., p. 236.

[11] P. T. Forsyth, <u>The Principle of Authority</u> (London: Independent Press, Ltd., 1913), p. 7.

[12] "Salvation" must be understood here in its broadest biblical use and not in the evangelical, narrow sense of regeneration alone.

FIVE

THE TRINITARIAN GOD

Jesus Christ is the one Word of God who reveals the trinitarian God as the first and final authority. The God made known by Jesus Christ is the trinitarian God. This means three things. First, Jesus in his identity as the Image of God is displayed in the New Testament as the one who makes known through himself the trinitarian God as Father, Son, and Holy Spirit.[1] Jesus' continuation in the Spirit in the early Church guarantees that this revelatory knowledge disclosed by the second person of the deity is continued through the instrumentality of the third person. The command of the Father means that his Word is his Son, or, that his Son can be identified quite accurately and appropriately as the Word of God.

But this God who reveals himself is also a God who remains hidden. The old Latin phrase, *deus revelatis, deus absconditas* "God is revealed, God is hidden," is appropriate at this point. God revealed is still the hidden God. That is, his self-disclosure shows mankind a person who remains full of mystery, as yet not dispelled, nor soon to be dispelled. The mystery of God remains long after all his secrets are told. The mystery is the depths of unexplored personhood, and the eternal character unencompassed by man even in the final redemption. This hiddenness of God is for our benefit; first negatively, in that we could not live in the visible disclosure of his full and awesome glory, and positively, in that his hiddenness preserves our own revelation of ourselves.

The hiddenness of God was a truth easily seen by the Old Testament community of faith. There we often find ourselves gripped as they were by the conviction, "No man shall see God and live." The Old Testament recognized this hiddenness of God in the utter majesty of a holy God, and understood that sinfulness meant that no

48

one could stand in his presence and live. Still we find the record showing repeatedly that God, in his revelation to these people, while not disclosing himself in an entirety that would literally slay them, does come to them in a real way, in personal encounter, and they do, in fact, live. But their lives are radically changed by his presence in that encounter.

In the New Testament we find that Christ has hidden God's glory even as he has manifested it. Thus, the New Testament authors record that Christ was the glory of God and explain the significance of this, but they do not develop greatly any idea of the physical visibility of this glory. Rather, this glory is seen in the ordinary, straight-forward account of the historical Jesus, who, in the course of his ministry and life and miracles, in spite of all the glory that attended him, nevertheless was not immediately perceived by all as being deity.

Indeed, from his own self-nomination as the Son of Man, through the opposition of the leaders of the Pharisees, and on through the reactions of the common people, it was perceivable that Jesus was indeed both unique and highly special. Yet it remained debatable, throughout the course of his life, as to what his nature was with regard to any divinity. In fact, even among his closest disciples his being confessed as Christ, the Son of the Most High, did not at first, perhaps, carry any implications that he was, in fact, God himself.

Even his disciples, in their confession and recognition that Jesus was the Son of the Most Blessed, had not yet fully recognized the fact of his true Godness. Nevertheless, with the coming of the Spirit at Pentecost, this truth was revealed. It then became a substantiating foundation to the early community. It was true what Christ had promised. He did remain, and continues to be with the Church.

In all of this, the hiddenness of God shows that God does not need us to be or to know himself. That is, God may remain apart from us and not have the actuality of his existence in any way diminished. God has created us, but we are not God, nor do we comprise in any sense any part of his essence. The fact that he has created us in his image and communicated to us things which are so characteristic of himself, as those things are given to us in Christ, is a gift and a behest, a part of his creation—but not he himself. God, though, has given himself to us in Christ, and even as we know ourselves in Christ, he has given the knowledge of himself to us in Christ.

Yet, on the other hand, this does not say that God does not know himself apart from us. Indeed, the Word of God in its eternal preexistence prior to the Incarnation and dwelling among men, was the Triune God in his self-knowledge apart from us. Nevertheless, though God does not need us to be or to know himself, he does show himself *for us*, and in showing himself to us in Jesus Christ, he reveals himself as a God who, in his freedom from us, is a God for us.

The God made known by Christ is the Eternal One. John, in his Gospel, points from the very beginning to the pre-Incarnate Son as the Eternal Word. This thought is picked up in the Pauline theology in the Colossian hymn of chapter one. Here the New Testament re-echoes the thought of the Old Testament, specifically the creation texts of Genesis 1 and 2. There God's Word, his creative activity in a personal intervention into the forces of time and space creates, forms, and molds the world and all therein. God's titular name as Creator is seen in close relation to his powerful Word.

God, who is thus self-enclosed, that is, removed, distinct, and completely non-contingent with creation, a God who does not need his creation, *nevertheless* has created.

If God does not need us, his name as Creator means he wills us. Creation, then, is not a necessary consequence of God's deity, but an expression of his freedom. God does not create us because he needs us; his name, Creator, means he wills us.

God wants us. This is the truth behind the doctrine of election, no matter what form this doctrine may take. God wants us specifically as his creation, and thus as his witnesses, but more particularly yet as his people, and most especially as his sons.

God creates us in his own image, that is, creation bears glory. That this glory has remained disguised by the fall does not change the fact that it continues to exist. In fact, creation has its hope in the hope of the redeemed, who in the fullness of their redemption revealed in the time of Christ, again unfolds the glory of creation itself.

God provides for us. The doctrine of providence emerges here. The God who does not need us, because he wills us, also wills to provide for us, and that care is continuous. Thus, even in the fall, God's judgment is displayed as a mercy, which, though it drives out Adam and Eve from the Garden, still cares for them. This, then, leads us to the doctrines of reconciliation and redemption, or the notion that God *pursues* us. The God who has wanted us in election, created us in his image, and provided for us in the fall is the God who pursues us this side of the fall. He pursues us by coming to us in the person of his Son. In this coming, and in the work that Christ accomplished on this earth in time and space, he both effects reconciliation, and initiates a redemption still awaiting its revealed fullness at the end of time. In all of these aspects, God reveals his character as being free from us, and also, predominantly, free for us.

The self-enclosed God, then, is also the self-disclosed. The revelation of God is in the Incarnation of God. The knowledge of God is not a knowledge of a God abstracted from us, or of a God who sets the wheels in motion and then contemplates it from afar, but a God who personally intervenes in his creation to redeem it in the Incarnation. The revelation of Jesus is caught by the confession, "Jesus is Lord!" But this is not any lord, any master, any sir. This is more than a respectful title of address to a learned teacher. This "Jesus is Lord" means that he is *the* Lord, the Old Testament God who revealed himself by the name Yahweh. That name itself means, "I will be what I will be." That is, it means freedom. But this is not freedom as arbitrariness. Rather, it is freedom with a purpose, one accomplished in Christ, and best known by the confession, "Jesus is Lord!"

Dietrich Bonhoeffer recognized the truth of this when he said, "God's will to rule is his will to love his church." [2] That is to say that the name Yahweh means freedom, but freedom for his people. That freedom expresses itself in his divine rule over his people. This is seen in the Old Testament through God's relationship with his people Israel in establishing a witness among the nations. It is continued in the New Testament by the witness of the Church to Jesus as its Lord. The Lordship of God means that in willing to rule God wills to love, because the best demonstration of his love in its practicality is precisely in his ruling.

God's self-disclosure is free, not coerced. That is to say, God's Lordship is not the result of any election by man, nor is it the result of any coercion by the Church. Rather, God freely chooses himself to be the Lord of his people, and no matter what any man may say, think, or do about this, it remains an unalterable reality. God's self-disclosure in revelation is free, and so, too, is his rule. Both God's self-disclosure and rule show God's love for his people. It is in both his freedom and his Lordship that love finds its direction and the power to be what it is, and to be what it is *for us*.

God's freedom in revelation means that he comes as he will, where he will, when he will. It also means that he is free from any bondage that man would assert toward him. He is free from man's bondage, and thus, free to bind himself to man. In fact, in his freedom from us, he finds his greatest delight in voluntarily binding himself for us. In this we see the picture of Jesus Christ as a servant. As Diogenes Allen has said, "Precisely because he does not need us, precisely because his status does not rest on us, he can serve us. He can wash his disciple's feet and not thereby cease to be Lord."[3] Bonhoeffer had a similar idea in mind when he wrote, " . . . by limitless serving God rules limitlessly over men."[4]

The revelation of God-in-Christ as servant demonstrates the truth of the controversial doctrine known by the name kenosis. This term derives from Philippians 2:5—11. There we see that the mind of Christ which believers are to have is seen in Jesus. Though he was in the form of God, he did not count that status as something to be grasped, but "emptied" himself, took the form of man, and man as a servant, and in his obedience to God became obedient even unto death, the death on a cross.

This servanthood of God, or this freedom of God for man, this work of God as savior of man is seen throughout the Bible. It is most prominent in the life, the work of Jesus Christ, and preeminently, of course, in those events of the Cross, Resurrection, and Pentecost. Nevertheless, in his teaching another thought closely aligned, and in no way opposite, emerges. For Jesus, in his teaching, the Kingdom of God was continually in focus. This Kingdom meant first and foremost the Kingship of God. The Kingdom of God is the realm that God rules. Kingdom, of course, means domain as well. This entails two elements: a place and a people. The people are more important than the place, but the place is particularly that wherein God himself is to be found dwelling in the midst of his people, recognized by his people and confessed as Lord by his people. That place is the household of God, his Church.

The God of both the servanthood of Jesus in his life, and the King proclaimed by Jesus in his teaching, is the God of good news. Jesus as the *Word* of God is, in all actuality, a *shout* of gladness. He came into the world as a town crier and in the midst of all the people, stood up and spoke. We see this in the story in

Luke chapter 4, at the beginning of Jesus' ministry when, in the synagogue, he takes the book, opens it to the prophet, and reads those words from Isaiah 61 that proclaim the acceptable year of the Lord, the delivery for the captives that is coming. Then he says, "this has been fulfilled today in your hearing." Thus, from the start, the message that Jesus preaches which is characterized by Matthew in his early chapters as "repent for the kingdom is at hand," is what John the Baptist had said, but more than what John the Baptist saw. For this news is not only news that one should repent because the Kingom is at hand, but more particularly, that the coming of this Kingdom means the coming of a God who in his freedom aligns himself with man by saving man and making man what he is in himself not, that is, righteous.

The good news of freedom that comes from Christ comes as the ethic of God's kingship. In all of this it must be remembered that the God proclaimed and demonstrated in Jesus is the one God. When Jesus is questioned as to what is foremost in the mind of God, he answers with that cry which is so characteristic of the best in Judaism, *Sh'ma* "Hear!" Hear that the Lord, the God of Israel is *one* God. If Jesus, in his identity with God, is seen to be divine himself, this does not mean that there are now two Gods, one in rivalry with the other, or even two Gods cooperating with each other, but that there is *one* God, and that the authority of the one God is *also the authority of Jesus*. But this, if recognized in and of itself, might nevertheless remain insufficient. Hence, we find James' warning in chapter two that even the demons recognize that God is one, and yet their only response is to shudder at the awesome truth of this. Rather, as Jesus saw, in answering and beginning with the Sh'ma, one might begin to proceed immediately to the *command* of God. Hence, Jesus' uttering of the Sh'ma is immediately followed by the great commandment, or what has been known also as the golden rule.

P. T. Forsyth once said, "There is only one thing greater than Liberty and that is Authority."[5] God in his freedom shows himself to be the well-pleasing *raison d'etre* of authority. God's complete freedom means absolute authority. Yet, we are told, and by Christ himself, that "if the Son makes you free, you will be free indeed." This thought is re-echoed in the teaching of Paul in Galatians where he asserts that it was "for freedom that Christ has set us free; stand fast therefore, and do not submit again to a yoke of slavery," (5:1) or a little later "for you were called to freedom, brethren; only do not use your freedom as an opportunity for the flesh, but through love be servants of one another. For the whole law is fulfilled in one word, 'You shall love your neighbor as yourself'," (5:13, 14). Thus, the freedom which God grants toward us and gives to us in Christ is a freedom not to caprice, but a freedom to one another. Or, as Luther put it, "There is no authority in the Church except to promote good . . . . Paul says to the Corinthians, 'God has given us authority not to ruin Christendom, but to build it up.' (2 Co. 10:8)"[6]

The Word of God as authority for us, then, means four important things. First, it comes to us as authority over us, revealed in the divine command, and summed up in that term, "*law*". Then, too, as a facet of law, and its natural consequence, authority is, second, revealed against us as divine *judgment*. But, third, authority is *for us,* and it is for us even in its judgment against us, for that judgment which is so unalterably opposed to us, and so clearly establishes our own frailty and the impossibility of our establishing our own righteousness, then points us to the righteousness revealed in God which is the sign of divine intervention. That God justifies himself and his authority is vindicated by his actions in Christ. Thus, fourth, the Word, which is God's Word, comes as God's "*Yes*" in Christ. This we have told to us by Paul in the first chapter of 2 Corinthians where he again asserts that God is in Christ saying, not "yes" and "no", as if there was caprice, but "yes" in a movement of freedom toward us, which inspires from us a grateful acknowledgement, and provides the foundation and basis for our saying "Amen". This Amen means that all the promises of God have found not "no", nor "yes" *and* "no", but *only* "yes" in Jesus Christ.

Finally, we must recall that the truth of the revelation of Jesus, who reveals the Triune God, means that the Triune God is the *one* God *known* in the Son as Father, Son, and Holy Spirit. The Triune God is the Father calling us, the Son coming to us, and the Spirit bringing us.

God's freedom for us means *our freedom* to serve. As he has been free and continues to be free to serve us in love, we are freed to love one another. This establishes the basis of his righteous commandment toward us, that we in word and deed love him and that that love be manifested especially in the love of one another. This love of one another reaches its own fulfillment in that love which comes freely from us toward those who oppose not only us, but who oppose us in their opposition to God.

[1] The Father and Spirit are revealed through the Son by their relation to him and interaction with him. I am not advocating Christomonism.

[2] Dietrich Bonhoeffer, Sanctorum Communio: A Dogmatic Inquiry Into the Sociology of the Church (London: William Collins Sons & Co., Ltd., 1963) p. 126.

[3] Diogenes Allen, "The Paradox of Freedom and Authority," Theology Today, Vol. XXXVI No. 2 (July, 1979), p. 173 (cf. S. K.'s parable in V. Ellers' The Simple Life).

[4] Bonhoeffer, Sanctorum Communio: A Dogmatic Inquiry Into the Sociology of the Church, p. 41.

[5] P. T. Forsyth, cited in Bernard Ramm's Pattern of Religious Authority (Grand Rapids, Wm. B. Eerdmans, 1957, 1959), p. 8.

[6] Martin Luther, "Christian in Society" I, Luther's Works Vol. 44 ed. James Atkinson (Phila: Fortress, 1966), p. 138.

SIX

THE FIRST AND FINAL AUTHORITY

Jesus Christ is the one Word of God who reveals the trinitarian God as the first and final authority. God in Christ is the alpha and the omega of both freedom and authority for man (cf. Rev. 1:8). His Word is the first as well as the final Word which mankind is to hear regarding all matters touching on Lordship. That authority which belongs to God is also that authority which is God. He is Lord, and he is himself authority.

The eternal God is also the eternal authority. He is the alpha and omega of authority in that he is the authority which originates all other authorities (cf. Romans 13) and he is that authority which will, at the end of time, be manifested as the boundary of all those authorities within time. The boundaries thus set by God were revealed in the historical Jesus. Beginning with the facticity of Jesus' very human existence, the Church argued that his Cross and Resurrection revealed and provided meaning to powers and authorities past and future. For the Church today, Jesus' past, in time and space, as terminated and fulfilled in the Cross and Resurrection, now explains his present as Lord over the Church and establishes a goal to the Church's future, namely, his return "in a like manner as he left."

God's primary authority is told in the first chapter of John's gospel: "in the beginning was the Word and the Word was with God and the Word was God." From the start, God's authority, with its attendant power to create and to save, is identified with the Word. This Word is God's own divine self by which he not only created all that exists, but also by which he established his dominion over it. His Word became his rule by gracious command.

The command brought forth a creation obedient to God by its very existence as the response to God's

56

demand. All creation was bounded by God's rule. Accordingly, the command to man must be viewed as given very specifically to *man in creation,* that is, to a created being already obedient by his very being. Man, then, was from the first under the rule of the Word of God and was so quite objectively. Man under God's authority is a given of creation and not a decision by autonomous reason, feeling, or will.

But the Word of God that created man and placed him among all creation addressed him in a particularly significant fashion. In so doing, God also spoke to all creation. Henceforth he would speak to creation only through man. God's first address to man established an *order* in creation. Man was given dominion over the rest of the created order. Thus, while God's first Word, bringing creation into being, set God's rule over all creation, his first Word to man elevated man above the rest of creation; but, as the second part of what God had said, this elevation was only to a place as God's Steward, and not to a rank alongside God himself.

God's authority thus retained its primacy. This primacy extends over the order of creation and also over all manifestations of authority within creation, both those exercised as a part of the natural order itself, and those created by man in his dominion over that order. The fall did not revoke the primacy of God's authority. Instead, it led to God's display of that authority as powerful mercy.

For man, the fall meant a corruption of his Stewardship. An unnatural tyranny by man followed the fall. But this tyranny carried with it the curses of a creation restless in its imposed bondage and in constant rebellious antagonism toward man. Only by the redemptive order is the creative order again glimpsed in its true beauty and harmony. In the redemptive order, creation once more looks in hope to man's salvation as the advent of its own liberation.

The primacy of God's authority has three corollaries to it. The first of these, of course, is also the most obvious: power. This is displayed by God's might, and yet it is also displayed by God's freedom. God's power is his freedom, and his freedom displays its power in God's might. The second corollary is order. This displays itself, not only in creation, but also in those mandates which God has issued in the ordering of man's dominion over creation. This order is itself, in a very important sense, creation. That is to say, God's authority is differentiated, delegated, and diffused in the order that is established by his creation. The third corollary is dominion. This is the Lordship of God over all things, and in a secondary sense, it is the dominion granted to man in the order of creation, as God's steward of all the good things that he has created.

These corollaries have their parallel on man's side. First, and the source of inordinate pride for man, is dominion. But this dominion is not carried out like God's. The Steward has cast off his humble garments for ostentatious rule. Rather than serving God, and even the natural order, mankind lords it over creation. Nor is the Church exempt from such a charge. Her continued rebellion, demonstrated in a widespread passivity to environmental concerns, is a crime against her first vocation given at creation to safeguard the creation of God. The redemptive order in which the Church stands is *not* a separation from the created order to which she also belongs.

The power of man is also all too evident. This power has mocked man's frailty and need for God whenever it has been linked to the enslavement of creation and not its liberation. The more man has changed his environment, the more he has displayed his impotency in insuring his own rule. Again the Church is not blameless. Her own power has too often been used to enslave and not liberate. The redemptive order to which the Church belongs and from which her power comes must express itself in the renewal of the created order.

It should not surprise us, in the light of these things, to find that the things in which mankind glories are its shame. This condition must remain as long as man mistakes his own authority in creation as the primary one. The Church, in relating consciously the redemptive order to the created order, can manifest a servant dominion and humble power that finds its source and boundary in the authority of God's Word.

This authority of God which is before all other authorities, orders and determines all other authorities, gives them their sense, their bearing, and creates their boundaries, is also the final authority. God's authority brings to an end all other authorities, and brings to completion the *telos* or purpose of every authority that there is. This finality of authority is shown again in the existence of God as his own Word, or as Jesus is called, the Word of God (cf. Rev. 1:8, 17:11-16).

As with the primacy of God's authority, so too, with its finality we must look to Jesus Christ. The Jesus of history preached of the advent of the kingdom of God. This rule by God, already intruding into the

58

world in Jesus, was the closing act of God's work. The kingdom of God is the redemptive order reconciled to the original order of creation. The authority of God is, taught Jesus, primal *and eschatological*. The original, pre-existent Word, incarnate in Jesus Christ, discloses the final, fulfilled reign of God.

This name, Word of God, not only means that Word which stands before, but that Word which stands *after*, and in standing after, it is the final Word which is to be heard. Thus, all that is seen and heard as God's "no", both in and outside creation is finally summed up in God's "yes"; a "yes" which contradicts any "no" that man night say, and any "no" that creation might now display in its bondage. This "yes" of the Word of God is an authority which again demonstrates not only its freedom, but its freedom for us, a freedom which moves from freedom toward freedom. For in its finality, this authority brings to creation and man in bondage both freedom and redemption.

This does *not*, of course, mean any necessary "restoration of all things" (*apokatastasis panton*). It *does* mean a restoration of the created order that clearly shows its connection to God's redemptive order. It *does* mean, too, that God's decision overrides all opposition so that all that is just, true, and beneficial for creation and man-in-creation results. God's authority, power, and glory are universally exercised in his dominion, but the finality of his rule also brings with it judgment.

The finality of authority, like the primacy of authority, carries with it three corollaries: The first of these is glory. The splendor of God is seen in the finality of authority. When all has been said and all has been written—when all is completed—then the reign of the glory of God is fully realized. A second corollary is restoration. This is effected not only in creation, but particularly in the reconciliation of God to man. This reconciliation is first the free movement of God to man, and then the gracious invitation to man, by the proclamation of the Church, for men to be reconciled to God. The third corollary of this finality of God's authority is his judgment, which, as is seen from the very beginning (cf. Genesis 3) is mercy. This mercy is again a sign of the gracious "yes" of God in Jesus, who displays his Lordship not only over against man but over against man in order to be *for* man. God's judgment is designed to lead all people to the cross, which is God's salvation (cf. Jn. 12:32).

Seen together, the first and final authority is not

two authorities but one. It is an authority which begins and stands before all other authorities and binds
them at the end of time, and yet continues, however in-
visibly, throughout the course of all time. That is to
say, that authority which from the beginning appeared so
powerful, so reasonable, and so beneficient, will again
appear as such at the end of time. No matter how invis-
ibly it may seem at this time to be that power, that
beneficience toward man, it is, nevertheless, the same
that it was first and finally. No other proof is needed
of this fact than the Scriptural claim in Heb. 13:8 that
Jesus Christ is the same yesterday, today, and forever.

There is a continuity of freedom, of authority, and
of God's people. This continuity is that the free God
who willed to create also graciously established his
authority over all and for all, and who now demonstrates
that most particularly and visibly in his people, but
not for his people alone, but through his people to all
people.

There is an open endedness to this first thesis that
is significant. God's authority is above all authority.
God's authority creates all other authorities. In the
Christological hymns of Colossians 1, and again in the
opening of Paul's letter to the Ephesians, we see that
all authority exists in Christ, is given to him, and his
name is the name that is established above all of these
authorities. The authority of Christ, or his Lordship
extends not only over the Church but through the Church
in benefit of all men, and also through the dominion of
man over all creation. But this authority extended over
all creation not only exists over creation but also *for
creation*. Authority, then, is for the freedom of creation, and against its permanent bondage. This again
calls glory to mind.

The authority of Christ as manifested in the Church
and for man is also an authority for order in creation.
This gives a proper place, although a relative place, to
the theology of the order of creation. In existing for
order in creation, this authority of the Lordship of
Christ stands against chaos. It is, in effect, a restoration of order in creation. Finally, this authority
of Christ in the Church for all men is also an authority
for the dominion of man in creation, and thus, against
the exploitation by man of creation. Exploitation demonstrates the fall and God's righteous judgment against
man, not against creation. That creation suffers as it
does, is not of its own doing, but it is because of man,
who in his dominion has enslaved creation and brought it
into the bondage that man precipitated against himself

60

in the fall.   Yet, God's judgment is seen also as his
mercy,   in that he who subjected creation, subjected it
in *hope*, a hope belonging to man, who, as he awaits his
final redemption in Christ also awaits a glorious release
for creation from its bondage.

SEVEN

THE WITNESS OF THE HOLY SPIRIT TO THE ONE WORD OF GOD

Our second thesis is that *the witness of the Holy Spirit to the one Word of God is, as the inscripturated Word of God, the mediating authority established for man by God.*

We must consider first the witness of the Holy Spirit to the one Word of God. To begin with, there are some important Scriptural data which must be examined with regard to this witness. Preeminently the Scripture on this witnessing ministry of the Holy Spirit is to be found in John 14 — 16. There the ministry of the Holy Spirit is seen predominantly in an objective sense. In John's Gospel the work of the Spirit is not emphasized in its inwardness in the believing community or the disciples. That *will* come later with Jesus "breathing in" the Holy Spirit to the disciples (John 20). But now the emphasis is on that work of the Spirit which comes as he stands outside the believing community, pointing that community to Christ. The key texts from John are these:

> *Jn. 14:15-17* "If you love me, you will keep my commandments. And I will pray the Father, and he will give you another Counselor, to be with you for ever, even the Spirit of truth, whom the world cannot receive, because it neither sees him nor knows him; you know him, for he dwells with you, and will be in you."
> *Jn. 14:25-26* "These things I have spoken to you, while I am still with you. But the Counselor, the Holy Spirit, whom the Father will send in my name, he will teach you all things, and bring to your remembrance all that I have said to you."
> *Jn. 15:26* "But when the Counselor comes, whom I shall send to you from the Father, even the Spirit of truth, who proceeds from the Father, he will bear witness to me . . ."
> *Jn. 16:7-15* "Nevertheless I tell you the truth: it is to your advantage that I go away, for if I do not go

away, the Counselor will not come to you; but if I go, I will send him to you. And when he comes, he will convince the world of sin and of righteousness and of judgment: of sin, because they do not believe in me; of righteousness, because I go to the Father, and you will see me no more; of judgment, because the ruler of this world is judged.

"I have yet many things to say to you, but you cannot bear them now. When the Spirit of truth comes, he will guide you into all the truth; for he will not speak on his own authority, but whatever he hears he will speak, and he will declare to you the things that are to come. He will glorify me, for he will take what is mine and declare it to you. All that the Father has is mine; therefore I said that he will take what is mine and declare it to you."

The Holy Spirit is sent by the Son at his petition of the Father. He comes after Jesus has departed this world. By his presence, the presence of Christ is continued. His work is preeminently a witness or preaching of Christ. This preaching of Christ will strengthen the community and comfort her. At the same time, this work of witness will provide the community with an answer for those times when it is brought before the magistrate and an explanation is demanded for its behavior and speech. This witness will also, at all times, provide a point of revelation to the world displaying God's righteousness and judgment, and making evident to the world its sin. This witness then, is a continuous proclamation undertaken by God himself. The instrumentality of the Holy Spirit's preaching will be what the community produces in its own word, whether written or spoken.

In Paul's writings we find a slightly different emphasis. The witnessing work of the Spirit for Paul is an inward thing. The Spirit is what God has given as an earnest of redemption. He is an indwelling spirit, an internal agent. By the Spirit comes power, the same power by which God raised Jesus from the dead. Through the indwelling of the Spirit, man receives the witness of God to his own relationship with God in Jesus Christ. This Spirit is also a spirit of comfort who preaches Christ, but here the emphasis is on a preaching of the Christ known preeminently by the individual within the believing community. Yet this Spirit is also a spirit who makes his witness and his proclamation of Christ known throughout the community by the gifts that he engenders. These gifts, meant for the upbuilding of the Body of Christ, all find their fulfillment in the proclamation or witness to Christ (cf. Ephesians 4, 1 Corinthians 12, 1 Corinthians 14).

63

The Scriptural data give us an idea both of the *extent*, and of the *character* of the witness of the Holy Spirit. In its extent, this witness is sufficient and concise. In other words, the witness says everything that *needs* to be said in order that the purpose of the witness be accomplished. That purpose is to point to Jesus Christ as the righteousness of God revealed for man accomplishing what man could not accomplish in himself. This is salvation. It is God justifying his own actions with regard to the depravity and the sin of man. The witness of the Spirit, and his preaching, is in this sense completely sufficient. There is no thing lacking necessary for man's salvation. At the same time, this witness is concise. It is to the point, for there is little time for extraneous matters. What is important is the significance of the figure of Jesus. What is important is the justification of the proclamation of the community. What is important is the encounter of this community with its God in Jesus Christ, and the invitation offered in that encounter to the rest of the world to be likewise included in the benefits of God's election.

The character of the witness of the Holy Spirit is objective, hortatory, trustworthy, and sufficient. It will be noted that not only is the extent of the witness sufficient, but its character is also sufficient. That is to say, its character is not exhaustive. It is brief. God, in his Word, says only that which needs to be heard, not all that would be heard, nor even all that one would like to hear, but only that which must be heard.

At the same time, this character is objective. It exists as a given and true reality, independent of what the world or the Church may think, feel, or decide about it. That character is also hortatory in its objectivity, for it is designed for a specific subjective response. This objective character demands of us a decision for it, not against it. It asks of the Church, and of the world, feelings and thinking that bring it into a consonance with Jesus Christ. This hortatory character of the witness of the Spirit is the source of the comfort and courage of the Church in her own testimony.

Finally, this character is trustworthy. By standing on this witness, the Church's own witness is established, and she finds a foundation in Christ that allows her to move steadily against the forces of the kingdom of this world and its prince, the prince of lies. Offering instead of deceit, truth and fidelity, the Church is an instrument of God against which not even the gates of Hades and death stand.

64

The goal or the direction of the witness of God's
Spirit is to the one Word of God. In the pursuit of
this goal the infallibility of the witness is glimpsed.
This infallibility is insured, in part, by the object of
testimony. God in speaking to us about himself, speaks
accurately, fully, and in every way trustworthily. The
infallibility of the witness rests not in the human instrumentality, but in the sovereignty of God. This sovereignty must not be understood statically as it is in
so many theories of inerrancy, but rather, dynamically,
in the continuing movement and freedom of God's Spirit.
He continuously elects faithful words to be his own Word.
He uses the righteousness of men in word and deed to
point, not to the righteousness in itself, but beyond
that righteousness to the righteousness of God revealed
in Jesus Christ.

The nature of infallibility is this: in its testimony, the witness of the Spirit will never lead anywhere but to Christ. No matter what it says, whether it
says it tangentally to the center, or directly to the
center, at all points it leads always, ever toward the
center, which is Christ.

Finally, the witness of the Spirit must be understood in the framework of the importance it achieved in
the time of the Protestant Reformation. The Reformers
all saw clearly the importance of this witness and its
work in establishing the authority of Holy Scripture and
of reviving the Church as a vital, preaching, witnessing
community, a community whose confession had the power to
turn the world upside down. Perhaps nowhere else were
the Reformers, Luther and Calvin, so closely agreed as
in their understanding of this witness of the Spirit.
From both of them, the Reformed and Lutheran traditions
in the creeds of the Reformation period expressed the
importance of this witness and made it clear.

The genius of the Reformation may be seen in that
for neither Luther nor Calvin was the doctrine of the
Spirit's witness a principal thesis from which other
doctrines were to be systematically deduced. Rather,
the Reformers worked from the text of Holy Scripture and
the witness of the Spirit was, as Ramm notes, "incipient
in their original doctrines and emerged at the proper
occasion."[1] The witness of the Holy Spirit was inextricably bound up with Scripture. To the Reformers it was
essential to understand Scripture as both witnessed to
by the Spirit and as *the Spirit's witness itself.* The
witness of the Spirit, therefore, is not something apart
from Holy Scripture. The teaching of the Reformers on
this witness surfaced where and when they expounded the
Scripture concerning this witness.

The Reformers worked in a context where high priority was given to the authority of the Church for religious certainty. Without completely rejecting the authority of the Church, the Reformers appealed to the authority of the Spirit's witness. It was the witness of the Spirit that gave Scripture a place above the Church for both Luther and Calvin.[2] Their understanding was carried over into the early Reformation creeds.[3] Along with the doctrine of the three-fold, one Word of God, the Spirit's witness supplied both an epistemological base for the Reformation and a context for biblically discussing authority.

What happened, then, in the generations after the Reformers? How did it come to pass that the Spirit's witness was again overshadowed in the Church? Ramm has written of the conflict between Roman Catholicism and Protestantism that, "The real life-and-death struggle was at two points: the relation of Scripture to the Church, and the source of the Christian's certainty that the Scriptures are the Word of God."[4] The Reformers developed one line of attack that made the Spirit's witness fundamental. Their successors pursued a different approach. Jack Rogers has observed:

> Calvin died in 1564. By that time the Roman Catholic
> Counter-Reformation had consolidated and focused its
> strength in a rejection of Protestant doctrines at the
> Council of Trent (1545-1563). In response to Trent, the
> second generation of Reformers adopted the methods of
> their adversaries in order to fight them. Post-Reforma-
> tion Protestants tried to prove the authority of the
> Bible using the same Aristotelian-Thomistic arguments
> which Roman Catholics used to prove the authority of the
> church. Melancthon, the successor of Luther, and Beza,
> the successor of Calvin, both endeavored to systematize
> the work of their masters by casting it into an Aristot-
> elian mold. Thus a significant shift in theological
> method occurred from the neo-Platonic Augustinianism of
> Luther and Calvin to the neo-Aristotelian Thomism of
> their immediate followers. A period of Protestant Scho-
> lasticism was thus launched on the European continent in
> the immediate post-Reformation period.[5]

A new context for the Protestant faith, one where the authority of Holy Scripture was pre-eminent, had emerged. But changes in Protestant thinking after the Reformers made inevitable a deemphasis on the Spirit's witness. Ramm has noted:

> Although post-Reformation dogmaticians on both the
> Reformed and Lutheran side carried over the doctrine it
> lost its vitality. The supernatural character of the

Scriptures themselves was so emphasized that the witness of the Spirit seemed to have no proper function. Liberalism had no means of doing justice to this doctrine, for it denied the supernatural revelation and redemption upon which it rests. Fundamentalism was only a step removed from liberalism, for in so emphasizing the verbal inspiration of Scripture and the inerrancy of Scripture it also embarrassed the role of the witness of the Spirit.[6]

From a different angle, Ramm has also observed:

> The subsequent history of the *testimonium* is a mixed one. Among the orthodox it suffered from four things: (i) it became identified with religious experience and so lost its real force as a persuasion; or (ii) in the development of a rationalistic apologetic there was no genuine place left for the *testimonium*; or (iii) a sense of balance was lost and the *testimonium* was interpreted as a formal validation of Scripture, or the validation of theological propositions without proper regard to Christ or salvation; or (iv) there was a failure to see its critical role in theological methodology.[7]

Today, there is a movement to recover the truth of this witness, to understand it again, and to assume for it once again, its proper place of prominence. Understandably, there is significant resistance in several evangelical sectors where Protestant Scholasticism provides the theological backdrop and where biblical inerrancy answers every question. But the wider conservative community, addressed as it is by issues demanding a more perceptive understanding and handling of authority, is returning to the Reformers for guidelines in the current situation. In view of today's impasse in evangelicalism over the issue of biblical authority it seems certain that a reattention to the doctrine of the Word of God and a new prominence for the role of the Spirit's witness must result. Such a move is a positive step in the direction of reformation and renewal in the Church.

[1] Bernard Ramm, The Witness of the Spirit (Grand Rapids: Wm. B. Eerdmans, 1959), p. 24. Hereafter cited as WS.

[2] G. C. Berkouwer, Holy Scripture, trans. Jack Rogers (Grand Rapids: Wm. B. Eerdmans, 1975), pp. 40, 41. Vol. 13, Studies in Dogmatics.

[3] See, for example, The French Confession of Faith (1559), article IV; The Belgic Confession of Faith (1561), article V; The Second Helvetic Confession (1566), chapter one; The Westminster Confession of Faith (1646), article IV.

[4] Ramm, WS, p. 11.

[5] Jack Rogers, ed., Biblical Authority (Waco: Word Books, 1977), p. 29.

[6] Bernard Ramm, A Handbook of Contemporary Theology (Grand Rapids: Wm. B. Eerdmans, 1966), p. 121.

[7] Ramm, WS, p. 26.

EIGHT

THE INSCRIPTURATED WORD OF GOD

The witness of the Holy Spirit to the one Word of God is, as the inscripturated Word of God, the mediating authority established for man by God. Part of the genius of the Reformation and its true heirs lies in the fact that they identified the witness of the Holy Spirit with that witness which is contained in Holy Scripture. This important step did several things in recapturing the spirit of the New Testament period. First of all, it affirmed the Bible as God's own Word. If in fact, the witness of the Spirit, that is, the Spirit's preaching of Christ, is identified with that preaching which occurs in Holy Scripture, then Scripture becomes the instrumentality of the Spirit. It becomes identical with his own Words, and hence, is truly God's own Word.

Any and all other attempts to understand Scripture as the Word of God standing outside this understanding are doomed to a static apprehension of Scripture as God's Word. Such a position in the Church has led often to a host of problems concerning the inspiration and authority of Scripture.

The second important matter established by identifying the Spirit's witness with the witness of Scripture rests in the affirmation of Scripture as the authority above both Church and tradition. This, of course, stems first and foremost from the fact that if Scripture is what God himself says through his continuing present and active ministry by the Spirit, then that Word must reign above the words of men which are established and continue through Church and tradition. And yet, there are three other factors contributing to this affirmation of Scripture as an authority above both Church and tradition. First, Scripture, by both its historical and theological proximity to the events it testifies to, has an accuracy and authority as a witness that no other witness can approach. Second, the authority of Scripture is closed and objective. This closed objectivity restrains the variant whims of the Church in any given time or place. Finally, Scripture has claimed for itself and has had recognized by the Church in every continuing generation the claim for its inspiration, or what might be termed its in-spirit-ation.

The doctrine of inspiration has been understood in more than one manner across the centuries. Some views lead to a very dynamic, continued operation of God's Spirit. Others tend to rest in a closed, static, inerrant document. The latter view has more often than not led to an understanding of the Scriptures as God-dictated words. The former view recognizes fully the free, sovereign act of God on behalf of man, and says that the integrity of man's own words is preserved in the electing by God of those words of men to be his own faithful witnesses. Such an understanding of inspiration as this does not in any way preclude infallibility, but it does argue that the infallibility of the witness rests not with its humanity, but with the electing God. That is to say, the full integrity of man as a fallible being is retained. There is neither glory nor rejection entailed in this. Simply stated, God is the one who chooses who will witness for him and when. This of course, leads to a wide variety of questions regarding both whether the Canon is open or closed, and the relative subjectivity or objectivity of the Scripture itself.

We have already affirmed that Scripture has its authority in part because of its closed objectivity. In regard to its inspiration, this means that God has continued to freely elect the words of Scripture as his own Words. We have confidence that this will continue to be the case. It remains the task of the Church in every generation to hear afresh this Word and to hear in this Word God's own voice. The existence of Scripture as the Word of God, its inspired quality, does not rest on the decision of the Church, however. It rests instead on God's objective decision. Thus, the Spirit continues to speak through Holy Scripture afresh in every generation, and will continue to do so until the return of Christ.

The authority of Scripture must also be directly related to its purpose. The purpose of Scripture, unfortunately, is often neglected or misunderstood, or deemphasized in the contemporary Church. Today there seems to be more attention given to the defense of the Bible (apologetics), or to the interpretation of Scripture, or, finally, to its application. Each of these matters have their place. Interpretation, especially, bears directly on an understanding of the purpose of

Scripture. Thus, for Luther, such things as Gospel and Law, or Justification by Faith, or the Centrality of Christ became important hermeneutical keys. The witness of Christ that Holy Scripture contains was rightly regarded by the Reformers as the singular, preeminent purpose of Scripture. This witness to Christ also explains the existence of Scripture as Canon. This objective standard and measurement evaluates all succeeding witnesses to Jesus Christ that occur in the Church and thus become a part of her tradition.

But what does all this say of the Bible as revelation? The Bible is rightly related to the doctrine of revelation by its name as the Word of God. As we have already seen, it is one of the forms of the one Word of God. It is so legitimately because it is the Spirit's own witness. Of course, the Bible as revelation cannot and must not be understood as such to be identical with that revelation of God which has taken place in Christ. Rather, it participates in that revelation by the close proximity it bears to it, and by its election of God to be the final, authoritative, objective witness to that revelation which occurs in Christ. Expressed somewhat differently we must see that the Bible in its connection to revelation is one with it, but not to be confused with it through fusion. Likewise, the Bible is distinct from that revelation which occurs in Christ, but must not be understood as separate from that revelation.

Finally, with regard to the Scripture's relation to revelation, the sacramental character of the Bible must be viewed. We have alluded to this character before. It means that Scripture, as a form of the one Word of God, is an *act* of God. The Bible carries with it the event of revelation. Revelation comes both *through* and *in* Scripture. By Scripture, God shows himself and brings the Good News of salvation for men and women.

Not everyone in the history of the Church has been agreed that this is truly the character of Scripture. Indeed, Donald Bloesch has written that,

> It is possible to discern three basic approaches to Scripture in the history of the church. The first is the sacramental which sees revelation essentially as God in action, and regards Scripture as the primary channel or medium of revelation. Here Scripture is thought to have two sides, the divine and the human, and the human is the instrumentality of the divine. In this category we include Augustine, Calvin, Luther, Spener, Francke, Jonathan Edwards, Pascal, and P. T. Forsyth. This approach also claims such noted representatives of Protestant orthodoxy as Flacium, Voetius, Gerhard, Bavinck,

71

Kuyper, and more recently Geoffrey Bromiley and G. C. Berkouwer. The second position is the scholastic, which understands revelation as the disclosure of a higher truth that nonetheless stands in continuity with rational or natural truth. The Bible becomes a book of revealed propositions which are directly accessible to reason and which contain no errors in any respect. The humanity of the Bible is regarded as an aspect of its divinity. Here we can list Protestant scholastics, such as Quenstedt, Wolff, Turrentin, and Warfield, as well as contemporaries like Gordon Clark, Francis Schaeffer, Carl Henry, and John Warwick Montgomery. Finally in the liberal-modernist approach revelation is understood as inner enlightenment or self-discovery: in this category are to be placed Schleiermacher, Herrmann, Troeltsch, Harry Emerson Fosdick, Tillich, Langdon Gilkey, Bernard Meland, Gregory Baum, J. A. T. Robinson, and Rudolf Bultmann.[1]

In the light of all this, it is hardly surprising that in our own time there has been much debate concerning the nature of Holy Scripture. Revelation has become a central topic of theological debate, and the authority of Scripture has been both challenged and questioned as rarely before. Indeed, in the sixties and seventies, the authority of Scripture became such an issue, especially within conservative Christianity, that the literature of American theology, and to some extent European, was literally dominated by the topic. Schubert Ogden noted that, "Protestant theologians from the sixties on have become increasingly critical of what James Barr has called 'the modern revival of biblical authority.'"[2] Of course, this is all right with Ogden, whose own position can be summarized by his conclusion that, "there is no sense, finally, in which the canon of Scripture is the sole primary authority for Christian theology any more than for Christian faith and witness."[3]

But Ogden and all who have wrestled with or against him in the liberal camp are hardly alone. The authority of Scripture has reached its most acute treatment in the seventies debate within the evangelical camp. As recently as 1979, Bloesch, a prominent evangelical, wrote, "as we seek to reaffirm biblical authority, there is a need to reinterpret this authority, particularly in light of the present day impasse in evangelicalism on this question."[4] In the light of this, it is not at all inappropriate to suggest that a reformulation of the authority of Scripture be attempted, and subjected to the current analysis both to the right and to the left. Therefore, the following propositions are set forward as guidelines to a reformulation of a statement on the authority of

Scripture.

I have argued for these theses elsewhere,[5] but they belong properly to a discussion of authority, especially that of the inscripturated Word of God. These propositions reject Ogden's pessimism. They offer instead positive steps to reaffirm basic biblical and evangelical convictions without alienating or separating conservative believers. Simply stated, these propositions are:

1. The authority of Holy Scripture is inherent.
2. The authority of Holy Scripture is apparent only within the Church.
3. The authority of Holy Scripture is the witness to Christ for the Church.
4. The authority of Holy Scripture is complete within the Church.
5. The authority of Holy Scripture is given for the proclamation of the Word of God by the Church.

With five such theses, a sound position on biblical authority can be established. This position will be both exegetically logical and evangelically consistent. When viewed as subordinate theses to those we are developing in regard to authority and the Church, it is evident that there is a mutual continuity, and a distinctly supportive character to biblical authority.

The authority of Holy Scripture is inherent. H. Jackson Forstman once remarked how, "Luther knew that believing in an inspired Bible settles no problems. As a matter of fact, it made problems for him."[6] Nevertheless, Luther did not give up inspiration and neither should today's Church. But this proposition embraces a full notion of inspiration, one which addresses not only the strict biblical sense of the term, but also the sacramental character of the Bible and its powerful independence from the necessity of apologetic proofs.

Biblical authority rests not in the Church's ability to demonstrate the logic of Scripture, or the scientific accuracy of Scripture, but in the Bible's own ability to persuade men and women that it bears reliable testimony to the work of God in the person of Jesus Christ. Yet, when we affirm the inherent authority of Scripture, we do not mean that the Bible has a magical quality within it. The inherent authority of Scripture can only mean the authority vested in it by its author, and therefore, the author's own authority. Accordingly, the authority of Holy Scripture rests in the authority of its human composers. But their authority was likewise invested in them by another. That it was God himself who gave them their authority is attested by their own confession and demonstrated by their witness to Christ. But this right and true authority given to them is proved by the witness of God's Spirit who continually testifies to the reliability of both the human testimony and the written record. No apologetic proof can supplant this witness by the Holy Spirit.

The authority of Holy Scripture is apparent only within the Church. If the inherent authority of Scripture indicates its inspiration, that inspiration is only attested by those who see the hand of God at work. Yet, while many admit to a certain degree, at least, of inspiration with regard to Scripture, the authority of the Bible is only functionally evidenced within the Church. Outsiders can cheerfully admit the quality of inspiration but still deny the power of the Bible's authority. Only within the Church does the fact of inspiration find its fulfillment by being coupled with authority. The Church and the world may both call the Bible inspired, but if the world can leave it at that, the Church, faced as it is by the inherent authority of Scripture, must act upon that inspiration by giving reverence to God and submitting to the Gospel.

The Church is marked by its position under God, as the elect of God through Jesus Christ. The authority of Scripture, as the authority of God, is above the Church. The Church's confession of the authority of Scripture characterizes it so that its people are called, not a people of "the book," but *Christians*. This is because the confession of biblical authority is the pointing beyond Scripture to the One who is pointed to by Scripture: Jesus Christ. But because it is only within the Church that God's work in Christ is known effectually, it is only within the Church that the rightful nature and character of Holy Scripture is apparent.

The authority of Holy Scripture is the witness to Christ for the Church. This witness established it above all other inspired men and books. But there are other men and books besides those we know in the Bible who we might call inspired and whose own witness to Christ is both eloquent and accurate. Yet we do not account them as equal to Holy Scripture. We cannot because they are separated from Scripture as secondary witnesses dependent upon a primary one. They lack the *proximity* of the Bible to the Word of God in Christ. Other men and books outside those known to us in the Bible have also been called inspired and have given witness to Christ. These were written at the same time that Holy Scripture was being formed. Some of them even enjoyed brief status as equals with Holy Scripture, as parts of the Bible. Yet

74

these, too, lacked the proximity of the Scriptures which have continued down to us today.

The proximity of the Bible to Christ is not merely a temporal matter, although we must not exclude temporality, since it is a right element in proximity. But it is only one element. Accuracy, or truth, is another element. Only true testimony is acceptable in the Canon. But each of these elements pale in comparison to the actual and final standard of proximity: the witness of the Holy Spirit.

It is because of the presence of God's Spirit in the Church that this community is the sole bearer of the sacred Canon. Holy Scripture is only apparent by the presence of the witness of the Holy Spirit. This witness guided the early fathers so that they were able to discern which books were attested by God as his own Word. This same witness continues to abide in the Church and to certify that the Bible is God's reliable witness to Christ. Because the Holy Scripture exists as a witness to Christ that only the Church can receive—and then only in submission and obedience—it is a characteristic mark of the Church. Its authority over the Church, that is, its existence as Canon, is based in its reliable function as that witness to Christ established above all others. As Canon, as the rule or standard to which the Church must base every final appeal, in at least all matters of faith and practice, the Holy Scripture functions as that authority designated by God as his own Word, his own answer to these matters.

The authority of Holy Scripture is complete within the Church. We may not think that Holy Scripture stands alone as the sole authority within the Church, but we must think of the Bible as the *final* and *sufficient* authority. Other authorities rightly have their place in the life of the Church. The tradition of the Church, including the writings of the Fathers, the decisions of the Councils, the confessions of the Creeds, the teachings of the Catechisms, and the insights of our present scholars all have a rightful place within the Church as guides possessing an authority that is correspondent to their faithful proclamation of Christ. The shepherding of Pastors in the local church life of the Church also carry this authority as those who proclaim Christ and are given the office of leadership. Yet each of these authorities is subject to the standard which measures all authority in the Church, namely, Canon—the Holy Scripture.

Even so, we are satisfied that apart from Creeds, Catechisms, and all other lesser authorities within the

Church, the Holy Scripture is always in itself and by itself the lone, sufficient authority given by God as the authoritative Canon for the faith and practice of the Church. If all we had was Holy Scripture, it would be enough. The Bible, under the witness of the Spirit, who enlivens it and causes it to become the Word of God again and again, is sufficient because it is complete. It is complete because it lacks nothing that is necessary for a man to know and believe concerning the work of God in the history of the man Jesus. The testimony of the Scripture is the testimony of God; this testimony is complete apart from any other testimony.

The authority of Holy Scripture is given for the proclamation of the Word of God by the Church. Earlier we said that the authority of Holy Scripture is the witness to Christ for the Church. We must now underscore this *"for the Church."* The witness to Christ is given to those who not only can but will receive it. It is given for the creation of the Church, its growth, and its sustenance. But beyond these, the witness to Christ that is embodied in Holy Scripture and that constitutes its authority is given for the Church to be used by the Church. Phrased somewhat differently, and more simply, the gift of Holy Scripture is to be used.

The Gospel, as the very power of God, is given a concrete witness in the Holy Scripture and a potentially loud and potent voice in the proclamation of the Church. Necessarily this presupposes the obedience of the Church in faithful and steadfast proclamation of the Gospel as it is recorded in the witness of Scripture. The Church has been commissioned, bestowed with a divine mission; this mission is inseparable from the existence and authority of Holy Scripture in her midst.

The purpose of Scripture is to witness to Christ, but it remains the peculiar character of the Bible that this witness is not fulfilled apart from the work of the Church. The Bible and the Church, the holy ones of God and the Holy Scripture are both of God and exist for one another. Their life is only in Christ. Without this kind of image the Church is faced with fragmentation. When the Scriptures and the Church are placed together—where they belong—they speak with an authority that causes the proclamation of each to be acknowledged as the wisdom and Word of God.

[1] Donald Bloesch, "Theological Table-Talk: Crisis in Biblical Authority," <u>Theology Today</u>, Vol. XXXV No. 4 (Jan. 1979) p. 455.

[2] Schubert Ogden, "The Authority of Scripture for Theology," <u>Interpretation</u>, XXX No. 3 (July, 1976) p. 243.

[3] Ibid.

[4] Bloesch, "Theological Table-Talk" p. 455.

[5] Gregory G. Bolich, <u>Karl Barth and Evangelicalism</u> (Downers Grove: InterVarsity Press, 1980) pp. 201-207.

[6] H. Jackson Forstman, "A Beggar's Faith," <u>Interpretation</u>, XXX No. 3 (July, 1976), p. 276.

NINE

THE MEDIATING AUTHORITY ESTABLISHED FOR MAN BY GOD

The witness of the Holy Spirit to the one Word of God is, as the inscripturated Word of God, the mediating authority established for man by God. We have already considered with regard to this thesis, first, the witness of the Spirit to the one Word of God, and second, the concept of the inscripturated Word of God, that is, the Holy Bible.

Now we must consider the witness of the Spirit and the Bible in their joint function as the mediating authority established for man by God. The need for some mediating authority within the Church has long occupied a place of importance among the Church's theological and practical problems. The question has been phrased in this manner by W. G. C. Proctor., "How is apostolic authority exercised in the post apostolic period? This is the critical issue in modern discussions of spiritual or ecclesiastical authority, which rest on the common assumption that absolute authority belongs to Christ alone and secondary authority to the apostles, but then see this authority exercised today in a variety of ways."[1] To get at this problem it is necessary to see the nature of the Church's original authority structure, and how that has been communicated down through the generations. Admittedly, there have been several perspectives offered by both Protestant and Catholic theologians.

The Scriptures indicate that Christ's authority was conferred to the apostles by the Spirit, both in Jesus breathing on the apostles the Spirit and by the events associated with Pentecost. But how, then, is the apostolic authority transmitted to those who succeed the apostles? This problem was faced by a Church in a sense quite ill-prepared for a continuing existence beyond the first or second generation. The expectation of the imminent parousia dominated the Church in its formative period. But, as this expectation was replaced by the realization that the Church would remain in the world longer than it had originally anticipated, such problems as abiding authority in the Church assumed more and more importance.

Some have suggested that the transmission of apostolic authority is indicated in Scripture by such events as the baptism in the Holy Spirit, or the ordination of office conferred by the laying on of hands, or by inspiration, or by the gift of apostleship bestowed by God's Spirit and recognized among the churches, or perhaps by a simple ecclesiastical election. Thus some might argue that the apostles transmitted their authority to episcopal successors. Others have argued that the Church is itself authoritative. Or that there is some authoritative apostolic tradition that has existed alongside that recorded in the New Testament documents. Thus the first interpretations of the early Church, while retaining a distinctive authority, nevertheless exist beside later, complementary, contemporary expressions of the Church's decisions from age to age. Accordingly, there remains throughout the generations a continuous dialog and interaction of authorities in the Church. All of these can be conceived to be under the direction of the same Holy Spirit.

In light of the fact, as we have mentioned earlier, that the Church is a charismatic institution, it seems wise to return to Weber's understanding of this kind of institution, and the way in which it solves the problem of what happens to the leaderless group. This problem was answered first by the disciples assuming places of leadership when Jesus died. That leadership was conferred by the advent of the Spirit. But what about the problem that remained for the post-apostolic Church? It was, too, in very important senses, a charismatic institution. How, then, were the apostles to be replaced? Weber has listed six principal types of solution to this problem. The first of these is to simply search for a new charismatic leader to replace the old. This could have happened if the disciples had sought a new Messiah figure after the death of Jesus, or it might have happened by the early Church turning from the leadership of the apostles to the leadership of other charismatically gifted individuals.

The second manner of solution involves a revelation by God that is manifested through a technique recognized as legitimate by those who are seeking a successor to the leaders who have departed. Thus, God might have in some manner, perhaps by the bestowal of gifts recognized within the community, or in some other fashion, utilized the search of the Church to hand-pick, as it were, those who would succeed the apostles.

The third manner of solution involves designation by the original of a successor. Thus, those favored by the apostles, as for instance, Timothy and Titus were favored by Paul, would assume a place of great leadership within the community. This is very close to the fourth manner of solution, which is a designation of the successor by the leaders, together with a recognition of these leaders by the community. This solution differs from the third chiefly in that the former might present itself as an imposition of the will of the leader upon the followers without regard to the followers' own desires. The latter not only involves selection by the leader but also consensus agreement by the community.

The fifth manner of solution involves a conception of charisma as a genetic quality transmitted by heredity. Thus, for instance, in Islamic religion, the descendents of Mohammed were those recognized as the leaders of the spiritual community. There is no firm parallel to this in the history of the early Church. Instead, the progeny of the disciples was recognized as a spiritual, and not a physical one. This, then, leads to a sixth principal type of solution where charisma is conceived as a quality ritually transmitted to another person. This would lend credibility to the idea that apostolic authority was conferred by such rites as the laying on of hands, even as the rites of baptism, or ordination to office assumed a role of great importance in the conferring of charismatic qualities to those who received them.[2]

Personal leadership within the Church may have occurred in different location by different of these ways. Thus, for instance, authority may have been conveyed by the operation of inspiration, or by the apostolic gift given by the Holy Spirit, or by the laying on of hands, or by a combination of these things. But ecclesiastical offices, as time went on, became more important as the charismatic nature of the Church gave way to patterns of traditional authority. Also, with the passing of time the role of the Spirit in transmitting authority by way of the Scripture assumed greater prominence.

This process, however, was slow. The Canon of the New Testament, for instance, was not immediately formed. The letters gained acceptance to varying degrees over a period of time. Even a hundred years into the Church's history, the authority, relatively speaking that is, of various New Testament documents was disputed, and not universally accepted. Then, too, as Eusebius records, the oral tradition of the Church retained a great importance

80

within the Church, and in some quarters was quite long in being replaced by the written authority of Holy Scripture.[3] Nevertheless, there came in time to be more and more of an emphasis on the objective qualities of Scripture and the necessity of a fixed Canon whereby all authorities within the Church would be measured and contained.

As this occurred, the importance of hermeneutics, which had existed from the first, assumed an ever more central place. Scripture gained an importance which it maintained despite the gradual political necessity of the central authority of the pope which eventually occurred. Thus, this authority was by no means absent in the time of the Reformation when Luther and those who followed him appealed to the Scriptures against the ecclesiastical and other political authorities.

It was part of the genius of the Reformation that it recognized and assigned such prominence to the role of the Spirit in his transmission of authority by means of Scripture. The solid standard *sola scriptura*, that is, "Scripture alone," expressed the Reformers' conviction of the normative authority within the Church. This authority measures and bounds all other authorities.

The character of this mediating authority has both a vertical and horizontal dimension. Vertically, it is from God to man. That is, Scripture occupies a place beneath God and above man. This has been expressed in theology through such ideas as Gospel and Law, or commandment and promise. In its horizontal dimension, the Bible exists as the word of man among men and women who are equal in Christ. That is, Scripture belongs within the province of the Church. It is, of course, in a historical sense, the product of the Church. Nevertheless, its nature is not confined to a subordinate position by the fact that it was constructed by human hands. For this is a Word which has been elected by God, and as the Church has recognized from the beginning, originated with God. The Reformers saw and made quite clear once again, that the witness of the Spirit in his own preaching of Christ is exactly identical to this witness contained in these written words. Thus, the Scriptures became the means whereby the apostolic authority of the beginning times in the Church continued to exist throughout every generation of the Church.

That apostolic authority first contained within the apostles themselves now came to rest within the words of Scripture. What then is the extent of that authority? Its extent, answered the Reformers, is delimited by its purpose. That is, the authority of Scripture exists in a commensurate degree to its purpose. That purpose is, as Luther expressed it, to point or to witness to Christ. So the Scripture's identity with God as his Word makes its authority equal to his own. The claim that the Holy Scriptures must be an authority established above all human authorities and all authorities within creation is so because this is God's own Word. Being his Word it says that its authority is *his* authority, or conversely, that his authority is *this* authority.

The Scripture's identity with man makes it an authority subordinated to God's. That is to say, although its authority is equal with God, the Bible assumes a place beneath the person of God himself, and the character of God disclosed in revelation in Jesus Christ. The suitability of Scripture to occupy this place as a mediating authority is demonstrated by, first, its divine election. God himself has said that *it* is what he himself has chosen to be the instrumentality whereby he has established an authority for man to abide by. Secondly, as recognized on this side, Scripture maintains a unique objectivity as a historical record and as the confession of the Church that has guided all of the confessions in each successive, contemporary generation.

Thus, we must conclude with two questions put to the Church by Luther. First, "what can the Church decree that is not decreed in the Scriptures?"[4] Second, "does it displease you that anyone should sit in judgment on the decrees of the Church although Paul enjoins it? What new religion, what new humility is this, that you would deprive us . . . of judging the decrees—of *men*, and subject us in uncritical submission— to *men*. Where does the Scripture of God impose this on us?"[5]

These two questions strike at the very heart of the Bible's work as a mediating authority. The mediation is first the delimitation by God of all avenues of access to himself and of all manner of speech and conduct within the Church. Scripture mediates by making clear what comes from God's side and by setting forth what is proper to man's side. It is true mediation in that here God and man meet, albeit on God's own terms.

This mediation is, second, between the Church and the world. Inasmuch as her own members are still in the world, too, the Bible mediates the Church to the Church as well as the believing community to the world outside. Thus the Bible judges the proclamation which daily functions in ruling the Church. The Scriptures keep calling the Church in the world to a being as the Church which is not of the world. This mediation within the community reemphasizes the importance of the Bible's place as

Canon.

This second aspect of mediation is also evident in the control exercised by Scripture over the missionary work of the Church. The Church must speak and act toward the world as the Bible decrees and permits. This means not only an adherence by the Church to the *content* of the Scriptures but also an adherence to its *form*. However, I do not mean Church language punctuated by "thee" and "thou" and "shalt not." Rather, loyalty to the form of Scripture means addressing our generation as each author of Scripture addressed his own time and people. The mediating authority of Scripture demands a contemporaneity of the Church's speech and conduct.

[1] W. G. C. Proctor, "Authority," <u>Baker's Dictionary of Theology</u>, ed. E. F. Harrison (Grand Rapids: Baker Book House, 1960) p. 81.

[2] Max Weber, <u>On Charisma and Institution Building</u>, ed. & intro. S. N. Eisenstadt (Chicago: Univ. of Chicago Press, 1968) pp. 55-57.

[3] This Eusebius cites in his <u>Ecclesiastical History</u>, Vol. I with regard to the testimony of Papias-trans. K. Lake (Cambridge: Harvard Univ. Press, 1965 pp. 292-293).

[4] Martin Luther, "Career of the Reformer" III, <u>Luther's Works</u>, Vol. 33, ed. Philip S. Watson (Phila: Fortress, 1972), p. 22.

[5] Ibid., p. 23.

TEN

THE PROCLAMATION OF THE CHURCH
IN HER ADHERENCE TO THE SPIRIT'S TESTIMONY

The proclamation of the Church in her adherence to the Spirit's testimony, is, as the translated Word of God, the functional authority among God's people. We are now confronted by the place of proclamation in the Church. We have already seen the importance of the Holy Scriptures within the Church as the mediating authority established by God through the witness of his Spirit, and the necessity for hermeneutics thereby created.

Proclamation, like Holy Scripture, is rooted in the one Word of God. More specifically, the origin of the Church's proclamation is in the command of the Lord, and in his example. Not only the Great Commission, but also prior, provisionary commissions are aimed at the spread of the Gospel as the publishing of what God has said and also done. Christ's own public ministry, in which he "went about all Galilee, teaching in their synagogues and preaching the gospel of the kingdom and healing every disease and every infirmity among the people" (Mt. 4:23), becomes the model for the early Church (cf. Acts 3). Thus the legitimacy of Church proclamation was a settled issue from the beginning.

But we must see the need, strongly supplied by the Apostle Paul's argument in Romans, for the place of proclamation. In Romans, Paul insists that the Gospel necessarily involves the need for continuous proclamation in the Church. Proclamation has its proper place within the community of the faithful, first by virtue of its election by God. It is elected by God as his own Word. Proclamation, together with Christ and the Holy Bible, exists as one of the forms of the one Word of God. To be more specific, the proclamation of the Church exists as one of the two elements of the Gospel. Thus, in the New Testament, the Gospel is conceived first as all that God has done in Christ, that is, as an objective reality

85

quite independent of man's thoughts, feelings, or decisions concerning it, but then, second, and perhaps somewhat more subjectively, it is the proclamation by the Church with regard to these events. Without this proclamation, Paul says, the Gospel could not have the power or reality that it does.

The preaching of the Church also occupies a prominent role in redemption (cf. Rom. 10:8—17). In proclamation, a man is confronted by God himself. This is not simply a claim upon man by the conveyance of information about God. It is a confrontation that tells the truth about both God and man. The truth is that man must hear, receive, and gladly embrace the Gospel. A redemptive decision has been made by God who now calls man to also decide. This is Church preaching.

But it is also the witness of the Spirit of God. Through proclamation the Spirit, in his election of the Church's words, takes them as his own, and personally addresses individuals and communities, calling them into an encounter with God wherein a decision is mandated. Proclamation then, occupies a place of centrality to the life and function of the Church. By it, the Church is constituted in mission.

In its assembly, the Church is first and foremost characterized by the preaching of the Gospel. This is the highlight of every assembly of the Church in her worship. The sermon ranks first and foremost among the functions of the assembled Church. This element of proclamation is also seen in the continuing character of the Church's celebration of the sacrament of the Lord's Supper. This is recognized by Paul, when, for instance, in his instruction to the Corinthians he notes that, as often as this is done the Lord's death is celebrated until he returns.

Proclamation also occupies a place of centrality in the life of the Church when the Church is not gathered. When the members of the believing community are not assembled in worship, but are going about their business in the world, their proclamation still constitutes the decisive character of the Church. This is accomplished in her confession of Christ, in her witness to him alone, and in her participation in God's redemptive work.

But we must ask a very important question. What is, in fact, the possibility of proclamation in the Church? As Barth phrased it in the 1920's after the collapse of liberalism, how is it possible that a man commanded by God to speak for God can actually do so? How can a man speak for God? In this connection, Dietrich Bonhoeffer observed that, "even if the man who preaches does not belong to the *sanctorum communio,* and will never belong to it, the fact that he uses and must use the forms developed by the objective spirit means that the Holy Spirit can employ even him as an instrument of his activity."[1]

In other words, the preaching of the Church, while hopefully always involving the faith of the preacher, and the faithful giving and receiving of the believing community, nevertheless does not rest on these being present. This is contrary, of course, to the Catholic notion of the authority of the office of ministry. The possibility of proclamation in the Church rests not with man then, but solely with God. It is the work of God's own Spirit that takes these words and makes them the instrumentality that brings a man into personal encounter with the God of redemption.

The history of proclamation in the Church is the history of the Church itself. In fact, it might be said that the history of the Bible is the history of proclamation, for both Old and New Testaments consist of proclamation. They are to be understood as more than historical records, or collections of ancient documents, whether these be conceived of as saga, legend, myth, or history. They are more, these documents, than poetry and prose. They are, in fact, proclamation: the witness and testimony of believing communities through successive generations to the same God. The character of proclamation as the very lifebeat of the Church was recognized by Jesus himself in discussing with the disciples the inevitability of proclamation, which is founded in confession (cf. Mt. 16:13-20).

The power of proclamation in the Church is such it affects two spheres, bringing them together in the same direction toward God. In the first sphere, within creation, proclamation announces that the creation which is subjected in futility by the fall of man is so by one who has subjected it in hope. Creation awaits the liberation which takes place even in the process of proclamation itself. Through proclamation the created order is brought near to the order of redemption.

This process is facilitated in the Church whenever biblical, Christ-centered preaching addresses, for example, environmental concerns. Such preaching, mostly absent in the conservative community, is not only legitimage, but actually necessary as a part of the Church's missionary vocation. Proclamation addressed to man-in-creation can both awaken so-called "social conscience" and practically apply the Gospel to concrete and urgent matters affecting everyday life. The work of the Church is a promotion of the union (without fusion) of redeemed and created orders wherein there is not two but only one order of authority.

In the sphere of redemption, proclamation announces the glad tidings of freedom to those who are held captive, and in that announcement, actually helps bring it about. In this sphere, Luther was of the opinion that, "in matters which concern the salvation of souls, nothing but God's word shall be taught and accepted."[2] Such a statement presupposes, of course, that other words *might* be taught and accepted. But these other words are foreign to the Gospel and must be resisted. In both redemption and creation, there is only one Word "whom we are to hear, whom we are to trust and obey in life and in death."

The power of proclamation in both of these spheres rests on the legitimate authority behind it. Thus it is of utmost importance that the Church continually be recalled to an adherence in her proclamation to the Holy Spirit's testimony. It is, after all, the power of the Spirit of God that is at work when the power of proclamation is felt. This is most fortunate since it is the Spirit who continually rescues the Church's preaching. By the grace of God the Holy Spirit moves men of faltering lips.

Finally, the propagation of proclamation lies at the heart of the nature of the Church as an outreaching community. Both Israel and the Church have been elected by God, not in an exclusive sense, but in an inclusive sense. This inclusiveness is communicated and made known by the proclamation of the believing community.

Proclamation, then, becomes a principal means of creating and maintaining the unity of the believing community. This is borne out by such Scriptures as Hebrews 13 and Ephesians 4, which link the proclamation of the Word of God quite closely with genuine spiritual leadership, and the maintenance of unity in the Church. Thus, I think it is correct to observe, "when a unity founded on the mission of the church is strengthened by the content of the gospel and actualized by proclamation, an apologetic of the Christian faith surfaces that has no need or use for philosophical hypotheses designed to safeguard the authority of the church's work. An evangelicalism united in the faithful proclamation of Christ need to claim authority, it is authority."[3]

This truth is particularly important to emphasize in today's Church. Apocalyptic and apologetic fevers rage throughout evangelicalism, often overshadowing other important labors, especially with regard to preaching. Even where the subject of proclamation is approached by attention to biblical authority, actual discussions on the place and authority of preaching are usually left aside. A one-sided preoccupation with apologetics vis-á-vis preaching is hardly desirable yet appears to be precisely where the recent past has led us. We all need to be reminded again that apologetics is not the primary mission of the Church. The vocation to which we all are called is the faithful witness to Christ.

The mission of the Church can be variously characterized and summarized. Indeed, all the confessions, catechisms, and creeds of the Church in one fashion or another serve as forms of the proclamation of the Church. Nevertheless, the simplest form, the most fundamental form, and the form by which the Church has been characterized in every generation is summed up in the three word universal confession, "Jesus is Lord!" This confession, Paul assured the Corinthians, can only be uttered under the guidance and power of the Holy Spirit. That is, whenever these words are said, they are words which the Holy Spirit himself agrees with, and that the Holy Spirit himself will and does say.

Therefore, the speaking of this confession does carry in itself an authority and power not confined to ordinary speech. Without at all becoming magic, Christian confession transcends the limitations of mere human speech in its role as God's instrument. By this human language, that most basic and necessary, as well as most powerful of all human facilities is given dignity, meaning, and purpose within God's gracious salvation. Frail and feeble words can, by God's hand, become instruments of reclamation and redemption. So the preaching of the Church, when and as it adheres to God's own sermon, is brought to a practical, functional authority in the life of men and women.

[1] Dietrich Bonhoeffer, <u>Sanctorum Communio: a Dogmatic Inquiry into the Sociology of the Church</u> (London: William Collins Sons & Co., Ltd., 1903) pp. 162-163.

[2] Martin Luther, "The Christian in Society," II, <u>Luther's Works</u>, Vol. 45, ed. Walther I. Brandt (Phila: Muhlenberg, 1962) p. 106.

[3] Gregory G. Bolich, <u>Karl Barth and Evangelicalism</u> (Downers Grove: InterVarsity Press, 1980) p. 180.

ELEVEN

THE TRANSLATED WORD OF GOD

The proclamation of the Church in its adherence to the Spirit's testimony, is, as the translated Word of God, the functional authority among God's people.

We have already observed that a man may speak the words of God quite apart from any inward connection to them. This point is made again by Dietrich Bonhoeffer. Considering the purpose of preaching, Bonhoeffer writes,

> If our starting-point is that preaching has the purpose of working on subjective spirits, subduing them to God's lordship and making them members of the *sanctorum communio*, that it is testimony to Christ, and not to one's own faith, then its effectiveness is mediated by the objective spirit, for it is plain that a purpose can be achieved without the man who is pleading its cause being inwardly connected with it.[1]

Bonhoeffer here retains the necessary emphasis on the objective work of God's Holy Spirit, and the fact that the preaching by men of the Church remains first and foremost the preaching of God's own Word by God's own Spirit. He notes this purpose is to accomplish in those who hear a submission to the Lordship of God, and an inclusion into the community of the faithful. Also he notes that such preaching is, in itself, testimony to Christ. This testimony is not self-directed, towards one's own faith, but is directed toward the object of that faith, namely God. Nevertheless, while the efficacy of preaching rests with the objective Spirit and not with the one who preaches, it is still true that within the Church, the necessity of a faithful congregation, and the necessity of a faithful preacher are not minimized.

Indeed, as we consider specifically the nature of the translated Word, we find that God has granted a prominence and importance to the work which is involved by

91

man in the task of preaching. Jean-Jacques Von Allmen, in his book, <u>Preaching and Congregation,</u> notes in a chapter on "The Two Poles of Preaching," that there are five theses that must be respected with regard to this translated Word of God. These are:

> *First,* if God speaks, it is in order that He may be understood. *Second,* the Word which God spoke to the world was spoken in another language and in another time than our own; it is, therefore, our duty to translate it and make it present. *Third,* the text of the Word which we have to translate and make present is preserved in Holy Scripture, the canonical witness of the apostles and prophets. *Fourth,* to translate the Word we must know two languages; to make it present, we must know two epochs. This knowledge cannot be achieved without love. Finally, *fifth,* without the work of the Holy Spirit, the Word which God has spoken to the world in His Son cannot be effectively translated or made present.[2]

In the light of these theses, and in the light of the reality of the necessity of translating God's Word to succeeding generations within the Church and outward to the world in a variety of cultures through time and space, it becomes indispensable that the Church turn her keenest attention to the matters of the translation of the biblical documents and to their right interpretation. Thus, hermeneutics involves two elements: translation, which to some degree will always involve commentary, and the work of exegesis.

In turning our attention first to the nature of the task of translation, there are several important matters which must be noted. Primary, of course, are the very basic problems confronting the translator. First of all he must know the language. This is rather self-evident. But, in knowing the language, one must know that language in terms not only of exact equivalents to words, but also idiomatic phrases, the complexities of grammar, and the usage of different terms, phrases, and thought patterns at various times in the culture in which that language grew and developed. This, then, means that the work of the translator is also the work of one who must engage in exegesis and commentary.

As Nida has pointed out, "in trying to interpret the meaning of an ancient document, one must attempt to see it in terms of that particular historical period in which it carried the message which one now wishes to reproduce."[3] Nida also notes that, "perhaps some of the greatest difficulties in Bible interpretation have arisen not from a proper application of exegesis, but from a

92

tendency toward eisegesis, that is to say, a tendency to read into the text more than is actually there. Personally I feel quite certain that St. Paul would be astounded to know about the variety and extent of interpretations which people have seen in his writings."[4]

Fortunately, the very nature of the task of translation imposes such strict bounds upon the translator that his possibility of rendering the text so as to irretrievably damage its meaning is virtually excluded. The words are there and they must be translated. But the words themselves impose bounds upon the translator which effectively hinders too radical interpretation. This is not to say that translators have not completely missed the meanings of words, or cannot; but there is a safety margin present in the texts themselves which can assure and comfort the believing community as scholars responsibly undertake the task of interpretation through translation.

The existence of many varied translations of the Bible into English, for instance, should not imply to the community that the task of translation is either hopelessly arbitrary, or subject to complete freedom. Rather, the believing community should be grateful for the receipt of so many translations that have resulted from loving labor, and careful attention by scholars dedicated to reproducing as closely as possible all of the eternal message of God's Word in contemporary forms. The task of translation undertaken by these men is not to overturn any earlier works, as for instance the venerated King James Version, but rather to update these versions on the basis of more complete evidence and thus more effectively communicate in contemporary terms God's truth. By this, people, in hearing and receiving that truth, may have their own lives brought increasingly into conformity with the Word of God.

The propriety of discussing both translation and exegesis with regard to the authority of proclamation should be obvious. These labors provide the connection between the Bible's mediating authority and preaching's functional authority. Translation and exegesis undergird the legitimacy of any given proclamation in the Church. They carry an authority of their own derived from their position between the Bible and proclamation and their identity in union with both. Thus it is not improper to seek and to speak of "authoritative" versions of the Bible, or "authoritative" exegesis.

Exegesis must be viewed in much the same manner as translation. Those who translate the Scriptures, and those who interpret them, either through their work in the pulpit, or the production of commentaries, or in the teaching of classes, have one and the same goal. They aim to bring the Word of God to the individual in his own concrete historical situation. It is the central task and purpose of hermeneutics, and its principal problem as well, to bridge the historical gap of time and space between the original writing and hearing of that Word and the contemporary translation and hearing.

Unfortunately, it must be said from the first that not all who practice the work of exegesis or the work of translation are responsible in their efforts. There are those who, in their interpretation of Scripture, employ quite suspect models of exegesis, and whose motives are less than pure. There are many who, in the interest of one thing or another, have perpetrated an irresponsible treatment of the biblical texts, and in so doing have lead the flock of God astray. The Scripture contains abundant warnings about such men and their practices. Nevertheless, hermeneutics must be regarded as a necessary and a possible task. Exegesis can be done and can be done responsibly. The need for exegesis is indisputable and indispensable.

I would not wish to deny the possibility that an individual can gain a sufficient knowledge of Scripture simply through the reading of a sound translation of the Scriptures. Nevertheless, it must be observed again that even in such an act exegesis, or commentary is involved. If this is true, then one need not fear seeking responsible exegesis, for such exegesis will add to his knowledge, his apprehension, and his understanding of any given text. To be sure, once again we must note that not all exegesis is sound, nor is even sound exegesis able to guarantee that all of its results will remain undisputed throughout the course of time. Exegesis, like the work of translation, has grown and developed over the years. As new evidence presents itself, understanding of the text can be advanced.

There are problems, of course, involved in exegesis, Perhaps the problem which presents itself first, and yet is perhaps (at least in Protestantism), not often considered as a problem, is what Luther pointed out, namely, no sole authority for interpreting Scripture is substantiated in Scripture.[5] God has not ordained one infallible interpreter of Scripture. Thus, Protestantism has rejected the Catholic notion of the infallibility of the pope when he speaks in his official capacity as Peter's successor. Rather, Protestantism, from Luther on down, has always held to the necessity of individual study of the Scriptures with a diligence that produced a variety of biblical scholars and a variety of systems and conclusions of interpretation.

Does this, then, mean that there is more than one interpretation to a text of Scripture? No. Rather, all those who do their work as responsibly as possible can argue, and argue rightly, that there is only one interpretation of the text, although the apprehension of that one right interpretation, because of the problems presented in the work of exegesis, may not always be certain. By and large, however, the interpretation of the text of Scripture is something that scholars can agree on. It is principally in the area of finer points of exegesis that there is room for great debate and controversy. Nevertheless, this need not discourage those who embark in the work of exegesis. Rather, they may delight themselves in the diversity and find satisfaction in the labors of those who, with great diligence, have pursued the knowledge of the Word of God.

Exegesis involves its workers with several presuppositions. When one comes to the Bible, he or she necessarily brings certain presuppositions. This is not, in and of itself, a bad thing. These presuppositions, in fact, may be divided into two classes. There are, first, those which are both unnecessary and undesirable. These are also, quite unfortunately, often unavoidable. In other words, we are all very fallible, and often unaware of pre-determinations in studying the Bible. We may inadvertently bring some undesirable prejudice to the text. The best hope here is to come to Scripture in humility, and in complete dependence on God's Spirit. Then, too, as prejudices are brought to awareness, they must be forcibly ousted.

The second class of presuppositions is of those that are both very necessary and desirable. First among these, of course, is our presupposition that Jesus Christ stands at the center of Scripture and the purpose of the Scripture is to point us to him. Unfortunately, this presupposition often appears quite avoidable. It is often strenuously ignored; but it is this presupposition that gives us rightful confidence. This confidence is our assurance that God's Spirit *does* teach (1 Jn. 2:20-22, 1 Co. 2:9, 10), that Christian confession *is* the Holy Spirit's testimony as well, and that the Church *is* in one voice with God, the apostles, and prophets when she declares with Scripture that Jesus Christ is Lord.

It is best to keep presuppositions as few as possible since the scientific nature of the investigation of the Bible must allow one to hear Scripture on its own

terms.   If the witness is reliable, it must be heard.
At the same time, it can and should be maintained that
presuppositions are to be found even in Holy Scripture.
Christians presuppose the presence of Christ precisely
because he is there, and they continually run full tilt
into his presence whenever reading Scripture rightly.
The laws of interpretation are, therefore, themselves
suggested by Scripture as it presents itself as an object of inquiry. Students of the Bible put questions to
it in order to hear it.   In all of this, however, no one
may become a judge of the Bible, for that is certainly
not science at its best.   All must remain learners and
importantly, learners judged by Holy Scripture.   There
is no room, then, for that superficial coming to Scripture which is often (and wrongly) called   "devotional"
reading and study.   Truly devotional reading and study
of Scripture is, as the dictionary puts it, a "zealous
attachment" to the Bible that will not let go until the
text has spoken, and had its complete say, to the very
limit of one's present ability to hear and receive, and
not to the limit of what one is willing to give in a
"quiet time."   There must be no question whatsoever as
to who submits to whom: Christians must submit to the
Bible and be captured by it until it lets them go.

The Church recognizes that she must come to Scripture in faith, with humility and with confidence,   in
glad commitment, doing her best to hear the Word.   If
there is no gladness, there is no rightness in her approach—for she is come to hear the Gospel, the Good
News.   She must hear it in gladness, and serve God with
great joy and thanksgiving, or she does not hear it properly.

Proper use of the Bible also must distinguish between interpretation and application.   The former aims
at explanation, while the latter intends an administration of the meaning. Thus, interpretation is the setting
forth of the meaning of the text as intended by its author.   The interpreter seeks to understand the message
in the same way the writer did.

Application is the appropriation of the meaning so
that it has unique and particular relevance to the one
receiving the message, but not so as to in any way dis-
tort the original meaning.   There are right and wrong
applications, just as there are right and wrong interpretations. But while there can be only one right meaning for any text, there well may be more than one right
application for any given text. The test of an application is whether or not it reflects an appropriation of
the author's meaning in such a way as to produce faithful

96

obedience in the personal setting of the hearer. This obedience is correspondent to the faithful obedience produced in the hearers of the original message, and that intended by the author.

Interpretation is the author's meaning addressed to the community and each individual, and so understood as the author intended; application is the author's meaning appropriated in a manner agreeable to the author's intent. Interpretation and application are in union without fusion, and distinct but not separate. No one has rightly interpreted Scripture without application, and there can be no right application apart from interpretation; but the two are not the same. Speaking as confessors of Christ Jesus, and from this unique perspective, it must be said that interpretation *points* to Christ, application *moves* toward Christ.

The Church continually reviews her work by the most fundamental laws of interpretation. The foundation for these is the Christian presupposition that Christ stands at the center of the Bible and that the Scriptures seek to direct all to him. As Luther put it, Scripture must be read, "in favor of Christ." This can *never* mean reading Christ into the Scriptures! Accordingly, as Luther so rightly saw, the first law which corresponds to this first presupposition is that Scripture interprets Scripture (*Scriptura sui ipsius interpres*). The witness must speak for itself. If anyone would find Christ, it must be because he is there. The self-interpreting character of the Bible was the reason Luther insisted that each believer interpret the Holy Scriptures for himself rather than allow the Church to determine this for the believer. Of course, Luther did not mean what he is often thought to have meant, namely, that "my interpretation is just as good as yours, so let's both be right, shake hands, and go our separate ways." Luther demanded that every believer study the Bible for himself so that it might be manifest most clearly that the Holy Scriptures have but one meaning, and each must relate correctly to it, both as individuals as well as as the Church.

The self-interpreting character of the Scriptures means, then, that the Bible must be interpreted according to its literal sense. This does not, of course, mean that when the text speaks of hills clapping their hands, that the mountains in Judah actually did so. On the contrary, the literal sense means the ordinary sense, that is, the sense which is normally indicated by the terms when used in that particular fashion. In this way, one can treat metaphors as metaphors, parables as parables, and so forth.

Several interpretive laws follow from this. First, interpret the whole of the Bible by its every part, and every part by the whole; second, interpret every part within its proper contexts; third, interpret the Old Testament in the light of the New Testament; and fourth, interpret the less clear from the perspective of the more clear. Each of these laws shows the self-interpreting character of Holy Scripture, and in fact, they overlap each other.

The utilization of these laws in a proper fashion calls for an unyielding self-discipline. There is no short-cut to proper understanding. The task of interpreting Scripture demands patient, careful attention. Scripture will prove itself clear, coherent, and cohesive, if it is attended to fully, with patience and close attention.

I do not wish to deny that the interpretive process is aided by the abundance of tools which can be brought to it. Knowledge of the original languages, of textual criticism, of higher criticism, of sophisticated techniques to uncover the author's situation--all these are helpful. But no person may be excused by lacking one or the other, or even all of these tools. The Scriptures are given so that each may be pointed to the Lord Jesus Christ. None need fear that the Bible will fail to do this, if only there is a commitment in faith to God's Spirit, coupled with diligent labor in study. God has given to each the capacity to work with patience, and in humble dependence, from a distinctive confessional standpoint.

Faithful exegesis not only produces results that are desirable within the community of faith, it also carries with it a certain weight of its own authority. This weight must not, as the temptation often presents itself, be used as a club. The right interpretation of a passage of Scripture must not be used for less than noble means. The task of exegesis, like that of dogmatics, presents itself in the service of the Church, not the overmastering of the Church by any one individual or group. Thus, the authority of exegesis is, like the authority of Jesus Christ himself, the authority of a servant, who in seeking to serve the Church, upbuilds her.

Hermeneutics carries with it not only the task of interpreting the Word of God and making it present so that it might be understood, but also the task of application. The cruciality of application cannot be either underestimated or underspoken. The need for application is, of course, self-evident. Without application, the message of Scripture, no matter how well understood, fails to produce the kind of righteousness in human behavior that is well fitted, and formed to the image of God in Christ, with which believers find themselves marked by God's action through his Spirit.

There are problems with application as well. Not all applications are right ones. There is the need for careful attention to the applications made, that they flow fittingly from the text of Scripture. As with exegesis, there are certain presuppositions that must be carefully adhered to. Again, first and foremost, all applications must be designed to lead the believer toward Christ. In fact, any application which does not lead the believer in this direction is a wrong application. But there are applications which, in their phrasing, may lead a believer in such a direction that movement toward Christ is far from evident. Thus, it is the responsibility of all who study Scripture to apply their understanding to themselves in such a fashion that there is a genuine, discernable movement toward Christ, a movement made evident and well understood.

Good application will show itself in the practical means of confession and love toward one another in the Body of Christ, and also toward those outside the Church. These are the results of right application: first, the confession of Jesus as Lord. Second, demonstrable actions of love. Application may be seen in the areas of both identity and vocation. First, one's identity is as a Christian, and second, one's vocation is in the service of the Church, and through the Church to the world as part of God's redemptive work.

There is an authority, too, to application. Indeed, it is the most concrete and immediate of authorities in that it calls for an instant personal accountability. The one who hears the Word must do it. The application of the Word thus has in it both the authority of promise to those who obey, and judgment to those who rebel. But this authority, like the authority of exegesis, is relative. It, too, is an authority that displays itself like the authority of Christ--in service, not in self-exaltation. Indeed, it is he who humbles himself who finds himself glorified by God.

Finally, in considering the translated Word of God, we are brought inevitably to the relationship of the Word of God in Holy Scripture to the sacraments of the Church, baptism and the Lord's Supper. These sacraments are preaching too. They likewise are a translation of the Word of God in every generation. Thus, baptism and the Lord's Supper are physical acts where God communicates grace to his believing community. They act continuously to preach Christ, and serve to preach Christ precisely in this sacramental fashion, that brings this Word of God, this one Word who is Jesus Christ, into immediate, existential presence and encounter with the believing community.

Accordingly, the sacraments also enjoy an authority in the Church as instruments of the Word. As translators of this Word, they belong to both Scripture, and more particularly, to proclamation. Together with translation and exegesis, especially as these are joined in the sermon, the sacraments guide the whole life of God's people, teaching, sustaining, and moving them toward Christ.

[1] Dietrich Bonhoeffer, <u>Sanctorum Communio: A Dogmatic Inquiry in</u>to the Sociology of the Church (London: William Collins Sons & Co., Ltd., 1963) p. 162.

[2] Jean-Jacques Von Allmen, <u>Preaching & Congregation</u> (Richmond: John Knox Press, 1962) pp. 20-31.

[3] Eugene A. Nida, "Issues & Insights in Bible Translating," <u>Theology News & Notes</u>, (March, 1977) p. 5.

[4] Ibid., p. 3.

[5] Martin Luther, "Christian in Society" I, <u>Luther's Works</u> Vol. 44, ed. James Atkinson (Phila: Fortress, 1966) pp. 133-137.

TWELVE

FUNCTIONAL AUTHORITY AMONG GOD'S PEOPLE

*The proclamation of the Church in its adherance to
the Spirit's testimony, is, as the translated Word of
God, the functional authority among God's people.* We
have seen both that the proclamation of the Church is
the Spirit's own testimony, and that this Word of God
needs to be translated in successive generations of the
Church. Now we must turn our attention to the fact that
this translated Word of God is the functional authority
among God's people. This brings us to a careful attention to the problem of the Sermon. Dietrich Bonhoeffer
observed that, "in the sermon, God's claim of authority
is made plain to his congregation. The congregation is
the society of authority. But the preacher himself does
not have this authority—this belongs to the Word which
he speaks."[1] Or again, "the church rests upon the Word.
The Word is the absolute authority present in the church.
It is indeed present only in the word of the church,
that is, in represented, relative authority, but it is
still the norm directing the church, in accordance with
which the church also 'directs itself.'"[2]

The functional authority of preaching in the Church
is in making mediated authority present and relevant.
There are two elements to this that must be noted carefully. First, proclamation dynamically retains the original, charismatic presence of Jesus Christ. Proclamation
as the Word of God is God's own Word, God's own presence
among his people. This is why, as Bonhoeffer observed,
the congregation may be called the society of authority.
In this society where the authoritative God is present,
authority is present also. The preacher, though, is not
the one who has this authority. The Word which he bears,
that is, *God's* Word, is this authority. Thus, the problem of the continuing authority of the Church from the
apostolic to the post-apostolic period was answered in
part, not only by Scripture, but also by the proclamation

102

of the Church. This proclamation being identified with the Spirit's witness meant that the presence of Jesus Christ himself through his Spirit would continue. Additionally, proclamation together with dogmatics contemporizes the eternal address of God to man so that it is both personal and relevant to all those who hear it in every generation.

Proclamation has the responsibility, together with dogmatics, of making this Word a translated Word of God. When this Word is translated, it becomes a truly functional authority, and not an authority which operates either hiddenly or obscurely. Proclamation serves as a primary function of authority in an important manner through becoming the basis of leadership in the Church (cf. Hebrews 13). Again, two elements must be observed: first, God's Word is the instrumentality of leadership, and it is intimately linked to unity; second, the role of spiritual gifts is tied closely to their function with regard to this proclamation of the Word of God. This role of gifts and their differentiation is a distinction in the midst of unity (cf. Ephesians 4). With regard to the specific offices of the Church, and those who fulfill them, Luther noted that, "these are the men whom Christ called his officials and council. They administer the spiritual rule; that is, they preach, and they care for the Christian congregation."[3] This emphasis on a functional rule by proclamation is quite in keeping with the New Testament.

Again with regard to such leaders, Luther observed, "now Christ did not mean that we should listen to them in all they say and do, but only at such a time when they present his word to us, the gospel, and not their own word, his work and not their own work. Otherwise, how could we know whether their lies and sins were to be avoided? There must be some rule as to what extent we are to hear them and follow them. Such a rule can not be established by them, but must be imposed upon them by God, a rule by which we can direct ourselves . . ."[4]

Accordingly, proclamation as the functional authority among God's people means, in part, integrity in the vocation of leadership. Yet Christian leadership must bear the character that Luther so clearly saw when he said,

> (A)mong Christians there shall and can be no authority; rather, all are alike subject to one another . . . . Among Christians there is no superior but Christ himself, and him alone.
> What then, are the priests and bishops? Answer: their government is not a matter of authority or power,

but a service and an office for they are neither higher nor better than other Christians . . . Their ruling is rather nothing more than the inculcating of God's word . . . for Christians must be ruled in faith, not with outward works.[5]

Perhaps with Hebrews 13 in the back of his mind, Luther advised leaders in the Church to "remember that you must take the lead and conduct yourselves in such a way that your life can be an example to the people and that they can follow in your footsteps."[6] Then again Luther said, "a pastor must not only lead to pasture by teaching the sheep how to be true Christians: but in addition to this, he must also repel the wolves, lest they attack the sheep and lead them astray with false doctrine and error."[7] Obviously, this is to be done by the ministry of the Word of God.

Proclamation as the functioning authority in God's Church is, as Luther in agreement with the New Testament saw, indisputably tied to truth. In fact, through even casual observance of the New Testament, continued exhortations to avoid futile disputations and endless and meaningless controversies are obvious. Believers are rather to dedicate themselves to true sayings, not in the interest of sterile orthodoxy, but rather in the interest of propagating the dynamic ministry of inculcating the Word which produces faith in those who hear it (cf. Romans 10). Proclamation is not a witness to oneself, but is, rather, a pointing to the one whose name is told in the most basic of all proclamations, the confession, "Jesus is Lord!"

Leadership is, in its most fundamental characteristic, witnessing leadership. True leadership within the Church is by those who take the front in standing forth in Christian testimony. This witnessing character keeps the nature of leadership in the Church linked to the servant manner of the Lord Jesus. The Church knows not only the service of those who are following, but also the subordination of her leaders to the Word which they proclaim. In this subordination their function is described by the New Testament as setting an example for those who follow.

Thus, Luther could note, "Scripture makes all of us equal priests, . . . but the churchly priesthood which we now separate from laymen . . . is called "ministry" (ministerium), "servitude" (servitus), "dispensation" (dispensatio), "episcopate" (episcopatos), "presbytery" (presbyterium) in Scripture (II Tim. 2:24). Here he (St. Paul) calls Timothy a servant of God in the special sense of preaching and spiritually leading the people . . . .

104

In I Corinthians 4 (:1), 'Dear brethren, we do not want people to regard us as more than servants of Christ and stewards of his spiritual goods.'"[8]

In all of this, there must be a constant retention of the fact that among God's people proclamation as a functioning authority means not only an integrity in the leadership, but also an agape submission by the people. Luther described this submission in various ways. He says, for example, that, "where you see that your neighbor needs . . . there love constrains you to do as a matter of necessity that which would otherwise be optional and not necessary for you to do or to leave undone."[9] Again Luther writes, "a Christian should be so disposed that he will suffer every evil and injustice without avenging himself; neither will he seek legal redress in the courts but have utterly no need of temporal authority and law for his own sake. On behalf of others, however, he may and should seek vengeance, justice, protection, and help, and do as much as he can to achieve it."[10]

Luther recognized that temporal authority is instituted for the protection of the people and the control of evil. Christians, though, do not need this, because they are, by the fact that they are Christians, bound by grace, which demands much more than temporal law demands. It demands love. Therefore, Christians look out for the good of their neighbors, not their own good. The Christian will suffer injuries because his concern is for the other person. However, he does not allow injustice to proceed against another person because of that same love for others. Christians support the institution of government because it is God's will, and because in supporting it, they look out for the interests of others. This looking out for the interests of others might be an adequate summary of what Paul says in Romans is the essence of the law; loving one another, or what Luther summarized in this simple statement: "everyone is under obligation to do what is for his neighbor's good . . ."[11]

If being a good neighbor is desirable for all, it is essential to leadership. But this involves service both by the leaders and those who follow. Luther, in commenting upon the discussion of leadership in First Peter, addressed both leaders and those who follow in God's Church. He observed that, "those who are young obey those who are old, in order that those who are in a subordinate position may always humbly obey those who are above them . . . . Such old people should be endowed with knowledge and understanding in the Holy Spirit . . . . . If they themselves are fools and understand nothing, no good government will result . . . . . If they have understanding, it is good that they rule the youth."[12]

Again, Luther wrote, "those who are young should be subject to those who are old, yet in such a way that the latter, who are above the former, do not consider themselves lords but deign to obey if a younger person happens to have more understanding and knowledge."[13]

Agape submission among God's people to the functioning authority of the Word of God is seen in, first, consent to the truth. This is carried forth by a joining of the people in a united confession of the Word of God. Second, submission comes in considering and following the example of those leaders who show their leadership by presenting faithfully the Word of God. Individuals must follow their example by a responsible submission to the Word, not blind loyalty to their leaders. The Church requires a responsible obedience to the Word of God that is borne by the leaders to be a people under God's commandment and promise. This means that rightly regarded leadership in the Church, that is, agape submission, is leadership which looks beyond self-service to the respectful submission of those whose own lives is marked by a service to the Word of God, and a burden of bearing that Word before, and to, all who are in God's Church.

Finally in this regard, it is well that we consider this comment by P. T. Forsyth on the ministry:

> The Church provided and provides the *personnel* for an institution already created for it by God's Spirit. And it modified its form. It did this as the need arose for filling a place that could strictly never be filled again—the place of the apostles, whose companying with Christ, and their gifts of normative revelation from Him, had been quite original, unique and historically intransmissible. The strict successor of the apostle is the New Testament, as containing the precipitate of their standard preaching. It is not the ministry that is the successor of the apostolate, but the ministry *plus* the true apostolic legacy of the Bible—the ministry *of the Word*. The ministry is the successor of the apostles only as the prolongation of their Bible—as the nervous system spreads the brain. The ministry of the Word is, therefore, not a projection or creation of the Church. The authority of the ministry is not drawn from the Church—only its opportunity is—else the message of the Word would be no message to the Church but only its soliloquy, the Church calling to its own soul, "Bless the Lord, O my soul"; and not the Church receiving the call and Word of God. What does come from the Church is the recognition of an authority it cannot confer, and the provision of opportunity. The word authority is ambiguous. It

may mean the ultimate equipment, commission, and *elan* by the Spirit, or it may mean the license given by the Church, and its call to exercise the gift in its midst— especially for life. In ordination the two things must meet—the man's call (not by religious sensibility but *by the gospel*) and the Church's seal of it—the authority of the Spirit in the man, and the recognition of it by the Church. There is the creative and sacramental authority, and there is the judicial and licensing authority.

The Protestant minister is a surrogate of the apostles rather than their successor. But it *is* in the wake of apostles that he stands, with their soul in his as the Bible is in his hand. His effectiveness is therefore apostolic in its kind. It lies in what made an apostle an apostle—in the gospel as an act and power of person on person. It is evangelical. He is a successor of such apostles functionally if not canonically, evangelically if not statutorily. The apostles appointed no canonical successors. They could not. They were unique. Through personal contact, they had been trained by the earthly Christ for witness, and endowed with a fontal power of interpreting Him. That was their prerogative. But the apostolate in that limited sense died with the last of them. It was by its nature incommunicable. Christ gave no canon for its perpetuation. The ministry was an ordinance of Christ rather than an institution, with the atmosphere of a gift rather than the regulations of a fiat. Christ ordained a ministry, the Church ordains ministers. And the expectation of a near *parousia* made a scrupulous provision for successors to the apostles seem unnecessary; the necessity only arose when that expectation died away, and some substitute had to be found for apostles now gone. The apostles could not send as they had been sent by Christ.

The ministry is, therefore, not the canonical prolongation of the apostolate any more than the Church is the prolongation of the incarnation. The Church is the product of the incarnation, and the ministry is a gift to the Church. It is not the prolongation of the apostolate but a substitute, with a like end, and on its base. The prolongation of the apostolate and legatee of its unique authority (I have said) is the New Testament, as the precipitate of the apostolic preaching at first hand. This is the minister's charter. The apostolic continuity is in the function, not in the entail; in the eternal Word proclaimed, not in the unbroken chain prolonged. It is in the message, not in the order of men. A hitch in the conveyancing therefore matters nothing. The apostles were not chosen by the Church, but when they died out a ministry arose which was; and which, under different conditions, performed the like function of preaching, spreading, and consolidating the gospel as interpreted by the apostles once for all. Christ chose the apostles directly, the ministers He chose and chooses through the Church. The Church does not always choose right; but then Judas was in the twelve. The apostolate was not perpetuated, and certainly not self-perpetuated; but it was replaced by another instrument for the same purpose at the motion of the same Spirit. It was replaced not by a prolongation but by a mandatory to administer its trust—by the minister of the Word. For that Word the apostles had authority by a unique call direct from Christ but mediated through the Church and repeated generation after generation—the function of being the living sacraments of a gospel the apostles gave.[14]

The minister, *because of the sermon,* because of the office and vocation of proclamation enjoined upon him, occupies a position of tremendous responsibility. But this need not be a singular responsibility. Proclamation ought to be a work shared by all. Those who, by God's grace, excell in this work should lead God's Church and "receive honor" (1 Tim. 5:17). The functional authority of the Church rests in the work of God's Spirit, and because it does, the work of men and women in the Church is freedom in humility and love.

[1] Dietrich Bonhoeffer, <u>Sanctorum Communio: A Dogmatic Inquiry into the Sociology of the Church</u> (London: William Collins Sons & Co., Ltd., 1963) p. 165.

[2] Ibid., p. 173.

[3] Martin Luther, "The Catholic Epistles," <u>Luther's Works</u> Vol. 30 ed. W. A. Hansen (St. Louis: Concordia, 1967) p. 132.

[4] Martin Luther, "The Christian in Society" I, <u>Luther's Works</u>, Vol. 44 ed. James Atkinson (Phila: Fortress, 1966) p. 52.

[5] Martin Luther, "The Christian in Society" II, <u>Luther's Works</u>, Vol. 45 ed. Walther I. Brandt (Phila: Muhlenberg, 1962) p. 117.

[6] Luther, <u>Luther's Works</u>, Vol. 30, p. 137.

[7] Ibid., p. 135.

[8] Martin Luther, "Church and Ministry" I, <u>Luther's Works</u>, Vol. 39 ed. Eric Gritsch (Phila: Fortress, 1970) p. 154.

[9] Luther, <u>Luther's Works</u>, Vol. 45, p. 98.

[10] Ibid., p. 101.

[11] Ibid., p. 97.

[12] Luther, <u>Luther's Works</u> Vol. 30, p. 138.

[13] Ibid., p. 139.

[14] Pt. T. Forsyth, <u>The Creative Theology of P. T. Forsyth</u>, ed. Samuel J. Mikolaski (Grand Rapids: Wm. B. Eerdmans, 1969) pp. 198--200.

THIRTEEN

THE APPLICATION OF AUTHORITY

The preceding chapters have developed, to some degree, the concept of authority in the Church. Yet there
remains a second substantial part to an approach to this
subject. The elaboration of theses about authority, so
that a rough theory is constructed that pokes into this
and that corner of thought as it develops, must be shown
more concretely in specific application. A theory that
is inapplicable will have limited use. In our own time,
it seems necessary, as well as highly desirable, to re-
think authority in the Church along the lines already
suggested. There still remains, however, an application
of these ideas to the problems that are pressing in our
own time.

It might, however, be unclear as to the necessity
of having elaborated the theses *prior* to particular applications. In other words, some justification of our
approach must be made. The elaboration of these theses
has taken place in a rather systematic form, and somewhat
apart from any specific applications to today's problems.
This course has been followed for three reasons.

The first of these reasons is clarification. The
theses, at best, present a starting-point. By elaboration, this beginning can be not only extended, but also
clarified. In this manner each thesis, which is a constituent part of an integrated, unified point of embar-
kation, is set in its clearest sense and shown in its
principal direction. This clarification occurs not only
by discussing each thesis in greater analytical depth
and systematic relationships, but also by particular concrete application. Analysis and synthesis have occurred,
now application must follow.

Likewise, elaboration apart from application has,
to this point, been used in order to amplify each thesis.
A conscious drawing of attention to the theses themselves
apart from their applicability to specific problems, can

allow a careful examination of the theory as it is shaped more or less 'purely' (that is, distanced from particular applications). In this manner, the logic and reasoning at the theoretical level are more fully disclosed. Thus, even should the theory prove quite pragmatic, it could, on solid theological grounds, be rejected. Of course, the opposite is also true. Should the theory to this point seem viable, but prove itself unworkable, it must be seriously questioned.

A third reason for my course thus far is more complex than those already indicated. While the elaboration has been somewhat involved, it was necessary to permit various implications of each thesis to show themselves. At the same time, the interrelatedness of all the theses emerged more forcefully. Thus, as specifics were spelled out, a genuine, if rudimentary, theory developed. This, in itself, is a substantial justification of the theses because it displays their appropriateness to the development of a genuinely Christian understanding of authority and the Church. With application added, the theory is tested, and hopefully further validated to an acceptable degree.

The course of my elaboration has followed a broadly repetitive and synthetic approach, so that the theory of authority is not viewed in a theological vacuum. Rather, this theory must be seen in some of its many essential connections to the whole of Christian theology. In this manner, it should be seen that the theory of authority in the Church has both an appropriate and a necessary place within the broadest context of Christian theology, which exists to serve the Church in her mission. The fault of all too many discussions of the concept of authority is that they have been removed from the theological framework in which they should naturally and normally be found. I have attempted to correct this in the elaboration which has preceded. Now it remains to take this theory and to also show its essential connections to the practical Christian theology that must meet and handle critical issues in a given time.

This leads us then, to the testing ground of specific issues. These issues could be placed in one or both of two categories: first are those issues of continuing urgency in every generation. In the chapters that follow, these are represented by topics like Church government, political involvement, and marriage and the family. The second class of issues which will be discussed are those issues of urgent contemporary concern. These include the ordination of women and biblical inerrancy.

111

In examining these issues, a particular eye is kept on the evangelical community. As a member of the conservative theological community, I am particularly concerned with those issues and perspectives that most involve the current evangelical generation. Nevertheless, I believe that my theory and its applications have things to say to all parts of Christianity. At the same time, I will admit that it is to the evangelical community that I speak first and foremost. It is my hope that in these applications the evangelical community will find itself challenged, reassured, and brought to a new awareness of its responsibility to address the whole of Christianity along systematic and biblical guidelines.

The process that I shall follow in the application of this theory of authority is simple: each issue will be related to each thesis. In this relation, practical notations will be offered. Thus, as a specific issue is brought to the front, it will be seen in its inward and specific connection with each form of the one Word of God. Thus, beginning with the one Word of God, Jesus, who reveals the trinitarian God, and proceeding through the mediating authority of Scripture and the functional authority of Church proclamation, every issue will be brought into the searchlight of its relation to authority in the Church.

Finally, there remains a note to be offered to the reader: in these chapters a very important and specific role is left to those who read this. This role is to *use these generalized applications as catalysts for reform and renewal* in their own country, local church, and home. By this I do not mean simply *change*. In too many parts of the country and in too many spheres, both in the local church and in the home, there is entirely too much change and not enough reform or renewal. The task that is presented to this generation is not simply change, but a more positive movement to bring the Church into conformity once again with the biblical witness, which is the Spirit's own sermon.

FOURTEEN

CHURCH GOVERNMENT

Church government, as the structure of authority in
the Church, should conform to the legitimate authority
existing in the Church. Thus, ecclesiastical authority
should be a demonstration of the Word of God. The Barmen
Declaration, commenting on Mt. 20:25-26, reminds us that,

> The various offices in the church establish no rule
> of one over the other but the exercise of the service
> entrusted and commanded to the whole congregation.
> We repudiate the false teaching that the church can
> and may, apart from this ministry, set up special lead-
> ers . . . equipped with powers to rule.[1]

In this chapter, such a contention shall be pursued by
comparing the issue of Church government to the three
forms of the one Word of God.

To begin with, some justification of the selection
of this problem may be necessary. It is probably obvious
that Church government is a continuing necessity, and
also, a problem in the Church. Ecclesiastical politics
has spoiled more than one task that the Church has undertaken in her past. J. Oswald Sanders, writing in his
book, Spiritual Leadership, notes that, "the overriding
need of the church, if it is to discharge its obligation
to the rising generation, is for a leadership that is
authoritative, spiritual and sacrificial."[2] This thought
is by no means new, and has been echoed repeatedly in
the Church's past. However, Church government, although
it is a continuing problem, is also one that has a specific applicability to today's situation.

Today's churches, conservative and liberal alike,
are marked by highly transient congregations. This tran-
siency is combined too with a ready willingness to leave
a church that does not measure up to the specific needs
or expectations of the individual believer. This general
lack of commitment for a long period of time to a specific

local church has created a temptation to compromise the essential characteristics of Church leadership. This is not to say that such a nature is true of all believers nor that such a temptation has corrupted all church leaderships; rather, it is to recognize that powerful forces are at work against the rightful course of authority in the Church.

There needs to be a return today, particularly in the evangelical churches, to the kind of outlook esteemed by Martin Luther. Luther was convinced that, "all Christians are truly of the spiritual estate, and there is no difference among them except that of office."[3] Luther wrote that, "those who are now called 'spiritual', that is priests, bishops, or popes, are neither different from other Christians nor superior to them, except that they are charged with the administration of the word of God and the sacraments, which is their work and office. . ."[4] This kind of viewpoint would do much to help correct an undeveloped evangelical ecclesiology.

As I noted much earlier, it is of paramount importance that across the broader reaches of the evangelical community a sharper assessment of the Church's nature and role be formed. While evangelical literature abounds with popular expositions on the Church, not enough serious attention has been focused on the full biblical picture of the Church. Such crucial ideas as the priesthood of all believers have been abandoned to particular denominations and not embraced as a part of the evangelical outlook. As long as this continues to be the case, there will also continue to be an unnecessary and unfortunate *artificial* separation between evangelical clergy and laity.[5]

It would seem today that too many believers see an almost metaphysical difference between themselves and those hired to discharge the office of ministry. They must rather see that all believers are truly of the spiritual estate, and all have been given to the same task. Nevertheless, there is a difference, a difference which creates an order from which a structure of authority becomes discernable. This structure rests in the fact that there are those who have been given to the Church by God, who have been called by God and charged, as Luther put it, with the administration of the Word of God and the sacraments.

To understand the proper structure and character of Church government, therefore, demands a return to the consideration of the one Word of God. First, the relation of the Church government to Jesus, the one Word of God, who reveals the trinitarian God as the first and final authority must be examined closely. The Church must begin with Jesus, for he is the primal form of the Word of God. In so doing, she turns first to that most basic connection she maintains to the Word of God, which is that of the believing community to the object of its belief, namely God.

The Church must always recall that it was Jesus who was her maker. Jesus originated the charismatic Church. This Church, through the agency of the continuing presence of the Holy Spirit, which meant also the continuing presence of Jesus, was a Church marked both by a giving of gifts and the operation of these gifts. This charismatic Church was a Church filled with vitality. In the course of time, the pressures of a developing tradition often worked against this vitality, and a stagnation occasionally resulted. Nevertheless, Church government in our own time will be best understood, not simply in its relation to the Church tradition that developed, but also in returning to the origin of this Church as a charismatic Church.

By this I do not wish to be understood to mean that the so-called Charismatic Renewal of our own time is the best or final word on the true nature of the Church. I do believe that this renewal has been a genuine renewal, and has offered insights important to the reformation of the evangelical church. At the same time, I also believe that the charismatic Church means more than the operation of spiritual gifts. It means, first and foremost, the free reign of God's Spirit in His witness to Jesus Christ as the foundation of the life of the Church, and more specifically, of Church government itself.

This brings us to the necessity of the trinitarian God to Church government. The biblical testimony makes clear that God, Father, Son, and Holy Spirit, is the one both who founded and who perpetuates Church leadership. It must be seen, however, that in our own time the work of the trinitarian God is *still* a necessary work. It was not only necessary at the time of the founding of the Church, but also today. The trinitarian God continues his active work of upgirding the continuing ministry of the Church. This includes, of course, the work of the Church's government.

The trinitarian God is necessary to Church government, first, in the legitimization of Jesus' authority. It is the work of God, that is, the Triune God, to testify to and to substantiate Jesus' Messianic authority. Thus, for instance, it can be seen in the narrative of his baptism that Jesus submitted himself to the Baptist and the testimony of God came by the voice of the Father heard from heaven, and the Spirit descending like a dove. Jesus' baptism was, therefore, more than that of a man consecrating himself to a renunciation of sin and the service of God. The submission of the Son of God was a self-attestation of his divine ministry. This testimony was corroborated by John the Baptist. But more, it was powerfully and eloquently attested by both Father and Spirit.

The works and words of Jesus were likewise marked by the seal of God, who witnessed and affirmed them even as he also did them. This accounts for the accurate (if not understood) perception by many people that Jesus had about him an air of authority not common to the religious teachers of the day. His messianic authority could be glimpsed in his remarkable charismatic ministry. Later, the same gifts and witness of God placed on Jesus would be bestowed by him upon those who were his disciples and apostles.

The crucifixion, however, presented as we have seen, a tremendous dilemma to those followers. He, whom they had followed, and who they, in an insight presented by the Father, had recognized as the Messiah, the Son of the Most High, was now dead. However, the resurrection answered this dilemma. The resurrection again showed that the work of Jesus and his authority is wholly a work of the Triune God. This Jesus, who had been crucified, died not as a mere man but as a truly divine person. He gave himself up for death, and by the gracious hand of his Father, was raised from the dead.

The resurrection however, presented its own dilemma. Would Jesus, or would he not, continue in his resurrected form as Lord of the visible Church? Jesus' Ascension only complicated matters. But Pentecost presented the answer to this dilemma as the promise of Jesus was fulfilled. His presence as Lord on earth would be by the stewardship of the freely serving Spirit of God.

There is, of course, a temptation at this point to confuse Jesus with the Holy Spirit. Indeed, the Holy Scriptures speak of the Spirit as the Spirit of Jesus. Nevertheless, what should be seen here again is a work of the Triune God, and this work is a legitimization of Jesus' authority, wherein each, Father, Son, and Spirit, work without fusion or confusion, but in genuine union.

Secondly, the Triune God is necessary to Church government in continuing Jesus' authority. This is done, first of all, by Pentecostal baptism. Pentecost presented the advent of the Spirit as not only the vital life-force of the Church itself, but also as the establisher of the disciples. They would be no longer timid in every moment, but now would move out with a force and a power not their own. Now is the promise of Jesus confirmed. The Spirit gives voice to those disciples who, when brought before men, wonder what to say. What they can, and will say is, of course, the Spirit's own sermon, a testimony to the messianic Jesus.

In addition to this receiving of the Spirit, and complementary to it, was also the bestowal of charismatic gifts upon the Church. These gifts are seen in a double movement in the New Testament. They are, first of all, freely given by the Spirit at his own discretion, and include gifts seemingly both natural and supernatural, although all are preternatural in their origin. Then, too, these gifts are viewed, as by Paul in Ephesians 4, as the bestowal of *persons,* and specifically, as persons attached to specific offices of Church ministry.

But basically, Jesus' authority is continued by the fundamental testimony of the Holy Spirit. This sermon, this confession, this witness, this proclamation, becomes the characteristic mark of the Church, and the means by which she is identified and guides herself. No one can say, "Jesus is Lord!" except by the Spirit, for this is his sermon, and always the truth which comes from God.

Finally, the Triune God is necessary to Church government in the legitimization and continuation of authority in the Church. In an interesting passage from the First Epistle of Clement to the Corinthians, four statements are offered concerning this very thing:

1. The Apostles received the Gospel for us from the Lord Jesus Christ, Jesus the Christ was sent from God.
2. The Christ therefore is from God and the Apostles from the Christ. In both ways, then, they were in accordance with the appointed order of God's will.
3. Having therefore received their commands, and being fully assured by the resurrection of our Lord Jesus Christ, and with faith confirmed by the word of God, they went forth in the assurance of the Holy Spirit preaching the good news that the Kingdom of God is coming.
4. They preached from district to district, and from city to city, and they appointed their first converts, testing them by the Spirit, to be bishops and deacons of the future believers.[6]

But many factors were engaged in this process. The Apostle Paul writes of the model and mind of Jesus (cf. Phil. 2:1—11). Although the historical Jesus is gone, he still reigns historically in the presence of the Holy Spirit, and his historical presence in the Incarnation is still looked back to by the Church as the ultimate model for its own thinking and behavior. Those who would be leaders must be scrutinized in light of Jesus himself.

The continuing historical presence of Jesus by the advent of the Spirit presents the important historical motif of the Church "in Jesus." This thought reminds the Church continually of the necessity of her own life being the life of her founding Lord. The leaders of the Church, then, must also be in Christ. They must have his life borne out in theirs. Their rule is really his.[7]

Last, the trinitarian work in selecting, equipping and commissioning believers must be seen. This can be viewed in several different fashions including a process which begins with the election by the Father of the Son. This election by the Father of the Son means the acceptance and approval of believers who are sealed by the Spirit in the Son. Or, this might be seen as an elevation of the Son by the Father in order to give the gifts of the Spirit for the maturing of his body, the Church. Or again, this could be viewed as a commission by the Son from the Father to be carried out in the power of the Spirit. No matter how it is viewed, the work of the *Triune* God must be glimpsed. He who has saved his people continues to save them by daily provisions.

The authority of the Triune God fixes boundaries upon Church government. This can be examined in several different manners. For instance, the Father's role is to enact the first authority which is the foundation of the Church itself. The Son reveals this authority of the Father and carries it out in his own obedience. But the Holy Spirit continues this authority in the Church until the final Parousia. This Parousia, or Second Coming of Christ, is itself a final and complete look at the authority of God as that authority which is revealed in the Son and exists both first and finally, always undergirding, shaping, and retaining the full power of the Church.

The boundaries of this authority fixed by the Trinity occur in three dimensions. The first of these is purpose. The fixing of purpose for Church government is to display in the created order the redeemed order. Thus we see in Scripture that believers, and most particularly leaders (cf. Heb. 13:7; 1 Peter 5), complete the suffering of Christ. Leaders function as stewards, or as shepherds, following the model of Christ. These, and other ideas presented in the New Testament, as well as the actual operation of the Church offices and gifts, demonstrate once again the redeemed order of God's work breaking into the created order. Nowhere is this more evident than in Church government where a spiritual authority inheres within the worldly forms of ecclesiastical politics.

The second boundary that God sets upon Church government is the fixing of limits to Church government. The Church must not usurp the place of the Word. Its function, rather, is to point to that Word as those submitted to it. Thus, Church government finds a place subordinate to the Word, and in its existence as that which displays the redeemed order in the created order, Church government has its limitation as a witness and not as the thing itself.

Finally, the third boundary is the fixing of a duration to Church government. Church government has not always existed, nor will it always. It is by its very nature a 'lame duck' government, transitory in nature. The duration of Church government is fixed between the Incarnation and the Parousia. Jesus' rule between these points is conducted by his stewards, that is, leaders in the Church.

Church government must be seen also in its relation to the second form of the Word of God, the Bible, the inscripturated Word of God. Thus, it must be seen that the Bible is, first, the foundation of the confessing Church. Second, the Holy Scriptures are necessary to Church government. Finally, the Bible as the Word of God for man exists for the benefit of man and the true conducting of Church government.

To say that the Bible is the foundation of the confessing Church by no means proves that this is the case. For here we are confronted with a basic problem. Church proclamation created the New Testament. Then again, the Old Testament Scriptures existed prior to the existence of the New Testament Church itself. There was already in existence, not only an elect people of God, but also a designated body of literature considered to be 'holy scripture.' The New Testament Church retained a continuity with this prior elect community by continuing to recognize its special status and adopting its Scriptures as their own, but then added to these through their own proclamation, uniquely centered in Jesus Christ. Nevertheless, this problem still exists. How can it be that the Bible, both Old and New Testaments, is viewed as the one foundation of the confessing Church, when it is at the same time a product of that Church?

The solution to this problem can only be that Holy Scripture, as Canon, fixes, judges, promotes and defines all proclamation both prior to itself and after itself. Irrespective of its origin, the Canon is established by

God as superior to that which comes before it in the way of proclamation, and that which will come after it. Thus, although it is historically a proclamation of the Church that can be fixed to a definite point in time and space, it rises above that historicity by its election from God still retaining the full character of that historicity. But now it has become the history that defines all other moments and movements in the history of proclamation.

The necessity of the Scripture to Church government rests precisely in its being that proclamation which is truly of man and of God, that judges as well as defines all other proclamation. Simply put, the necessity of the Bible is as the Canon established above the Church. The place of Canon cannot be underestimated. The role of Scripture as Canon is a necessary and direct result of its relation to the Word of God.[8]

The Bible established as Canon the testimony of the apostles and the prophets. Scripture, in being *their* written testimony spread their authority and defined it. In being their *written* testimony, it continued their authority after them. Thus, it characterized post-apostolic leadership in apostolic fashion, and, at the same time, allowed for the testing of Church government and its leaders. All those who would follow the apostles and prophets must have their own proclamation, character and offices defined by the model established and continued in the record of Holy Scripture.

The necessity of the Bible to Church government is also seen in the boundaries it establishes. The first of these is in limiting access to God. It does this in a two-fold manner: it first restricts the authority of Church government to that given by God, as an objective, abiding, living witness to the Word of God. This inscripturated Word of God established forever the rightful boundaries of Church government. Then, in accordance with this establishment, Scripture tests Church government by its self-limitation to that given by God. Thus, the Church, in taking Holy Scripture and submitting to it, is judged and judges herself by it.

The Bible also mediates the Church to herself and to the world. Scripture does this by first fixing an abiding testimony of the Church's developing identity. The Church understands herself in accordance with the pictures given to her by the first proclamation of the community. Then, second, the Scripture fixes the mission and missionary method of the Church. All successive generations of the Church return to the Holy Scriptures to find there the record, not only of the Great Commission, but also of the actual practice of the Church as she expanded and moved out into the world, literally turning it upside down.

Finally, the Bible is, as the whole Word of God, also God's Word wholly for man. It is this no less than Christ or the preaching of the Church which exists for man. In being for man, the Bible must also be allowed its freedom over against man. The Scriptures must be viewed truly as Canon, not simply as a tool to be used or abused in accordance with its master. Rather, the Bible must overmaster the Church, so that its true and free character *for the Church* can be seen. This character of being for the Church and for her government is in providing to the governing body of the Church an abiding record and model that can shape and refine the character of a continuing godly, witnessing community in the world.

Church government must be seen in its relation to the third form of the Word of God, the proclamation of the Church. This proclamation of the Church is the functional authority of Church government. It is so, again, in three connections. First, the translated Word is the foundation of the ruling Church. Second, the proclamation of the Church is necessary to the functioning of Church government and finally, this functional authority provides for the process and structure of Church government.

The translated Word as the foundation of the ruling Church is evidenced in two facets. First, the translation of this Word is the principal work of the ruling Church. It is the unique character of Church government to translate the Word afresh in every generation to those who follow that leadership. Second, this translating work delimits and defines both the character and task of Church government. Inasmuch as the principal work of the ruling Church is to translate this Word of God, it must limit itself to *this* task, and in so doing, will find its character shaped uniquely by this task itself. The result can only be a Church government which is at the same time a preaching body.

Thus, it is virtually self-evident that preaching is necessary to Church government. In this connection, three facts must be noted. First, without proclamation there is no Church, and therefore there is no government in the Church. Second, it is by preaching that the Holy Spirit continues the charismatic presence and authority of Christ and his prophets and apostles. Third, preaching preserves the servant character and steward role that Jesus manifested and gave to his followers as a commission.

This servant character, this stewardship role, is

121

carried out by the process of functional authority in Church proclamation. It is so in four different dimensions: these are charismatic leadership independent of any given office, traditional offices within the Church, the sermon, and the congregation's responsibility.

It remains true, as Sanders has said, that, "leadership is influence, the ability of one person to influence others."[9] This influence is not contingent on office alone. Indeed, as we have seen earlier, it was charismatic leadership that brought about the origin of the Christian Church. Again, it was charismatic leadership that formed the structure of Church government in its earliest period. Finally, it is my contention that it is charismatic leadership that is again needed in a vital role in order to recover the dynamic of true Church government in our own time. This charismatic leadership is defined by its consciousness of a divine mission, and by its rigorous, even radical following of the model of Jesus Christ, and its adherence, strictly, to the confession of the early Church, centered in Jesus Christ. This does not mean a fundamentalistic narrowness. It does, in fact, mean precisely the opposite: an openness to the world in order to serve it by a faithful proclamation that translates the timeless Word into a Word which is contemporary, relevant, and yet full of the force and power of the Spirit's own testimony.

A renewed emphasis on charismatic leadership by no means diminishes the necessity or importance of the traditional offices of the Church. It will, I believe, help to keep those traditional offices in proper perspective. In our own day and age, these offices have often fallen prey to a 'hardening of the arteries.' Because they are without checks or balances, they tend to become repositories of every grievance within the Church. It will be, therefore, necessary to look closely at the foundation and conception of these offices as contained in Scripture, and as practiced in the Church (see next chapter).

But the service of the Church, her fulfillment of stewardship, is seen uniquely in her ministry of preaching. The visible success of the Church in effecting redemptive change in herself and the world to which she ministers has always been related directly to her vigor in faithfully preaching the Gospel. By the preaching of the Church the Holy Spirit works mightily. The sermon becomes the focal point of the worshipping assembly's eager attention. Here God will again address them, sustaining, comforting, and exhorting them. They will be renewed.

The sermon also occupies a unique place within the

process of Church government. It is, as it were, the central point of the functional authority of Church government. In its concentration solely in the hands of one or two men in the local congregation, the inherent temptations to a domination by man, and not God, is vastly accentuated. For this reason, if for no other, today's local churches should be encouraged to broaden and develop the notion of the sermon, the responsibility of the hearers, and the sharing of the responsibility of preaching among the elders of the Church. The sermon, it must be recalled, is God's own Word. It is, therefore, a task to be approached with great seriousness. The fact that the sermon receives so little attention in the wider life of the community by being analyzed, rightly obeyed, and scrutinized in accordance with the other two forms of the Word of God, indicates a primary reason why authority within the Church today is as confused and troubled as it is.

Finally, there is the responsibility of the congregation which cannot be overemphasized. It is the responsibility of the believing community, as not only *hearers* but also *doers* of the Word, to listen attentively to the proclamation of the Church and relate to it in a twofold fashion. First of all, this congregation must listen as those committed to hearing and obeying the one Word of God in life and in death. But, second, this congregation must hear this Word as one that is spoken by human lips. Therefore, it must hear this word as those committed to a critical discernment so that this human word is continually being reformed and refined in light of the first two forms of the Word of God, Jesus Christ and Scripture.

References Cited—Chapter Fourteen

[1] John Leith, ed., <u>Creeds of the Churches</u> (Richmond: John Knox Press, 1973), p. 521.

[2] J. Oswald Sanders, <u>Spiritual Leadership</u> (Chicago: Moody Press, 1967), p. 16.

[3] Martin Luther, "Christian in Society" I, <u>Luther's Works</u> Vol. 44, ed. James Atkinson (Phila: Fortress, 1966) p. 127.

[4] Ibid., p. 130.

[5] Even the so-called 'body life' movement has, for the most part, failed to correct this gap. This is largely due to the inordinate elevation of the pastoral-shepherd (pastor-teacher) gift, and its usual connection to a specific office and on-staff, paid position.

[6] "The First Epistle of Clement to the Corinthians," <u>The Apostolic Fathers</u>, tr. K. Lake (Cambridge: Harvard University Press, 1912) pp. 79-81.

[7] This ought not, however, to be misunderstood. Their rule is not exactly identified with his. Jesus must rule in them and through them. But they must continually submit themselves to him as also parts of the Body and not co-heads over the Church.

[8] In the wake of renewed discussion by evangelicals of issues related to biblical authority, it seems appropriate to request that the idea of Canon be given renewed affirmation, exposition, and prominence.

[9] Sanders, <u>Spiritual Leadership</u>, p. 19.

124

FIFTEEN

THE OFFICES AND MINISTRY OF THE CHURCH

From the beginning the early Church was a charismatic Church. Pentecost, with the outpouring of the Spirit, set the tone. The whole structure of the Church,
including her government, was characterized by both the
supervision and the energizing assistance of the Holy
Spirit. Spiritual charismata, or 'gifts',[2] were graciously given by the Spirit ("who apportions to each one
individually as he wills," 1 Co. 12:11). These gifts
were very likely the forerunners of the later development
of offices in the traditional sense.

However, it is important that the distinction between gifts and offices not be unduly emphasized. John
Knox has observed:

> Sometimes a distinction is drawn between the "charis-
> matic" ("Spirit-given") ministry in the early church and
> the "institutional" ministry. But if such a distinction
> was made by others in the primitive period—which seems
> rather dubious—it certainly was not made by Paul. The
> ministry was in every part charismatic; and if by "insti-
> tutional" one can mean "contributing to the growth and
> orderly functioning of the church," it was also in every
> part institutional.[3]

This union between gift and office is critically
important to perceive. The Church very early in her
existence recognized the possible distinction between
charismatic and institutional ministry. The apostles
addressed this possibility by stressing the union of the
two.[4] Later trends toward a traditional authority tended
to lose sight of a union with distinction. Increasingly,
the gifts were either identified with the assumption of
office, or ascribed a separate, and eventually inferior
role.

Properly understood, spiritual gifts and institutional offices complement each other. Even as the

institutional ministry suffers apart from a charismatic
base, so, too, the gifts fall into disorder without the
structure and the assistance afforded by offices in the
Church. The Church today can be renewed by once more
embracing God's still freely given grace. Knox is correct in observing the earliest New Testament situation,
one which ought to continue to inform our understanding
and practice today:

> We are not dealing with formal offices, but with func-
> tions for which persons were as certainly spiritually en-
> dowed as for prophecy or healing. Indeed, the "deacons"
> and "bishops" of Philippians are almost certainly to be
> identified with the "helpers" and the "administrators" of
> I Co. 12:28 and with the helpers of several kinds and the
> "presidents" who are mentioned in Rom. 12:6-8; and it is
> scarcely open to question that Paul thinks of these per-
> sons as being "gifted" as certainly, and in the same
> sense, as the "prophets" and "teachers," not to speak of
> the workers of miracles and the speakers with tongues.
> In I Co. 12:28 they are mentioned, indeed, between the
> healers and the ecstatics. What could more clearly indi-
> cate that Paul thinks of them as exercising a "charisma-
> tic" function? The same meaning is no doubt to be seen
> in the fact that the administrators (or bishops) are men-
> tioned only after the helpers (or deacons) in the same
> passage, and that in Rom. 12:6-8 the "presidents" are
> placed between two classes of helpers—those who contrib-
> ute and those who show mercy. There are no distinctions
> of "inferior" and "superior" among these workers in the
> churches. They are all recipients and agents of the same
> Spirit; and whether some of them always exercised the one
> kind of function or the other (that is, superintending or
> helping), or whether all of them at certain times exer-
> cised both functions, they were equally members of the
> body of Christ, equally indispensable to its proper and
> effective functioning, and therefore equally significant.[5]

Any distinction among Christians resulting from
office-holding is false and damnable. Spiritual gifts,
functions of ministry, and the priesthood of believers
are all interdependent concepts. Where one or more is
lacking the Church suffers. Indeed, all three are fixed
in union at the same point: the Holy Spirit. He gives
gifts to all believers to do the work of ministry that
benefits each participant and recipient.

The structure of the Church, especially her government, depends on the Spirit's use of all three components.
The priesthood of all believers incorporates every Christian in an equally meaningful participation in the ministry of the whole Church. All believers confess the
same Lord. They all have a share in this ministry. But

all the functions of ministry, in all their variety, are inextricably tied to this one equalizing and fundamental ministry of proclamation. Every function of ministry exists to promote and to facilitate the preeminence and centrality of the proclamation of the Gospel. The Spirit's own sermon on the lips of all believers is the goal of each and every function of the Church, although this is as often indirectly aimed at as directly approached.[6] The gifts, too, are given to aid in this ministry, and not as extraneous boons of God's providence.

Donald Bloesch is surely correct in urging, "if we are to have spiritual renewal in our time, the church must be open again to the specific gifts and charism given by the Spirit of God for the purpose of ministry in the world."[7] Scripture states that "the gifts and the call of God are irrevocable" (Rom. 11:29).[8] The Bible advises that "as each has received a gift, employ it for one another, as good stewards of God's varied grace" (1 Pet. 4:10). These gifts are important, not incidental, and Scripture warns, "Do not neglect the gift you have" (1 Tim. 4:14). If the gifts fall into disuse, believers are exhorted "to rekindle the gift of God that is within you" (2 Tim. 1:6).

Both believers who have been installed in an office and those who have not are equally the beneficiaries of God's gifts. As Hans-Helmut Esser has observed, "it is inconceivable to Paul that there should be any Christian without some gift of grace. At the same time, a single individual may be characterized by more than one gift of grace."[9] Bloesch stresses the indispensability of these gifts by reminding us that "what is important to recognize is that all believers share in the ministry and mission of our Lord Jesus Christ through the charisma they have received. All ministries, including those exercised by a special commission (eg., pastor, teacher) are charismatic."[10] No gift should be excluded from its role in the total work of the functional authority of proclamation in the Church. At the same time, any unrighteous utilization of any gift should be rebuked.[11]

All spiritual gifts can assist the government of the Church. Yet, there are certain gifts more obviously paired to so-called leadership functions. Knox noted, for example, that "of the several ministries of the local church it is natural that those of 'administrators' and 'helpers' should have been the first to receive official status. These are the least obviously spiritistic of them all, the most clearly susceptible of being filled by human election or appointment."[12] Knox has contended that Paul's reference to "bishops" and "deacons" at Philippi is to "those members of the Philippian church who have proved to have administrative gifts—gifts of wisdom, efficiency, and tact, some in planning and oversight (the "bishops" or rulers), others in actually performing the various particular tasks belonging to what may be called the 'business' of the congregation (the "deacons" or helpers)."[12]   Knox also cautions that "one must not make the mistake of identifying these with the formally elected or appointed, the ordained, officials of a later period."[13] Yet, it was those who exercised these gifts that (probably) were granted "official" status through ordination to the governing of the Church.

There are at least twenty spiritual gifts mentioned in Scripture.   While some are, perhaps, more obviously related to specific ruling offices, and need closer attention at this point, all are useful to the governing of the Church. In particular, the gifts of administration (or governing, *kubernāsis*), apostleship (*apostolos*), helps (*antilāpsis*), leadership (or ruling, *proistāmi*), shepherd (or pastor, *poiman*), service (or ministry, *diakonia*), and perhaps knowledge (word of knowledge, *logos gnoseos*), wisdom (word of wisdom, *logos sophias*), and teaching (*didaskalia*), are pertinent. Of these, administration, leadership, shepherd, and service require more elucidation.[14]

The gift of administration is mentioned in 1 Co. 12:28.   Some have equated this gift to that listed in Rom. 12:8, although the word is different (*proistāmi*). The Greek term is related to that used of the steersman or helmsman of a ship (*kubernātās*, Ac. 27:11).   It could suggest, then, a governing of people by their skillful coordination as they labor together.   Some have taken the term figuratively, rendering it "wise counsels," and thereby suggesting a government by sound guidance rather than by fiat. The gift benefits from a recognized office and functions best where it is "officially" recognized and permitted its proper measure of authority.

The gift of leadership is mentioned in Rom. 12:8. The Authorized Version renders the Greek term, "to rule." The usage of *proistāmi* presents several related ideas. Demosthenes, Euripides, and others used it to designate the function of a protector or guardian. Superintending or presiding over something or someone is the sense of the word as used at 1 Tim. 5:17 or 1 Th. 5:12. At Tit. 3:8, 14, the term means, "to care for, give attention to."[15] The meaning is obviously close to that of administration. This gift is served also by being wielded from an office like that of elder.

When *proistāmi* and *kubernāsis* are jointly considered,

which is surely reasonable, a picture of leadership is developed that stresses factors common to both and in line with New Testament thought on shepherds, elders, and deacons. This leadership comes as a gift of grace. The gift calls only incidental attention to itself. Its purpose is to *serve* others whether by coordinating their efforts to mutual advantage, affording guardianship, or rendering some other form of aid. Leadership is, at Rom. 12:8, qualified by the idea of "diligence" or "earnestness" (*spoudā*). The image is of a confident, optimistic, eager person who genuinely cares for others and who hastens to help them (cf. 2 Co. 7:11, 12; 8:7, 16, 17, 22; also Heb. 13:17). From Scripture the idea of the Christian leader is sharply delineated by the following considerations:

1. The leader is one appointed to give aid to the Church. This appointment is first from God, and carries with it the gift of God's gracious equipping of this person to this vocation (Eph. 3:7; Col. 1:25; I Pet. 5:2, 3; Heb. 13:17, etc.).

2. The service of the leader is first and foremost the guidance and equipping of persons by the proclamation of God's truth (1 Co. 12:28; Eph. 4:16, 17; Heb. 13:7; also, Tit. 1:7-9; 2 Co. 4:5, etc.).

3. This assistance puts persons above tasks (Rom. 12:8; 1 Pet. 4:10; Eph. 4:12-14, etc.).

4. This ministry is a genuine leadership through positive direction and surehanded guardianship (Rom. 12:8; Heb. 13:17; 1 Th. 1:6-10; Gal. 1:6-12, etc.). The leader, by personal submission to the Gospel, and frequent acquaintance with it, is able and willing to undergo the vicissitudes accompanying the gift and position and steadfastly continue to direct the Church to Christ.[16]

The gift of being a shepherd is mentioned in Eph. 4:11. Like the gifts of apostle, evangelist, and teacher, this gift is named in terms of a person. Similar to the gifts of administration and ruling, this gift has its root meaning in the notion of a protector. In its proper rendering as a herdsman, or better, shepherd, the term occurs several times in the Gospels (Mt. 9:36; Lk. 2:8; Jn. 10:2, etc.). Metaphorically, the term is used of the presiding officer of any assembly (1 Pet. 2:25; Heb. 13:20; Eph. 4:11), thus, of Christ as the Shepherd of the Church, or of overseers in the Body.

Ezekiel 34 presents a sharply contrasting set of portraits of shepherds. Faithless shepherds are indicted because: they have fed themselves at the expense of the sheep (34:2, 3), taken wrong advantage of the fat and strong (34:4), not ministered to the weak or sick (34:4), neglected the crippled stragglers (34:4), allowed some to freely stray (34:4), refused to seek the lost (34:4), and have lorded it over the flock with both harshness and force (34:4). The predictable result was that "they were scattered, because there was no shepherd; and they became food for all the wild beasts" (34:5). These were false shepherds, for they had by faithlessness forfeited their positions.

God himself is the true and faithful Shepherd. He is committed to: search for his sheep, and seek them out (34:11), rescue them and thereby make one flock (34: 12), gather them into their own good pasture (34: 13, 14), personally shepherd them there and also cause them to lie down in peace and plenty (34:15), and reverse all the wickedness of the faithless shepherds by seeking the lost, bringing back the strayed, binding up the crippled, strengthening the weak, watching over the fat and the strong, and feeding them all in justice (34:16). This picture, then, is a backdrop for the New Testament image.

Jesus, in Jn. 10:1-18, calls himself both "the door for the sheep" (10:7), and "the good shepherd" (10:14). Jesus knows each of his sheep by name (10:3). The sheep hear his voice, and trust him to lead them out (10:3). Jesus waits until all are safely brought out, and then he personally leads them (10:4). The sheep will only follow one they trust—and flee all others (10:5). Jesus is the truly faithful shepherd. He leads the sheep into rich feeding grounds so that they not only have life, but an abundant life (10:9, 10). He lays down his own life for the sheep, for he freely dies to protect them, unlike the disinterested hireling who flees in the face of danger (10:11-15). Jesus has only one flock, but that flock encompasses future generations of sheep, so that his death is not only for the living, but also for those who are yet to live (10:16, 17). He does all of this for the flock out of a loving obedience to the greatest Shepherd, his own Father. His Father's will is also Jesus' will so that nothing he does for the sheep is done from an unwilling compulsion (10:17, 18).

In 1 Pet. 5:4 (see 5:1—11), Jesus is called the *chief* shepherd. This simply means that every shepherd on earth among God's people is an "under-shepherd" to Christ, the chief shepherd of the one flock. That there are legitimately shepherds under Christ is clearly taught here in 1 Peter, but already suggested back in John 10 by Jesus' own words, "he who enters by the door is the shepherd of the sheep" (10:2). Christ the door, and the "gatekeeper" of the flock admits to the sheepfold those whom he has called and equipped to assist him in shepherding.

130

In Heb. 13:20, Jesus is called the *great* shepherd. This title comes in conjunction with the author's description of leadership in the Church. Jesus is the great shepherd in virtue of the suffering he has accomplished for the sheep (13:12), the example he has set for other shepherds (13:7), and the reality that his shepherd ministry is eternal (13:8). He is also the foundation upon which all shepherding is established (13:20, 21).

From Christ comes the gift and vocation of the shepherd in the Church (Ephesians 4). The gift is a person given by God to assist in the equipping of the saints, the work of ministry, and the building up of the Body of Christ (4:12). The shepherds work alongside and together with the apostles, prophets, evangelists, and others to bring these about. The labor continues "until we all attain to the unity of the faith and of the knowledge of the Son of God, to mature manhood, to the measure of the stature of the fulness of Christ" (4:13). Growth in the Church is "into Christ" and is facilitated by "speaking the truth in love" (14,15).[17]

The shepherd's ministry is further elucidated in 1 Pet. 5:1-3. The total work of the shepherd is neatly summed up in the charge, "tend the flock of God that is your charge" (5:2). But this work is qualified by three sets of opposing ideas. First, the shepherd receives his charge "not by contraint but willingly" (5:2). This means the tending of the flock is undertaken freely, as something rightly desired and not because of unrighteous pressure. Second, the shepherd takes his charge "not for shameful gain but eagerly" (5:2). This may appear to be an odd expression. It intends to teach that the eagerness of the shepherd is such that in tending the flock he has no time to plot ways of selfish gain from shepherding. Third, the shepherd accepts his charge, "not as domineering over those in your charge but being examples to the flock" (5:3). Shepherds must not engage in "lording it over" (NIV) the flock, taking advantage of their status or position. Rather, they are to be examples, even as Christ has been the great example (cf. 1 Pet. 2:21-25).

As with the gifts of administration and ruling, that of being a shepherd can flourish when exercised in an office of the Church. No one should suggest, however, that an office is necessary for the gift, for offices are not preconditions to gifts. It is far more likely that the office (or offices) of bishop and elder resulted from the logic of fully realizing these gifts, and others in a more structured, orderly, "official" fashion. In the same manner, gifts like those of helps or service may have helped suggest the permanent institution of the

131

deaconship.

The gift of service, or ministry, is mentioned in Rom. 12:7. The Greek *diakonia* is the same term used for a deacon in the Church. It means service, or ministering, especially of those under the command of others, and is rather broad in usage. The gift is very similar, and may be identical, with that of helps (*antilāpsis*), mentioned in 1 Co. 12:28. Perhaps the distinction between the terms is one of focus. Whereas the gift of helps is more person oriented and arises rather spontaneously, the gift of service is more task oriented and follows the directions of others.[18] Understood in this fashion, and given the eventual rise of offices in the Church, it is little wonder that "deacons" (servers) came to be the titled right-hand assistants of the bishops and elders.

One other word found in the New Testament is of particular interest and value in understanding the government of the early Church. Forms of the term *hāgeomai* are used in Heb. 13:7, 17, 23, meaning "to lead." The term in its various forms and other occurrences can mean also "to think," "to believe," or "to regard as," but it is its appearances in Hebrews 13 that are important to our consideration.[19] Büchsel, in Kittel's Theological Dictionary of the New Testament, offers the following summary:

. . .ἡγούμενοι, mostly in the plural, is used for the leaders of the community in Heb. 13:7, 17, 24. In the greeting in 13:24 the ἡγούμενοι are mentioned before the ἅγιοι. The community is obviously divided into those who lead and those who are led. In 13:17 they are pastors responsible to God. God has entrusted the other members of the community to them, and therefore they owe them obedience. The founders of the community, who have died (as martyrs?), are also among the ἡγούμενοι, and they are set up as examples of faith (13:7).[20]

Both Judas, called Barsabbas, and Silas are designated by this term (Ac. 15:22). Its usage in the early Church vis-à-vis the *episkopos* or *presbuteros* is uncertain, although Büchsel writes that, "in Lk. 22:26 the ἡγούμενος is contrasted with the διακονῶν and is parallel to the μείζων ἐν ὑμίν."[21] But what Büchsel does not point out is the qualifying clause placed in Heb. 13:7 after the admonition, "Remember your leaders" (*tōn hagoumenōn humōn*). This clause, *humin tōn logon tou theou*, "those who spoke to you the word of God," appears to clarify leadership in the Church in contradistinction to a specific office.

Of course, officers of the Church have their ruling

132

delineated in large part by the verbal ministering of the Word. This fact is true of bishops (1 Tim. 5:17) and deacons (Ac. 6:3, 5; 7:2—the example of Stephen[22]) alike. But in Hebrews, attention is called *first* to this distinguishing ministry. Then, likely on the basis of this, that leadership is "considered" (*anatheōrountes*) in light of the "outcome of their life." Their faith, displayed in life and word, is to be imitated (Heb. 13:7). Quite possibly, it is the ministry of the Word that is their "keeping watch over your souls" (Heb. 13:17). Certainly there is sound ground for asserting that their authority as leaders rests in their connection to this Word.

Whatever connection that might be made between these leaders in Hebrews and elders in the Church[23], the relationship of the leader to his authority to lead is seen in terms other than the status and power inherent in an office. This does not preclude the possibility that such leaders were normally and naturally invested in an office. What this might suggest, however, is that charismatic authority still predominated over the increasing tendencies toward traditional authority, and that this authority was linked less to any status of the leader and more directly to his function as the representative (as apostle, disciple, etc.) of Jesus Christ himself.[24]

Thus, it appears eminently reasonable to suppose the prominence of spiritual gifts and the ministry of the Word in validating authority during the earliest period of Church government and during the gradual transition to more formal, traditional patterns of authority. There should not be thought a radical separation between gifts and offices. The wielding of the former suggested the desirability of the latter. As offices grew in function, power, and importance, the gifts were gradually relegated a lesser role. The spontaneity of expression customarily accompanying the manifestation of gifts was given an increasingly minor place in the developing, orderly liturgy of the Church structure. Knox reminds us, however, of the great difficulties that must be faced in trying to describe the organization and function of ministry in the early Church. He states that, "these difficulties are so grave, and with our present resources so definitely insurmountable, that a clear picture of the early ministry is simply beyond our reach."[25] At the same time, some helpful points do surface. Knox notes, for instance, that the rise of monepiscopacy "does not clearly emerge till the opening years of the second century."[26]

George H. Williams has observed that the term *ordinatio* seems to have been coined first by Tertullian in respect to ecclesiastical functions. In fact, Williams contends, "deaconesses, subdeacons, acolytes, exorcists, and lectors were not in most places in the mid-third century considered truly clerical."[27] Yet there were an abundance of "lesser" ecclesiastical posts, including doorkeepers, gravediggers, and the acolytes who, among other duties, ran clerical errands for the presbyters.[28] Williams observed from Cyprian (c. 200/210-258) that the Church, in that time, exercised the power "of choosing their bishops, presbyters, and deacons and rejecting the unworthy."[29]

Two offices are of particular concern to us. Since it is not practical to fully outline the history of all these offices, it is the simpler task of brief description that must be pursued. The office of elder (jointly considering *episkopos* and *presbuteros*), and that of deacon (*diakonos*), are the principal ones of Church government, especially at the local church level. The terms are biblical ones (Ac. 6:1; 1 Tim. 3:1-13; Tit. 1: 5—9, etc.), although it is disputed as to whether their use in the New Testament reflects actual offices. The functions or status of these elders and deacons are not precisely spelled out, but qualifications are set forth.

The elders (also called bishops or presbyters, in accordance with specific Greek words), are present in both the Old and New Testament period Judaism as well as in the early Church. The terms *episkopos*, *presbuteros*, *kubernāsis*, and *prohistāmi*, each designating either a function or status of leadership, may be intimately related at the very practical level, but *presbuteros*, in particular, has become the common word associated with general eldership in the Church. It is used of Christian leaders in Acts, the Pastorals, and some of the Catholic (General) Epistles.

Lothar Coenen writes that "besides meeting general personal and moral requirements, they have the special tasks of exhorting, and refuting objectors. In other words, they continue the juridicial role of elders in the synagogue in the form of a presiding group."[30] Their functions were multiple in "ruling" the people, but the New Testament advises, "Let the elders who rule well be considered worthy of double honor, *especially those who labor in preaching and teaching*" (1 Tim. 5:17). It is of paramount importance that an elder "hold firm to the sure word as taught, so that he may be able to give instruction in sound doctrine and also to confute those who contradict it" (Tit. 1:9).

In the Didache (or, "The Teaching of the Twelve Apostles"),[31] both bishops and deacons are said to also render to the Church "the service of prophets and teach-ers."[32] Prophets "speak in the Spirit," but, "not every one that speaketh in the Spirit is a prophet; but only if he hold the ways of the Lord."[33] Teachers likewise exercise a verbal ministry of the Word. The Church is advised that "if he teach so as to increase righteousness and the knowledge of the Lord, receive him as the Lord."[34] Bishops and deacons, as well as prophets and teachers, are "honored ones" who are not to be despised. Yet, unlike the "charismatics," the bishops and deacons are men "appointed" by the Church.[35]

The offices of elders and deacons both underwent changes. A distinction in elders resulted in bishops, and under them, the presbyters. Among deacons the ques-tion of the ministry of women surfaced. Deaconesses were eventually accepted in some parts of the Church, but not all.[36] The deacons were subordinated to the elders from the first, and characterized as being "as eyes to the bishop, carefully enquiring into the doings of each mem-ber of the church."[37] They served the elders in a va-riety of functions. But the early hints of the New Tes-tament concerning elders and deacons were becoming less recognizable.

Samuel Southard has argued that, "according to Paul, the ministry has its primary authority in its function-al service."[38] But as the functions of ministry, and especially the ministry of the Word, became centered in the offices of the Church, a gradual shift occurred with regard to the perceived locus of authority. Moreover, the ministry of the Word, rather than accentuated by this shift, suffered from competition with other facets of the ruling offices. The centralizing of ministry and author-ity set aside the priesthood of all believers. In a pen-etrating analysis, Bloesch has summarized:

> By the beginning of the third century the role of bi-shop became more liturgical in character. The titles "priest" and "high priest" were now applied to the min-istry of the bishop, a practice which had earlier been strictly avoided. The first Christian writers to use the words *priest* and *high priest* of the church's minis-ters were Tertullian and Hippolytus. Küng makes this astute observation: "A genuine sacralizing and ritual-izing took effect, especially from the fifth and sixth centuries on: fading of the ministry of the word into the background, the cultic-ritual activity of the minis-ter as the real priestly work, reification of liturgical authority, a special holiness and dignity proper to the office holder."[39]

The Constitutions of the Holy Apostles (late fourth

135

century), which built on the Didache, is a prominent example of the great attention and reverence accorded the subject of Church leaders. But even earlier could be found such remarkable statements as this: "it is clear that we must regard the bishop as the Lord himself."[41] While charismatic ministry in the priesthood of all believers enjoyed Church favor in some circles even into the third and fourth centuries, its subordination was inevitable. Authority moved from the immediate power of the Holy Spirit to the Church herself. The offices had become more authoritative than the functions of ministry, and eventually this power apart from the Word corrupted the ministry of the Church.[42]

The Reformation represented only a partial recovery of the New Testament situation. The Reformers placed the center of authority outside the offices of the Church. The Holy Spirit's work was accentuated and, in connection with biblical authority, took a decidedly objective cast. The priesthood of all believers was reaffirmed and the laity were given privileges long denied them.[43] Preaching replaced the Mass as the high point and center of the Christian worship assembly, though the verbal proclamation was paired with the proclamation inherent in the sacrament (cf. 1 Co. 11:26). Yet the Reformers gave little serious attention to spiritual gifts, and left many misconceptions of the offices of the Church intact.

Luther, with brilliant insight, saw the interdependent connections between preaching and the priesthood of all believers. He said, "Since he is a priest and we are his brethren, all Christians have the power and must fulfill the commandments to preach and to come before God with our intercessions for one another and to sacrifice ourselves to God."[44] Nor is the duty of Church elders (*presbuteroi*) any different. "These are the men," said Luther, "whom Christ called his officials and council. They administer the spiritual rule; that is, they preach, and they care for a Christian congregation."[45] Again, Luther says of the author of 1 Peter, "he calls those men elders who have had an office and have preached."[46]

However, Luther certainly maintained a "high" view of the offices of Church government. He taught:

> Scripture makes all of us equal priests . . . but the churchly priesthood which we now separate from laymen . . . is called "ministry" (*ministerium*), "servitude" (*servitus*), "dispensation" (*dispensatio*), "episcopate" (*episcopatus*), and "presbytery" (*presbyterium*) in Scripture . . . . (II Tim. 2:24). Here he (St. Paul) calls Timothy a servant of God in the special sense of preaching and spiritually leading the people.[47]

For Luther, "every minister or spiritual regent should be a bishop, that is an overseer or watchman so that in his town and among his people the gospel and faith in Christ are built up and win out over foe, devil and heresy."[48] In the midst of all his duties, thought Luther, "this is the chief responsibility and duty of the bishop: the ministry of this Word."[49] This is not just his preeminent *task*, but literally assumes a place above the bishop. For, while the bishop may exercise the ban, "no one may ban someone or himself be banned from hearing the gospel and the sermon."[50] Deacons, too, "were men who also preached occasionally."[51] At every point these offices are viewed from the vantage point of the ministry of the Word.

Nowhere is this more true than in relation to the authority of those who rule in the Church. Luther forcefully exclaimed:

> Among Christians there shall and can be no authority; rather all are alike subject to one another . . . . Among Christians there is no superior but Christ himself, and him alone.
> What, then, are the priests and bishops? Answer: Their government is not a matter of authority or power, but a service and an office, for they are neither higher nor better than other Christians . . . Their ruling is rather nothing more than the inculcating of God's Word . . . for Christians must be ruled in faith, not with outward works.[52]

Here rule in the Church can be conceived as belonging to the Word of God. This rule can be expressed in and through any believer. But it is especially evidenced —or ought to be—in those ordained to the offices of Church government. These offices are offices of *ministry*, the ministry of the Word, and those who fill these offices are *servants* of the Word, ruling by their example of faith and being ruled by the Word they speak.

Calvin, in his Institutes, well expresses this understanding:

> We are now to speak of the order in which the Lord has been pleased that his Church should be governed. For though it is right that he alone should rule and reign in the Church, that he should preside and be conspicuous in it, and that its government should be exercised and administered solely by his word; yet as he does not dwell among us in visible presence, so as to declare his will to us by his own lips, he in this . . . uses the ministry of men, by making them, as it were, his substitutes, not by transferring his right and honour to them, but only

137

doing his own work by their lips, just as an artificer uses a tool for any purpose.[53]

Thus, Calvin can infer from Scripture "that the two principal parts of the office of pastors are to preach the Gospel and administer the sacraments."[54] Moreover, Scripture indicated to Calvin that "to all who discharge the ministry of the word it gives the name of bishops."[55]

The power of the Church is for "edification" and those who wield this power must consider themselves "to be nothing more than servants of Christ, and, at the same time, servants of the people in Christ."[56] Calvin warned that "whatever authority and dignity the Holy Spirit in Scripture confers on priests, or prophets, or apostles, or successors of Apostles, is wholly given not to men themselves, but to the ministry to which they are appointed; or, to speak more plainly, to the word, to the ministry of which they are appointed."[57] Calvin wrote:

> Here is the supreme power with which pastors of the Church, by whatever name they are called, should be invested—namely, to dare all boldly for the word of God, compelling all the virtue, glory, wisdom, and rank of the world to yield and obey its majesty; to command all from the highest to the lowest, trusting to its power to build up the house of Christ and overthrow the house of Satan; to feed the sheep and chase away the wolves; to instruct and exhort the docile, to accuse, rebuke and subdue the rebellious and petulant, to bind and loose; in fine, if need be, to fire and fulminate, *but all in the word of God.*[58]

This dynamic notion of ministry did much to reform the Church. Both Luther and Calvin restored preaching to its rightful place. The universal participation of believers in Christian ministry received new impetus. Even the role of spiritual gifts was acknowledged.[59] But at this latter point, the Reformers refused to pursue the New Testament witness far enough. The essential role of spiritual gifts was overlooked. The roots of traditional offices in charismatic authority was left an undeveloped idea. The result was the quick return of Protestant orthodoxy to a situation inwardly similar to Medieval Catholicism, if outwardly different.

The formal role accorded the sermon was not enough. In time, doctrinal expositions, replete with learned expositions of the finest theological points, began to call attention more to the preacher than to the Word preached. The office of pastor became the locus of authority in the local church; he was the holder of the keys which unlocked the meaning of Scripture.[60] Then, too, apologetics became a wider practice as the "new age" called biblical authority into question. Preaching often became preoccupied with vindicating the Bible, "proving" its message rather than proclaiming it. Thus, today, we are forced to ask as seriously as does Barth, "Is not the very fact that so wretchedly little binding address is heard in the Church accountable for a goodly share of her misery—is it not perhaps *the* misery?"[61]

The recent Charismatic Renewal has refocused attention on the Holy Spirit and spiritual gifts in both Protestant and Roman Catholic circles. No longer are these matters confined to Pentecostal communions. Even in the moderate dispensational camps, spiritual gifts are being scrutinized afresh and often reinterpreted. The genuine potential to continue and extend the reforming work of Luther, Calvin, and others is tremendous. But, for the most part, the initiative has passed as spiritual gifts have been practiced increasingly apart from the central task of preaching the Gospel. Abuses that have accompanied Charismatic revival are often directly traceable to the absence of sound proclamation, and not because the gifts are themselves "demonic".

The evangelicals have seized recently the initiative in forging a faithful and intelligible statement on biblical authority. Their work can be furthered by diligent and creative labor in understanding the interface existing among charismatic ministry, Church proclamation, and the priesthood of all believers. Movements in evangelicalism accentuating the involvement of laity are to be applauded. But they need also to be cautioned to conform to both the freedom of service inherent in manifesting spiritual gifts, *and* the freedom of submitting to the order created by the Word of God.

This order means a *genuine* distinction between laity and pastorate. This distinction is not one of kind, so that the minister is viewed as a superior person, or even especially gifted or elect. The distinction is one of calling, and only then in part. All are called to participate in the ministry of the Word. All have gifts. All are priests. But to some has come a peculiar vocation, a call that separates them to the *regular* and the *periodic* tasks of preaching, of administering the sacraments, and of governing by their examples of faithful service. These individuals are distinguished by ordination. They are not *better* than others, or even different, yet they are uniquely marked by their ministry, and to them is given special honor and status.

However, the place of the pastor is characterized also by *union* with the laity. All are *simul iustus et*

simul peccator, "at the same time justified and a sinner."
All are called to be witnesses, and the Holy Spirit can
speak through anyone. Each person has a gift with which
to serve the whole Church. Not only pastors, but also
laity can be officers in the Church. On a given occasion
the unordained may preach or administer the sacraments.

The Church must move closer to this union, while
preserving the distinction. The traditional offices of
the Church must be successfully challenged to renewal by
the encouraging of charismatic ministry. "Unofficial",
spontaneous, Spirit-filled operations of spiritual gifts
and displays of leadership must be supported.[62] Freedom
within the order of Church government is needed. Rigid
conformity to established Church bureaucracy is misin-
formed. It tacitly assumes authority is finally located
in the Church herself, in her offices and liturgy. But
authority in the Church is the living Lord Jesus Christ.
He must reign!

The roots of traditional authority in a past where
charismatic authority was prominent must be more closely
examined. Whatever must be done to promote the centrality and preeminence of Jesus Christ *must* be done. The
preaching of the Gospel must regain its superiority over
apologetics. Intermittent opportunities for lay preaching could very well prove invaluable in increasing a general appreciation of preaching and closer attention to
the spoken Word. It might also challenge pastors to renew their own efforts.[63]

The biblical images of administrators, leaders, and
shepherds should all be presented in sharper perspective
to local churches. Various so-called "Shepherd Groups",
have proven very successful in renewing the total ministries of local bodies. Laity and pastorate can join
together in fruitfully exercising the constituent parts
of the total ministry of the Word of God. The offices of
the Church can themselves be reformed and renewed. On
the one hand they can be "demythologized", and reoriented
to concrete, simple, and practical service. On the
other hand they can be rightly honored as indispensable.
When Church officials commend themselves by their faithful examples, they should be commended by others. In all
these things, as the priesthood of believers, charismatic
ministry, and the Word come together, "we are to grow up
in every way into him who is the head, into Christ, from
whom the whole body, joined and knit together by every
joint with which it is supplied, when each part is working properly, makes bodily growth and upbuilds itself in
love" (Eph. 4:15-16).

[1] Hans-Helmut Esser, in The New International Dictionary of New Testament Theology (hereinafter cited as IDNTT), writes that "the manifold outworking of the one grace in individual Christians through the one Spirit is called by Paul *charisma*, a personal endowment with grace" (Grand Rapids: Zondervan, 1972; II, p. 121). Arnold Bittlinger, in his scholarly Gifts and Ministries, offers this definition: "a charism is a gratuitous manifestation of the Holy Spirit, working in and through, but going beyond, the believer's natural ability for the common good of the people of God" (Grand Rapids: Eerdmans, 1973; p. 18). In Kittel's Theological Dictionary of the New Testament, the salient point is made that these gifts are not "the eternal already present today." but "represent our future possession in provisional form" (IX, p. 405). That is, they have a duration fixed by the purpose they serve.

[2] These spiritual gifts are mentioned in several places in the New Testament, notably in Romans 12, 1 Corinthians 12 and 14, Ephesians 4, and 1 Peter 4. The Greek term translated "gifts" is closely related to the word meaning "grace".

[3] John Knox, "The Ministry in the Primitive Church," in The Ministry in Historical Perspective, eds. H. Richard Niebuhr and Daniel D. Williams (N.Y.: Harper & Row, 1956), p. 10.

[4] Originally, the "offices" were *functions* undertaken by persons with the appropriate spiritual gift. However, it is impossible to precisely ascertain at what point the function became "official", that is, recognized by a formal institution.

[5] Knox, "The Ministry in the Primitive Church," pp. 10-11.

[6] Hence, even such "minor" Church functions as collecting the tithe, or ushering, or preparing the Sunday bulletin, are all aimed at promoting and facilitating the one great work of Christian preaching, though admittedly less directly than, say, singing a hymn, or reciting the Creeds.

[7] Donald Bloesch, The Reform of the Church, (Grand Rapids: Eerdmans, 1970), p. 114. See also, Bloesch's Essentials of Evangelical Theology, II, (San Francisco: Harper & Row, 1979), ch. 5. Hereinafter cited as EET.

[8] This text is applicable to all of the spiritual gifts and the vocation that God gives.

[9] Esser, IDNTT, p. 121.

[10]Bloesch, EET, Vol. II, p. 109.

[11]There is no good reason, for example, why the improper use of tongues should be rebuked while the abuse of, say, the pastoral gift, is overlooked because of expediency or fear.

[12]Knox, "The Ministry in the Primitive Church," p. 19.

[13]Ibid., p. 10.

[14]My selection of these may appear somewhat arbitrary. Certainly apostleship and teaching were fundamental to the first offices of the Church. But these four are not used exclusively. I intend them to be case examples only. They are appropriate and somewhat less often examined than the two I have mentioned above.

[15]These senses are of *proistāmi* in the perfect, pluperfect, 2 aorist active, and in the present and imperfect middle; in the transitive tenses it means "to set" or "place before; set over" (see New Thayer's Greek-English Lexicon, p. 539).

[16]Because of a close relationship in submission to the Gospel, the leader is constantly confronted by the challenge to reform and be reformed; to renew and to be renewed. But the temptation to simply *change* is also present. Change, however, is not always right; reform and renewal are continuing processes.

[17]The spoken ministry of the Word is quite vital and very natural. One should speak the truth with his neighbor "for we are members one of another" (4:25). Talk that is "good for edifying" should replace "evil" talk so that "it may impart grace to those who hear" (4:29). It is the Word that is ministered by speech and act that most visibly characterizes the love of the Church.

[18]This is, admittedly, speculation on my part.

[19]For the information on this term, I am indebted to the article in Kittel's Theological Dictionary of the New Testament, Vol. II, pp. 907-909, by Büchsel.

[20]Ibid., p. 907. Interestingly, Büchsel notes that, "Reverent subjection to human officers with divinely given pastoral authority is now integral to Christian piety. This high estimation of office implies transition to early Catholicism, *unless it can be explained from an early regard for office*" (p. 907, italics mine, see his note 6).

[21]Ibid., p. 907.

[22] I recognize Ac. 6 cannot be used to "prove" the office of deacon. But the work of Stephen here appears to be a sound model of what, in fact, many early "deacons" did.

[23] The Epistle of Ignatius to the Trallians (AD 80-107) exhorts, with Heb. 13:17 in mind, "Be ye subject to the bishop as to the Lord, for he watches for your souls as one that shall give account to God." From the Ante-Nicene Fathers, ed. A. Roberts and J. Donaldson, (Buffalo: The Christian Literature Publishing Co., 1886), p. 66.

[24] As a sidelight, recall the connection between the gifts of the Spirit and the ministry of the Word which constitutes the Holy Spirit's principal work. Authority related to the gifts is also, and even predominantly, linked to Christian "Spirit-filled" proclamation. Cf. also the use of the verb *presbeuō* in 2 Co. 5:20.

[25] Knox, in The Ministry in Historical Perspective, p. 2. The fact that Knox himself believes that elders are a post-Pauline development in polity (pp. 19-23), should not dissuade us from accepting many of his observations. Rather, they must be understood as falling under his own warning. We simply are ignorant of many relevant facts necessary to understanding when, where, and how offices first came into being and exactly how they functioned.

[26] Ibid., p. 23. Knox adds the further comment that 3 John may be a protest against this development.

[27] George H. Williams, "The Ministry of the Ante-Nicene Church (c. 125-325)," The Ministry in Historical Perspective, p. 51.

[28] Ibid.

[29] Ibid., p. 49.

[30] L. Coenen, "Bishop," IDNTT, p. 199.

[31] The date of composition is uncertain. It has been assigned to anytime from late first century to sometime in the third century.

[32] "The Teaching of the Twelve Apostles," The Ante-Nicene Fathers, Vol. VII, ed. A. C. Coxe, p. 381.

[33] Ibid., p. 380.

[34] Ibid.

[35] Ibid., p. 381. Those appointed are to be "worthy of the Lord,

men meek, and not lovers of money, and truthful and proved."

[36]The Constitutions of the Holy Apostles speaks favorably of deaconesses, but the Council of Laodicea (A.D. 343-381) forbade
the appointment of any who were called presbytides (diakonssai
presbytides), and the first Council of Orange (A.D. 441), in
its twenty-sixth canon, forbade the appointment of deaconesses
altogether.

[37]Epistle of Clement to James, "Clementine Homilies," Ante-Nicene
Fathers, Vol. VIII, p. 220. The Clementine Homilies are
dated c. 200-250 A.D.

[38]Samuel Southard, Counseling for Church Vocations (Nashville:
Broadman Press, 1957), p. 49.

[39]Bloesch, EET, II p. 110. Bloesch quotes Hans Küng, Why Priests?
trans. R. C. Collins (Garden City, N. Y.: Doubleday, 1972),
p. 54.

[40]Ignatius to the Ephesians, "The Epistles of St. Ignatius," Ante-
Nicene Fathers, Vol. I p. 181. This letter has been dated
98-117 A.D. (Eusebius, 108 A.D.).

[41]Ignatius to the Philadelphians, "The Epistles of St. Ignatius,"
Ante-Nicene Fathers, Vol. I p. 261.

[42]The papacy, itself the logical result of the shift of authority
from Christ by the Spirit to the Church, was naturally the
focal point of the corruption that occurred. The Pope, as
the visible representative of Christ on earth, or as the
Apostolic successor, enjoyed the highest authority in the
Church because the Church had centered authority in her ministers (officers) of which he was the highest.

[43]This was especially true with regard to the ministering of the
sacraments. The Reformers recognized that, in principle, any
believer may administer baptism or conduct the Lord's Supper.

[44]Quoted in Bloesch, EET, II, p. 104. CF. the quote from D. Bonhoeffer (p. 71), "He has put His Word in our mouth. He wants
it to be spoken through us. If we hinder His Word, the blood
of the sinning brother will be upon us. If we carry out His
Word, God will save our brother through us," (cf. Eze. 33:
1-9).

[45]Martin Luther, "The Catholic Epistles," Luther's Works, Vol. 30,
ed. W. A. Hansen (St. Louis: Concordia, 1967) p. 132.

[46]Ibid., p. 133.

[47] Martin Luther, "Church and Ministry," I _Luther's Works_, Vol. 39, ed. E. Gritsch (Phila: Fortress Press, 1970), p. 154.

[48] Ibid., p. 155.

[49] Martin Luther, "Commentaries on 1 Corinthians 7, 1 Corinthians 15, Lectures on 1 Timothy," _Luther's Works_, Vol. 28, 3d. H. C. Oswald (St. Louis: Concordia, 1973), p. 286.

[50] Luther, _Luther's Works_, Vol. 39, p. 22. The "ban" was excommunication from Church fellowship and the sacraments.

[51] Luther, _Luther's Works_, Vol. 28, p. 295.

[52] Martin Luther, "The Christian in Society," II, _Luther's Works_, Vol. 45, ed. W. I. Brandt (Phila: Muhlenberg Press, 1976), p. 117.

[53] John Calvin, _Calvin's Institutes_, II, trans. Henry Beveridge (Grand Rapids: Wm. B. Eerdmans, 1970), pp. 315-316.

[54] Ibid., p. 320.

[55] Ibid., p. 321. Calvin prefaced this remark by writing, "In giving the name of bishops, presbyters, and pastors, indiscriminately to those who govern churches, I have done it on the authority of Scripture, which uses the words as synonymous" (p. 321).

[56] Ibid., p. 390.

[57] Ibid.

[58] Ibid., p. 395. Italics mine.

[59] See, for instance, Calvin, _Institutes_, p. 323, who writes, "Hence Paul, in the First Epistle to the Corinthians, when treating of the offices, first enumerates the gifts in which those who performed the offices ought to excel."

[60] This "power", then, could intellectually be based on the objective authority of Scripture, thus preserving the soundness of orthodox doctrine, and yet, in practice, come down to the "greater" authority of the pastor who, in sermon after sermon, demonstrated his (singular) ability to unfold the Word.

[61] Karl Barth, _The Church and the Political Problem of Our Day_ (New York: Charles Scribner's Sons, 1939), p. 83.

[62] I presume that merely disruptive displays are recognizable as decidedly unhelpful, as well as contrary to Scriptural

teaching and prescribed New Testament practice (cf. 1 Co. 14).

[63]Even permitting and encouraging lay participation in the public reading of Scripture and public exercise of prayer could be very helpful in reforming and renewing local congregations.

SIXTEEN

THE ORDINATION OF WOMEN

The ordination of women is a particularly controversial issue in the wider Church community today. It
presents its own peculiar and particular problems to both
liberals and conservatives. American society is growing
more aware of the significant abilities and potential
contributions of women. Various "women's liberation"
movements have sharpened the conscience of the populace.
In this climate the Church has been urged to reevaluate
its own utilization of women in ministry.

From the Roman Catholics to the charismatics, women
are finding new dimensions of service in the churches.[1]
Beverly J. Anderson writes that "the most publicly visible changes that women bring to the ministry are in the
area of leadership style."[2] She observes that "women
are modeling a style of leadership that acknowledges the
pain of ignored talents, dual standards and narrowly defined roles."[3] Anderson advocates the placement of women
in traditionally male-dominated roles and offices. She
argues, "it appears then that women clergy can be more
open to exploring leadership styles that are less hier-
archial and more fluid than those of the majority of
their male colleagues, who have been admitted to the
system as a matter of fact, expectation, and privilege."[4]

Barbara Brown Zikmund acknowledges that, *"women are
challenging traditional sources of religious authority."*[5]
She continues:

> Because classic interpretations of Scripture and church
> history have not accepted many forms of female leader-
> ship, the very presence of woman leaders emphasized the
> tension between Scripture/tradition and religious knowledge
> which comes directly from the Holy Spirit. This is not a
> new development in the history of the church. It was al-
> ways true that women were able to command religious author-
> ity when there was popular confidence in the power of the

147

Holy Spirit (eg. medieval mystics). Whenever women have moved into visible church leadership, the relative importance of Scripture and tradition has been reduced and the legitimacy of personal religious experience has been enhanced.

Not everyone, of course, will welcome such effects as the lessening of the relative importance of the Bible. But then, not all who are urging a greater appreciation and freedom for women in Christian service believe such an effect is either inevitable or desirable. Yet it is difficult to dispute that today women *are* challenging established, if not articulate and accurate, understandings of authority, *and* these understandings are routinely linked to definite Scripture-traditions. Thus, all too often, a link has been forged between sexism and superficial exegesis; but today the same is often true on the other side as well. The challenge to traditional authority has frequently utilized inadequate biblical exegesis and wrongly set aside the Canon in favor of cultural considerations or personal religious experiences.

The way out of this dilemma can only follow from pursuit of the one Word of God in its three-fold form. Marguerite G. Kraft, of Biola College, is correct in observing that "our job is to witness to Christ and the Word of God. If and when the women's issue arises from within the culture, then Christians in that culture need to look to God's Word for answers."[7] This means not only an appeal to the charismatic authority of Christ Jesus, but also proper consideration of the Canon and Church tradition. The functional authority of proclamation must also be examined. Together these three, Christ, Scripture, and proclamation constitute the Word which the Church must hear and obey.

There are many facets to the more general problem of the role of women in the Church. We cannot be afraid to admit the existence of genuine wrongs perpetrated against women who seek ministry. Joan Chatfield is uncontestably right in asserting: "That sexism exists in the world, in the church, in the special domain of professional mission endeavor is a reality."[8] Many men and women are now engaged in seeking justice for all. They have carried their cause into a multitude of arenas, including the "leveling" of language, so that it will not reflect sexual bias;[9] identifying social classifications and stratifying along sexist lines, in order to correct such wrongs; and ministry discrimination in the Church, such as forbidding the ordination of women. Responding to Chatfield, Virginia Ramey Mollenkott writes, "While I heartily agree with Chatfield that sexism is a diminishment

148

of history, policy, and economics,' I should like also
to call it by an older and simpler name: sin."[10] Clearly there is a legitimate application to be made in this
area of Jas. 2:1, My brethren, show no partiality as
you hold the faith of our Lord Jesus Christ, the Lord
of glory."

While my own focus is on the issue of ordination,
I understand the necessity of viewing this one particular
problem against a wider backdrop. Accordingly, I desire
to hear and understand what is said not only about ordination but all of these other issues as well. But I am
restricting the discussion for the most part, and only
hinting at my thoughts in other areas. Preliminary to
a consideration of ordination in relation to the Word of
God, then, must be a brief sketching of the arguments
raised in favor of ordaining women.

First, as observed earlier, the pursuit of ordination for women is admittedly part of a challenge to existing traditional patterns of authority in the Church.
This challenge, however, is being advanced by sensitive
men and women who respectfully insist on a wide reexam-
ination of the authority patterns of Church and society.
Their challenge incorporates exegetical and ecclesiastical work. It is not a monolithic challenge, but is represented by a wide variety of opinions all more or less
formally joined under the indictment of the Church that
sexism is a painful and sinful reality that must be confronted and overcome. Many issuing this challenge are
acutely aware of how they and others have been wronged.

Second, this challenge is based on a rejection of
all forms of discrimination arising from belief in sexual superiority of either male or female. The key biblical text cited is Gal. 3:27-28, "For as many of you as
were baptized into Christ have put on Christ. There is
neither Jew nor Greek, there is neither slave nor free,
there is neither male nor female; for you are all one in
Christ Jesus." Joan Chatfield offers the succinct summary: "National, racial, economic, and sexual supremacy
are leveled in Christ Jesus. National identities, racial
and economic differences, sexual distinctions remain. It
is superiority of the one over the other which is named
for what it is: a travesty outside the plan of God."[11]

Third, this challenge raises some particularly sharp
questions for men in the Church. Answering Chatfield,
S. Scott Bartchy states that "the basic question, as I
see it, that we Christian males must ask ourselves is
this: Are we willing to allow both Jesus' way of treating people and his teaching to criticize and revise fundamentally the uses of power that we have learned from

the world and regard as 'natural' because of our socialization as males?"[12]   Peter H. Davids likewise wonders
whether, "the roots of the problems addressed . . . might
lie more in the roles of men than in those of women."[13]
Davids continues:

> Women in church are asking for power, rights, hier-
> archy, and authority. This should make us uneasy not
> because the women are seeking equality in these areas,
> but because they thereby point out that the men exercise
> such "lordship." Where did the model of the servant
> community go? Who has heard the words of Jesus about the
> first being last, the leader the servant of all?[14]

Judy Alexander adds force to this query by stating
bluntly, "If the leaders are men, those men should serve.
If those who serve are women, their leadership should be
acknowledged."[15]

Fourth, this challenge likewise raises keen questions for women and all exegetes of Scripture. Chatfield
believes, "a scriptural focus will refine the vision of
men and women called to co-labor, sent into the field."[16]
Patricia J. Mortenson asks frankly, "Are women conscious
that God speaks to them through husbands and elders, but
also speaks directly and specifically to them through his
Word by his Spirit?"[17] Mortenson also asks questions of
critical importance not only for women but for the male-
dominated sphere of biblical exegetes as well. She ur-
ges that "perhaps we need to look again at Genesis in the
Hebrew and determine the meaning of the word 'helpmeet'.
Does it mean assistant, a helper for one who is the primary mover; or does it mean a strong partnership with
some variance in function?"[18] In citing Gal. 3:28, she
notes, "If the Holy Spirit is given equally to men and
women alike, and spiritual gifts are bestowed on both men
and women, what is the meaning and the implication of the
priesthood of every believer, male and female?"[19]

Fifth, the challenge, having raised critical questions, answers with strong assertions.   The first of
these, an unqualified rejection of sexism, has already
been seen. Often coupled with this, whether quietly or
loudly, is an indictment of the ecclesiastical hierarchy
which has either applauded sexism or stood mutely aside.
Thus Chatfield tersely confesses, "my church is not an
equal opportunity employer."[20] But, the challenge goes
deeper than the charge of sexism. Men in leadership are
all too frequently abusing their place, and now they are
being called to account. Alexander speaks for many when
she states, "When our leaders fail to follow Christ's example and to become servants, they sin."[21] She reminds
us that "authority is not equivalent to superiority."[22]

More positively, the challenge asserts there is a genuine need for the exercise of dogmatics, wherein the preaching and practice of the Church is carefully reevaluated in light of the Gospel. The challenge is, in fact, a call to reform, with particular attention to the serving of justice. It is for an acknowledgement, acceptance, and appreciation of the distinctive, but joint role to be played by women in Christian ministry. Chatfield speaks to this when she argues that "looking carefully at the New Testament theses, with an openness that is unhinged from a precluded agenda and from an habitual albeit unconscious acceptance of sexism, the message seems clear. . . . Jesus came to tell *us* the Good News, to allow *us* to participate in his mission."[23] Similarly, Mortenson writes:

> When women begin to understand that the entire Good News is for them, they will begin appropriating Christ Jesus in order that the fruit of his Spirit may be increasingly apparent in their lives. There will be greater development of their God-given gifts and a sense of partnership in the proclamation of the Gospel. Their participation in a more public type of ministry in leadership or decision-making roles will always be according to their recognized spiritual gifts which equip them for these roles.[24]

Sixth, the principal quality of this challenge lies in its vigor for a new implementation of charismatic authority and, to a lesser extent, charismatic ministry. The challenge to traditional authority is in the hope of recovering the mind and model of Jesus.[25] Appeals are made more often to Jesus than to the hard admonitions of Paul.[26] The role of the Spirit is accentuated and that of Scripture diminished. This does not necessarily mean a lessening of biblical authority, but a subordination of this authority to that of the Holy Spirit. The gifts of the Spirit become an important hermeneutical help. It is often pointed out that "Neither the gifts of the Spirit nor the natural gifts of leadership seem to have been given more to one sex than to the other. Nor is there any evidence in the New Testament that either the 'fruit' or the 'gifts' of the Spirit are sex-linked."[27]

Seventh, with particular relation to the issue of ordination, these considerations present a challenge to gladly accept qualified women into the offices of ministry. Since Jesus, and the New Testament, applaud women workers and unhesitatingly welcome them as partners in mission, the sexism of today's Church must be rejected as unbiblical. Inasmuch as a charismatic base underlies ecclesiastical offices, a refusal to ordain women appears clearly contrary to the nature and purpose of spiritual gifts. Where ordination is confined to men, will not sexism prove inevitable? Does not, in fact, such an occurrence mean precisely that the Church equates falsely authority with masculine superiority? Where, plead the issuers of this challenge, is any demonstrable evidence that women are less gifted or able to fulfill any of the offices of Christian ministry?

The answers to these questions cannot be spun out of hand. They demand a sensitive and honest hearing and appraisal. In accordance with both an understanding of authority as described by the Word of God, and the pertinent challenge to return to the founder of the Church to be corrected, we must turn first to the authority of Jesus. Is the ordination of women consistent with his authority? Does Jesus address the issue either explicitly or implicitly? Both Jesus' acts and his preaching must be instrumental in answering these two questions.

Certainly it is clear enough today that Jesus espoused what can only be regarded as a "high view" concerning women. The respect and place accorded to women in the teaching and ministry of Jesus are remarkable for a teacher of his day.[28] In all four Gospels a portrait of Jesus emerges that shows a man without pretense of any sexual superiority. The female nature is not regarded as in any respect inferior to that of man. In simple point of fact, women in the ministry of those surrounding Jesus occupy a prominent place.

But what, precisely, was this place? Several observations come readily to mind. *First*, no woman is listed among the Twelve. There is nothing in the Gospels to indicate that women enjoyed *all* of the prerogatives or responsibilities enjoined upon Jesus' male disciples. *Second*, despite the admittedly significant visibility of the women around Jesus, for the most part no mention is made of women being present when Jesus gathers the disciples aside for special instruction. *Third*, there exists no explicit teaching by Jesus upon which to base the inclusion of women into all of the specific and distinctive aspects of apostleship. It is true that no teaching in itself excludes women either, but two facts are clear: Jesus everywhere upholds the goodness and propriety of the God-established natural order, and women were *not* accorded the place granted men in apostleship. This latter fact, especially, must be explained, and no simple charge of cultural sexism would appear adequate. The revolution against sexism initiated by Jesus is continued in the early Church.

Fourth, a careful distinction seems necessary

152

between the *inclusion* of women into partnership with men in the Christian mission, and their specific sub-*ordinated* position. The question must be asked: do we have in the New Testament the record of a true revolution only half begun, or the subtle trappings of a more sophisticated sexism? Are women offered something with the right hand only to have it snatched away by the left? Or, is the precedent established with Jesus that true sexual equality rejects all notions of sexual superiority, but retains a created order wherein men have authority over women, but enact this authority in Christian *caritas*, that is, with all humility, gentleness, care and respect?

In all of the recorded interactions of Jesus with women no definite "ordination" to formal leadership (i.e., as a disciple, leader of others, head of formal tasks, etc.) can be pointed out. At the same time, women are appointed specific tasks (Jn. 20:17), enjoy individual instruction (Lk. 10:38-42), are not discriminated against in petitions (Jn. 11:28-44), and are singled out for praise as righteous examples (Mk. 12:41-44). Raymond E. Brown, in a study entitled, "Role of Women in the Fourth Gospel," has advanced some provocative ideas. Bartchy agrees with Brown's conclusion of a study of Jn. 4:38, about John's use of *apostellein*, that "this description of the missionary activity of the Samaritan woman modifies to a certain extent the thesis that male disciples were the only significant persons in the founding of the Church."[29] In view of the Gospel's accounts, one must agree. Women are not accorded a minor, insignificant place. Jesus includes them in the Great Commission. Yet some explanation must exist for the fact that none of the Twelve are women, and that the early Church did not appear to regard Jesus' example as indicating that they should occupy the most prominent roles of leadership.

It seems to me that Jesus, as the first form of the Word of God, as, properly speaking, the *one* Word whom we are to hear and obey, demonstrates clearly an opposition to sexism. He opposes any idea that women have a lesser place in his Church and her mission. But this Word must not be heard to say something more than what is clear. It does not clearly proclaim the same *offices* of ministry (formally speaking) for women as for men. Jesus must not be heard in opposition to his apostles and prophets. What appears clearly is that Jesus, in his disclosure of the Triune God as the first and final authority, delegates that authority in such a manner that three familiar conclusions must be formed. First, the authority of women, like that of men, is under God. Second, *God* sets the boundaries on any and all authority to be exercised

153

by women. Third, these boundaries, seen only implicitly during Christ's earthly ministry, are articulated more fully by the teaching of the New Testament writers.

What, then, does Scripture say? As a mediating authority, Scripture stands between God's authority and all authority exercised in the Church. It must be accorded its place as Canon and allowed to freely guide the Church in her thinking, speaking, and acting. Exegesis must be utilized with honesty and cautious care, following the basic premise of permitting Scripture to serve as its own best interpreter.

This last point is of critical importance. Many, on both sides, have accused opponents of biased or careless biblical investigation. Davids, viewing Chatfield's use of Gal. 3:27-28, notes it "is frequently used, as here, simply as a catchword for *our* theology. He proceeds to complain:

> Such exegetical weakness appears not only in feminist argument, but in much modern theological method: Scripture is apparently cited with a desire to find some legitimation there, but weak exegesis means that only superficial parallels at best are selected from the scriptural tradition . . . . Either we must do without legitimation from Scripture, giving it up as a lost cause, or we must do careful exegesis before doing theology.[31]

While Chatfield rejects Davids' criticism, his point is worth repeating: exegesis must create theology, and not vice versa.[32] Thus, the occasional suggestion to dismiss certain of Paul's texts on the grounds that these reflect only simple cultural expressions of a less enlightened view of women is hardly credible. The goal of theology is not, after all, to reproduce another culture. Rather, it is to speak to our own along the same lines of address utilized earlier in history and in a different culture. It ought also to be remembered that the biblical perspective, in both Old and New Testaments, definitely affords a higher view of women than that visible in contemporaneous, surrounding cultures.

The Scriptures do not represent, at any point, a depreciation of the status or work of women. On the contrary, at every point they represent a true liberation of women, though this liberation is itself conditioned completely by the authority of God. This is true as much for Paul as for Jesus. With Paul and the other New Testament writers, the charismatic institution of leadership means women enjoy the presence of the Holy Spirit, the outpouring of his gifts, and spiritual vocations as much as do men. But in Paul, the critical impact of redemption on the created order becomes most visible.

154

Paul's great pronouncement in Gal. 3:27-28 cannot be minimized. It strikes a profound blow for all humankind. Both male and female have a place *in* Christ. Alongside this can be set his parenthetical comment in 1 Cor. 11:11, "Nevertheless, in the Lord woman is not independent of man, nor man of women." Their mutual status in Christ means men and women are equally recipients of the benefits and responsibilities of Christian existence (cf. 1 Pet. 3:7). This includes, of course, spiritual gifts (1 Cor. 12:7, 11). It also includes mutual submission (Eph. 5:21) and respect, or consideration (Eph. 5:33; cf. 1 Pet. 3:7).

Herman Ridderbos, in his Paul: An Outline of His Theology, suggests that we are confronted by two viewpoints: "on the one hand the woman shares fully in the salvation given in Christ . . . on the other hand, fellowship in Christ does not remove the natural distinction between man and woman, and man's position of leadership with regard to woman."[33] These must not be regarded as mutually exclusive, but complementary (although existing in view of Rom. 8:18-25, i.e., in a setting where redemption is only partly unveiled). For Paul, the in-breaking of redemption restores the created order as a new creation, a new order under the revealed Lordship of Christ.

Thus the difficult texts, advising silence by women in public assemblies, are much more than concessions to an antagonistic cultural setting. Paul's 'theology of creation' is *Christian*; it understands the created order subordinated to the redemptive order manifested by Christ "in this present time." But redemption does not overthrow creation like a Gnostic putting off of the flesh. It restores and fulfills creation. The created order again serves to picture the redemptive order. Thus marriage reflects the covenant of salvation in Christ (Eph. 5:32). The authority of both State and Church reflect the reality of God's authority (Rom. 13:1).

Yet, the proponents of ordination for women appear to base their case on the "superiority" of Paul's insight in Galatians 3. They set an opposition between this and certain other texts. Krister Stendahl, in his, The Bible and the Role of Women, acknowledges that, "in all of the texts where the New Testament speaks about the role of women in the church, we have found that when a reason is given, it is always by reference to the subordinate position of women in the order of creation. This applies to her place in the home, in society, and even in the church, that is, when she is 'in Christ'."[34] In other words, equality in salvation is realized without the disruption of the created order, an order still retained by redemption.

But Stendahl views the matter somewhat differently. On the basis of Gal. 3:26-28, Stendahl supports what he conceives is a biblical "emancipation proclamation" for women. He argues, "something has happened which transcends the law itself, and thereby even the order of creation."[35] Thus, "if emancipation is right, then there is no valid 'biblical' reason not to ordain women."[36] This idea of a "transcending" of the created order is essential to those who favor ordaining women. Grace is superior to nature, and redemption to creation. Hence, the establishment of women as equal recipients of grace can only mean their equal privilege to receive ordination of the formal offices of ecclesiastical leadership.

Certainly the early Church struggled with the effects of redemption on the created order. Paul, especially, wrestled with this relation. But it is not tenable to maintain the apostle advocated a setting-aside or major revision of the created order. in fact, as Stendahl has observed, Paul appeals repeatedly to the created order in discussing the role of women in the Church (1 Cor. 11:2-16; 14:33-36; cf. 1 Tim. 2:8-15). To be sure, cultural considerations also enter. But these should not be viewed as dictating the policy set in the early Church. Rather, theological insight is expressed in appropriate, contemporaneous forms. So Ridderbos writes of Paul's advice:

> (T)he intention was to give expression to the distinc-
> tion between man and woman and perhaps also to the subjec-
> tion of woman to man. The deeper motive, i.e., the place
> that from the beginning God chose to ascribe to woman in
> her relation to man, therefore finds its concrete form in
> the manner in which it is proper according to custom that
> a woman conduct herself in public and is to know her place
> with respect to man. So far as this is concerned Paul is
> here apparently apprehensive, just as he is elsewhere, lest
> in the consciousness of its new freedom the church give of-
> fense to others . . . . On the other hand, it is clear
> that there is also a relativizing element in this appeal
> to custom and the "commune measure," insofar, that is, as
> the (sub-*ordinated*)position of women with respect to man
> is to be given expression in a manner that must be consi-
> dered appropriate for a certain time and culture.[37]

The Scriptures are not compromised by cultural demands and pressures. The task of Church proclamation is to preach the full Gospel, in all its integrity, but in contemporaneous forms of address. This, however, can only be accomplished if the Scriptures are understood. Thus Paul, understanding the law and the prophets, *and* the new revelation in Christ, faithfully adhered to the Gospel while still appealing to *God's* created order. The Church today must likewise know the Scriptures.

It appears to me that at least six facts clearly emerge from the Scriptural data. *First,* the order of creation subordinates woman to man but neither is independent from the other, although their roles are distinct (1 Cor. 11:2-16). *Second,* Jesus did not upset the created order, but clarified it in relation to himself and redemption. *Third,* there is no so-called "double standard particularism," that is, an equality between women and men in salvation but in no other way. Instead, woman is, ontologically, in every respect the equal of man. *Fourth,* there is a universal application of redemption to creation which is inclusive of men and women, not exclusive (Gal. 3:27-28; 1 Pet. 3:7; Rom. 8:18-25). *Fifth,* the order of creation is retained by the Church as a tool of her mission, thus explaining the display of redemption in created institutions like marriage (Eph. 5:22-33), and the importance of avoiding giving offense (Romans 14 & 15). Redemption intrudes into creation so that the latter may rightly manifest its interiorized covenant of grace and providence. *Sixth,* the ordination of women must be viewed as a misunderstanding of redemption to the created order *and* an abuse of authority. Such an act stands contrary to the plain statements of the New Testament.

What, then, can the Church proclaim? To this point in her history the Church has steadily resisted all attempts to grant women certain offices and ministries. John S. Pobee has asked, "Is women's liberation (which I distinguish from the dignity of the woman as one in the image and likeness of God) a basic ingredient of the Gospel?"[38] Thus far the Church has answered with a resounding "No!" But the tradition is hardly infallible and it has been rightly questioned. Too often the Church has practiced sexism and wrongly called distinction "superiority."

The Church today must return once more to the charismatic leadership of Jesus Christ *and* to a renewed fidelity to the Scriptures. This means recognizing and heralding the truth that the Gospel of redemption liberates women to Christian ministry. These ministries include the successful (if not always public) exercise of all the fruit and gifts of the Holy Spirit. Yet, it must also be acknowledged that a distinctive place and character is retained for women within the created order that the Church does not supercede but utilizes in her mission. Thus, as but one example, the exhortation still

157

stands to wives to be submissive to their husbands, "so that some, though they do not obey the word, may be won without a word by the behavior of their wives, when they see your reverent and chaste behavior" (1 Pet. 3:1-2).

There does not appear anywhere in the New Testament any prejudice against women participating in the proclamation of the Gospel through the utterance of a "prophetic" word. In fact, women are cited as having prophecied without rebuke (Ac. 21:8, 9), and they must certainly be included in Paul's discussion of gifts with the believers at Corinth (1 Corinthians 12 & 14). However, while all *can* prophecy, women are to exercise restraint and refrain from speaking in the public assemblies of the Church (1 Cor. 14:33-36; cf. 1 Tim. 2:11-12). This, Paul writes, is in accordance not only with the law (1 Cor. 14:34), but with the Word of God (1 Cor. 14:36). Paul sternly warns, "If any one thinks that he is a prophet, or spiritual, he should acknowledge that what I am writing to you is a command of the Lord" (1 Cor. 14:37).

Certainly such a command must not be viewed as a simple concession to culture! It is only understandable in light of the relation of redemption to creation. Women have as much freedom as men to privately spread the Good News about Jesus. Women, too, are called and characterized as Christian confessors, whose responsibility in the Church and before the world is to witness clearly to Jesus Christ, and him as *Lord*. When they do this they are exercising the highest authority, and truly serving as leaders. This is true charismatic leadership and not to be minimized. Alexander offers a timely reminder when she writes, "We all have roles requiring submission, and we all have roles of authority. In fact one person may be both an authority and a subject in different relationships to the same person."[39] We are to all "be subject to one another out of reverence for Christ" (Eph. 5:21).

Women can also serve in "official" capacities. For example, Phoebe, "a deaconess (*diakonon*) of the church at Cenchreae" (Rom. 16:1), is commended by Paul.[40] But the early Church developed the duties of these women along lines that kept them from formal leadership over men (cf. 1 Tim. 5:3-16; cf. the Didache). There are no indications of women elders, presbyters, or bishops. Likewise, no woman was permitted to become a prominent teacher or theologian. Their capabilities were to be utilized privately. In public the woman deferred to the man.

This deference can easily be misconstrued. It is not either a false humility or a divine right for the superior man. It *is* the created order. Women may, indeed *must* preach the Gospel. Nevertheless, under the strictures of Canon, and in accordance with the authority of God himself as revealed in Christ, they may, and indeed *must* refrain from doing this in the public assemblies of the Church. This does not reduce or abrogate their responsibility of coming prepared to participate in Christian worship (1 Cor. 14:26). It does delimit their proper avenues of expression.

The functional authority of Church proclamation is *not* served by women in the pulpit. Their presence there is an unnecessary offense, and contrary to Scripture. God's authority he purposed to be redemptively reflected through his own ordained, created order. I acknowledge that this is a hard word, and not by any means acceptable to many. However, I resist the charge that this position is sexist. Indeed, I want to offer a statement of reconciliation to those who cannot agree with what I have set forth.

It seems to me at any rate that we make too much today of the offices of the Church and not enough of the function of leadership that can be manifested by anyone in the priesthood of all believers. In the current situation in the Church the inordinate focus on the prerogatives of ecclesiastical office have not only resulted in controversy and confusion, but have hindered a right concentration of attention on the dynamic ministry of the proclamation of the Gospel itself. Only by recognizing that the Canon liberates both men and women to a free proclamation of the Gospel apart from the offices of the Church will there be any reinstatement of the charismatic nature and the corresponding power of the early Church.

There are still a host of subsidiary questions that remain. For instance, can a woman *ever* preach a sermon? Such a question can only be answered by inference and application of what has been outlined above. In accordance with the teaching of the Apostle Paul in 1 Corinthians, it seems clear to me that a woman, no less than a man, should be prepared to preach the sermon of Christ. It appears to me that she should come to the public assembly prepared to share a word of prophecy. Nevertheless, in accordance with the Canon, it also appears clear to me that the woman should *always* defer to the man in the exercise of that gracious privilege. Such a deferment is not a belittlement of the woman but is, instead, a joyful and gracious submission to the boundaries of authority given to her and to the man in their joint ministry under the leadership and Lordship of Jesus Christ.

Finally, I urge that evangelicals engage in profitable and positive ecumenical dialog and association with

other believers on this issue. For too long they have
occupied the role of bystanders who have criticized with
too little understanding, and too little positive, constructive dialog with others outside the evangelical per-
suasion. Now that evangelicals are being brought increasingly to face this issue within their own domain, it
becomes not only desirable, but literally *imperative* that
they open a fruitful dialog with those with whom they
must necessarily disagree. This does not mean a reen-
gagement of the old fundamentalist-modernist controversy,
but rather a humble willingness to see, to understand,
and still, where necessary, to respectfully disagree.

[1] Many Catholic churches now allow a greater role for women in the Mass. In Pentecostal and Charismatic circles, as well as many Wesleyan churches, women have long enjoyed ministries denied them in other denominations.

[2] Beverly J. Anderson, "Womanstyle: Eyes to See the Gifts in Others," The Christian Century, Vol. XCVI, No. 5 (Feb. 7-14, 1979), p. 123.

[3] Ibid.

[4] Ibid.

[5] Barbara Brown Zikmund, "Upsetting the Assumptions," The Christian Century, Vol. XCVI, No. 5 (Feb. 7-14, 1979), p. 127.

[6] Ibid.

[7] Marguerite G. Kraft, "Comment on: Women and Men: Colleagues in Mission," Gospel in Context Vol. 2 No. 2 (April, 1979), p. 20.

[8] Joan Chatfield, "Women and Men: Colleagues in Mission," Gospel in Context, Vol. 2, No. 2 (April, 1979), p. 5.

[9] Personally, I confess my sympathies about this language-changing labor are not too firm. I may be wrong, but I think most Americans still believe masculine pronouns are generally inclusive in meaning, subject, of course, to contexts. Peter H. Davids probably speaks for the majority when he states, "It is simply linguistically wrong to say that a word must carry all of its meanings all the time or that grammatical gender has anything to do with sexual gender." (Comment on: Women and Men: Colleagues in Mission," Gospel in Context, Vol. 2, No. 2 (April, 1979), p. 17. At the same time, I certainly do not desire to offend, and personally do not object to substituting the neutral "person" for "man."

[10] Virginia Ramey Mollenkott, "Comment on: Women and Men: Colleagues in Mission," Gospel in Context, Vol. 2, No. 2 (April, 1979), p. 21.

[11] Chatfield, "Women and Men: Colleagues in Mission," p. 8.

[12] S. Scott Bartchy, "Comment on: Women and Men: Colleagues in Mission," Gospel in Context, Vol. 2, No. 2 (April, 1979), p. 16.

[13] Peter H. Davids, "Comment on: Women and Men: Colleagues in

Mission," <u>Gospel in Context</u>, Vol. 2, No. 2 (April, 1979), p. 18.

[14] Ibid.

[15] Judy Alexander, "Servanthood and Submission," <u>Gospel in Context</u>, Vol. 2, No. 2 (April, 1979), p. 37.

[16] Chatfield, "Women and Men: Colleagues in Mission," p. 4.

[17] Patricia J. Mortenson, "The Role of Women in Missions," <u>Gospel in Context</u>, Vol. 2, No. 2 (April, 1979), p. 29.

[18] Ibid.

[19] Ibid.

[20] Chatfield, "Women and Men: Colleagues in Mission," p. 7.

[21] Alexander, "Servanthood and Submission," p. 38.

[22] Ibid., p. 37.

[23] Chatfield, "Women and Men: Colleagues in Mission," p. 7.

[24] Mortenson, "The Role of Women in Missions," p. 30.

[25] This is quickly evident in most of the authors I have cited in this chapter.

[26] Paul is championed, of course, for his true insight in Gal. 3: 27-28. Elsewhere he is reproached for being still culture-bound.

[27] Bartchy, "Women and Men: Colleagues in Mission," p. 16.

[28] It is impossible to imagine, for instance, that Jesus might pray, "Lord, I thank you that I was not made a woman'!

[29] Bartchy, "Women and Men: Colleagues in Mission," p. 16, with reference to Raymond E. Brown, "Role of Women in the Fourth Gospel," <u>Theological Studies</u> (36: 688-699), 1975.

[30] Davids, "Women and Men: Colleagues in Mission," p. 17.

[31] Ibid., p. 18.

[32] This is true even where certain necessary Christian presuppositions bear on exegesis, for these presuppositions are themselves products of exegesis (eg., the *sensus literalis*).

162

[33]Herman Ridderbos, Paul: An Outline of His Theology, trans. J. R. deWitt (Grand Rapids: Wm. B. Eerdmans, 1975), p. 460.

[34]Krister Stendahl, The Bible and the Role of Women (Phila: Fortress Press, 1966), p. 38.

[35]Ibid., p. 34.

[36]Ibid., p. 41.

[37]Ridderbos, Paul: An Outline of His Theology, pp. 462-463.

[38]John S. Pobee, "Comment on: Women and Men: Colleagues in Mission," Gospel in Context, Vol. 2, No. 2 (April, 1979), p. 23.

[39]Alexander, "Servanthood and Submission," p. 37.

[40]It is, admittedly, very doubtful that the "office of deaconess" is referred to here. But clearly Phoebe, and other women, occupied a role close to titular in nature. Later, the office of deaconess was formally recognized, although not in every place at every time.

SEVENTEEN

POLITICAL INVOLVEMENT

The authority of the Church and her mission will
necessarily bring her into a constant involvement and an
interaction with the strictures of the State in which her
mission is conducted. The Church, which is not of this
world, is always within this world. Thus, the authority
of the Church will always come into opposition to the
authority which rules in this world. While it remains
true that the authority of the State itself comes from
God, nevertheless this authority, corrupted as it is,
will again and again reveal itself in its opposition to
the authority of the Church. It therefore becomes a matter of great importance to examine the nature of the authority of the Church in its relation to the authority
of the State, or, to put it more simply, Church-State
relationships.[1]

Richard Mouw has criticized contemporary evangelicalism for being an "immature movement" in this sphere,
characterized by an "ongoing evangelical confusion about
the relationship between the 'personal' and the social
dimensions of human life."[2] Most evangelicals are still
uncertain as to how to best respond to a post-Watergate
era. The heralds of the new evangelical call to social
awareness must overcome this uncertainty. Evangelicals,
with their keen ethical sensibilities, require direction
in pursuing justice and comfort to the deprived and needy
of a complex society.

Yet, if there has been any one arena in which evangelicals have visibly surfaced in significant numbers,
it is in politics. To be sure, it is precisely at this
point that evangelical "immaturity" has often shown itself. But it is promising that the burgeoning attention
accorded evangelicals in the late seventies and on into
the new decade has been brought about in no small part
by evangelical action in national politics.

164

The proper relation between Church and State is, therefore, very much an alive issue. While evangelicals search for appropriate actions to take, more attention to the *reasons* behind such actions must be given. The evangelical community is divided by those who still advocate as complete a separation between Church and State as possible, those who are urging a more vigorous address of the State by the Church, and those who would seek to conform the State to a Christian ideal in the name of the Church. The relation of authority in the Church to that wielded by the State is once again assuming more importance. Evangelicals must be recalled to a theological examination of the problem.

Authority in the relation of Church and State must, as all other issues, be examined in accordance with the three-fold form of the one Word of God. Therefore, we must see the significance of Jesus' authority for this relation, the mediating authority of Scripture between Church and State, and the functional authority of the prophetic Church with regard to the State.

Jesus' authority in relation to the State displayed the significance of God's own authority. Jesus revealed the Triune God as the authority established above both Church and State. The State in its authority does not exist autonomously, nor does it exist above or below the authority given to the Church. While the State's authority is independent of the Church, it is still dependent upon the God who has given authority to the Church as well.

Jesus set an example for the early Church, that the Church and State are not opposed. This is not to deny the simple reality of the fact that the State and its authority frequently opposes the authority given to the Church. This opposition is more often seen in the simple non-recognition by the State that the Church has an authority which can in any way have a claim on the citizens of the State. Jesus, however, both in his relation to the State personally, and in his teaching about the State, stressed that the opposition that exists between Church and State must be one-sided. That is, the State must be that which was demonstrated by Jesus himself. Resistance must take place only within a positive sphere, where the Church works for the best good of the State and not in opposition to it. This understanding seems to lie behind those acts recorded of Peter, Paul, and the other early Church leaders in Luke's Acts of the Apostles.[3]

When the State opposed Christ, he overcame it in passive resistance. Though Jesus submitted to the State, he clearly demonstrated that the authority of the sacred,

165

or the redeemed order was superior over the secular, or created order, *within the Kingdom of God.*[4] In so doing, he did not evidence any disrespect for the authority of the State, but a clear recognition of the limitations of that authority.[5] Within the world, the Church is not superior to the State, but now God's kingdom is breaking more fully into the world and an envious State sees its reign coming to an end. Jesus' authority reveals God's boundaries before and after the State, and thereby sets limits to the State in its own exercise of authority.

Thus, both the history of the early Church, and the teaching of the Scriptures (both Old, and yet more particularly New Testament), demonstrates a continuation of the understanding focused in Jesus' own ministry and his teaching.[6] Oscar Cullmann observes that "there are . . . problems which are actually posed and solved by the New Testament. The question of Church and State is one of them: It is so closely bound up with the Gospel itself that they merge together."[7] In a certain sense, the same might be said of the Old Testament.[8]

The Scriptures thus function as a mediating authority between Church and State, and they do this in four dimensions. First, vertically, Scripture establishes the same one God above both Church and State. Second, in a horizontal dimension, Scripture presents a union and a distinction between the authority of Church and State. The distinction between these two is their purpose, or mission. The Church exists in a role unique from that of the State. Their union is in the character of each as servants of both God and man. Both Church and State err when they usurp a place of authority as those lording it over the ones under their jurisdiction. Third, Scripture is Canon over the Church, but not over the State. Scripture as Canon must therefore be exercised in the State by the *prophetic* Church. The Church has a role within the State by the exercise of Scripture, and the Church must therefore relate to the State by its exercise of Scripture. Finally, conflict between Church and State must be understood in such a way that the dynamic role of the Spirit's witness is fully incorporated. This witness is the promise that when the Church is called to account by the State, the Spirit himself will impell the Church to proclaim a faithful testimony to Jesus Christ. Likewise, the Church, in calling the State to account, must invoke this same faithful sermon and testimony.

A question naturally arises from this: where in Holy Scripture are *concrete* models to guide the Church? How, *practically* speaking, can the Bible serve as a mediator in the above-named dimensions? The answer to this query must consist in discovering biblical commands and suggestions, as well as recovering a biblical understanding. In the pursuit of this, I have been aided by such outstanding examples of biblical research and presentation as that offered by Daniel Lys in his searching article, "Who is Our President?"[9]

Lys works from the text of 1 Sam. 12:12 — "When you saw that Nahash the king of the Ammonites came against you, you said to me, 'No, but a king shall reign over us,' when the Lord your God was your king." From this text a pertinent sermon is constructed, one which offers a host of insightful observations. But first, let Lys set the background:

> The *historical background* is at least twofold. On the one hand Israel had so far constituted what Martin Noth calls an amphictyony, that is, a sacred tribal league, gathered around the central sanctuary of the Ark, expressing their common faith in the recital of the saving acts of God and obedience to the same divine law. Each tribe, however, was politically independent. When a tribe was in danger, God raised up a "judge" as a "savior" to deliver this tribe from the enemy (e.g., Judg. 3:9 f.). This charismatic leadership was limited in space and time. Attempts to make it hereditary had been either rejected (Judg. 8:22 f.) or a failure (Judg. 9). This could look like complete freedom, since "every man did what was right in his own eyes" (Judg. 17:6). But this was more than that: This was the reflection of the faith in God who, through holy war, and without recourse to human military designs, was able to deliver his people. Now a stronger danger threatens Israel in her totality. Saul appears as the charismatic leader for the whole sacral league, *and* is made king, in spite of the distrust uttered in 1 Sam. 10:27 (see also 11:12 ff.). Notwithstanding the establishment of kingship, it seems that the Northern Kingdom was unable to accept the idea of dynasty and longed for the ancient charismatic leadership. This fact would explain the numerous upheavals.[10]

The unique relation of Israel to the kingship is evident as far back as the opening of the decalogue. Lys notes, "since the great king is replaced by the Lord in the covenant formula, there is no longer any room left for any great king but the Lord, at least according to the theology of the Old Testament — and this will involve giving up also any foreign relations according to human patterns, and any human kingship."[11] Thus, "1 Samuel 13:14 opposes the present 'kingship' of Saul to the 'chiefship' of a man to come who is after God's heart."[12] Yet the kingship does come to Israel. Then, almost immediately, it reaches its greatest height in David.

Lys comments:

> In a certain way, David is the ideal king, called *nagid*, from the point of view of God (1 Sam. 23:30; 2 Sam. 5:2; 6:21; 7:8). The king is, as it were, demythologized. He is a human being, adopted by God (2 Sam. 7:14; 1 Chr. 28:6; Ps. 89:27; Ps. 2:7). He may be rejected if he does not act according to God's will. In fact, from the very beginning, (1 Sam. 13:14), there was a tension between the present, disappointing king and the king to come as a true one, who was expected at any new enthronement to be the good ruler through whom God *the* King could rule his people (cf., e.g., the expectation of a new David and the way Ezekiel 34 describes at the same time God (vs. 15) and David (vs. 23) as the "shepherd" of Israel). We could speak here of a "relativizing" of the idea of human kingship *and* of the "humanizing" of God's kingship. It is in this eschatological tension that Jesus came as *the* King—whose kingship is of a kind different from any human kingship, and whose name is definitely related to the idea of salvation (ysh') which runs through the Israelite pattern of leadership as the reason for the raising up of the judges. The function of the king as 'savior' is spoken of here only once (1 Sam. 9:16; cf. 10:27!; also 11:3 and 14:45); but above all God performs this function (2:1; 7:8; 10:19; 14:6, 29; also 4:3!).[13]

In view of these and similar considerations, Lys recommends that, "to witness to God's kingship means to live theocratically in a world where there is no theocracy—and where any theocracy, either worldly or churchly, would be respectively the pagan divinization of human institutions or the sin of a church confusing itself with God's kingdom and using God as a tool for its plans."[14] Lys is thus led to the key issue: "If a Christian wants to live his life as a unity where his faith expresses itself in his existence—if he wants to avoid having his life split into two parts: the part of God and the part of the world, the part of religion and the part of politics—then it is necessary to reflect with courage on the following question: How does the Bible help me to make my political choices?"[15]

Lys recognizes, "Since the Lord is the only God, he is also the God of the pagans (though they do not know that)."[16] This, Lys concludes, must mean two important things. First, "the destiny of the Lord is not tied to the political existence of Israel . . . . His destiny does not depend on the political success of Israel."[17]

"in fact," as the second matter, "the testimony of Israel to the Lord in front of the nations will be expressed in both victories and destructions . . . . Israel is then the servant and the witness of the Lord in her doom *and* in her salvation."[18] These ideas are to be manifested in the human kingship. "The Israelite king, if he was to be really the king of the elect people, was just the representative of the Lord, the mediator of the covenant . . . . The prophets had to remind the actual king that he was to conform his life to the pattern of the ideal king as God's image, and not try to resemble the earthly kings, that he was there as a king not for political success but for witnessing among the nations."[19]

Admittedly, the difficulties in applying Israel's situation to our own are in some respects formidable. But I agree with Lys that the Bible, even here at 1 Sam. 12:12, is instructive in encouraging me to ask questions about my political choices that I *can* answer. My answer is guided by the text. I am part of *God's* people. My first allegiance is to *his* kingship (Lordship). My place within the State is as a member first of the Church, and then, in the State, as a witness to the King of kings. This witness is mine to make regardless of the State's support or opposition to it, and also irrespective of the State's gain or losses. Frank Spina reminds us that "Israel the believing community has been around, even if at times only as a 'remnant', since the end of the Late Bronze Age (ca. 1200 B. C.), but no political structure, including the Israelite state, can make a similar claim; in fact, it is a rare state that lasts much longer than about three-hundred years."[20] Thus I am reminded that my proper place, as a member of God's Kingdom, is not contingent on the success of the State of which I am also a member.

Movement from text to sermon, like that afforded by Lys, both demonstrates the role of Scripture *and* the importance of preaching. By the sermon the Church is reminded of its place vis-á-vis the State. Also by the sermon the Church takes up her prophetic mantle. She now speaks not only to God, but for him. She does this, not by her own wisdom, but in the power of the Holy Spirit's own witness and, therefore, by the exposition of Holy Scripture. Thus her preaching is biblical preaching of a prophetic character.

But this also means that the functional authority of the prophetic Church rests solely on God. It is by his Spirit's testimony that the witnessing community is preserved, and preserved as such, even while the State is formed or passes away. But there are four salient

points that must be highlighted concerning the functional authority of proclamation in relation to the State.
These points form the basis of the different practical
actions undertaken by the Church in any State.

First, proclamation, by its very nature, asserts
the freedom of the Gospel from State dominion. Barmen
declares: "The commission of the church, in which her
freedom is founded, consists in this: in place of Christ
and thus in service of his own word and work, to extend
through word and sacrament the message of the free grace
of God to all people."[21] But this also means the *political* work of asserting *Christ's* kingship. Thus, Barth
writes, "This gospel which proclaims the King and the
Kingdom that is now hidden but will one day be revealed
is political from the very outset, and if it is preached
to real (Christian and non-Christian) men on the basis
of a right interpretation of the Scriptures it will necessarily be prophetically political."[22] Accordingly,
Barmen must insistently repudiate "the false teaching
that the church, in human self-esteem, can put the word
and work of the Lord in the service of some wishes, purposes and plans or other, chosen according to desire."[23]

Freedom from State dominion means freedom to be and
to become the liberated bondsmen of the Lord Jesus. So
Barth states succinctly, "The Christian community shares
in the task of the civil community precisely to the extent that it fulfills its own task."[24] And this task is
first the preaching of the Gospel of Jesus Christ. It
is, by its very nature, political and does not need to
be made more so by human intervention.[25] Alan Richardson
advises, "The Christian engaged in political activity,
whether at the national or local level, will view his
work as the service of God through the service of mankind. He will be humble and not count his Christian pro-
fession as conferring upon him superior political exper-
tise."[26] Christian freedom is always for the betterment
of the State even when it must resist the State.

The freedom of the Gospel from State dominion means
that a properly understood Christianity can never simply
be equated with a national religion. This is true even
in the other direction, where the Church assumes a dominion over the State and becomes the national political
order. Such a fusion, from either side, is dangerous.
Barmen powerfully addresses this very issue as follows:

> "Fear God, honor the King!" (1 Peter 2:17).
> The Bible tells us that according to divine arrange-
> ment the state has the responsibility to provide for jus-
> tice and peace in the yet unredeemed world, in which the
> church also stands, according to the measure of human

insight and human possibility, by the threat and use of force.

The church recognizes with thanks and reverence toward God the benevolence of this, his provision. She reminds men of God's Kingdom, God's commandment and righteousness, and thereby the responsibility of rulers and ruled. She trusts and obeys the power of the word, through which God maintains all things.

We repudiate the false teaching that the state can and should expand beyond its special responsibility to become the single and total order of human life, and also thereby fulfill the commission of the church.

We repudiate the false teaching that the church can and should expand beyond its special responsibility to take on the characteristics, functions and dignities of the state, and thereby become itself an organ of the state.[27]

Second, proclamation acknowledges the right of the State to wield authority, but it must be wielded for the sake of the freedom of the Gospel. In this manner the State, like the Church, must respect and yield to the authority and freedom of the Gospel. This is accomplished by the State at the precise point of its God-given charter: "Would you have no fear of him who is in authority? Then do what is good, and you will receive his approval, for he is God's servant for your good" (Rom. 13:3-4). This must be examined both positively and negatively.

Positively, the State upholds its authority virtuously when it enacts and enforces a civil order that does not hinder the Gospel, but, in fact, permits its full expression. Thus Rome, in its best character, afforded law, peace, and the Roman roads for the service of the Gospel. At their best, "rulers are not a terror to good conduct, but to bad" (Rom. 13:3). Also, it must be remembered that, "there is no authority except from God, and those that exist have been instituted by God" (Rom. 13:1). Luther expressed the opinion that, "when in Rom. 13 (:1) Paul says that the government is of God, this is not to be understood in the sense that government is an affliction . . . but in the sense that government is a special ordinance and function of God just as the sun is a creature of God or marriage is established by God."[28]

Government belongs to the order of creation. This order is not to hinder the breaking-in of the redemptive order because redemption gives meaning to creation. In the positive sphere Christians should acknowledge the State as given by God for protection, peace, and the restraint of evil. In return for this service by the State Christians serve the State through obedience, support, respect, honor, gratitude, and especially prayer (1 Tim. 2:1-2).[29] Luther himself believed that "preachers . . . should faithfully remind the authorities to maintain peace, justice and security for their subjects, to defend the poor, the widow, and the orphan."[30]

However, not all governments are what the Church might pray for them to be. Negatively, the State abuses its authority by denying its servant character and establishing a civil order that oppresses its people or hinders the Gospel.[31] Yet even such a State is still the servant of God. The Bible repeatedly describes wanton, pagan governments used by God to accomplish his own purposes (although they are ignorant of this).[32] Luther advised that Christians 'give the benefit of doubt' to the State: "if you do not know or cannot find out whether your lord is wrong, you ought not to weaken certain obedience for the sake of uncertain justice; rather you should think the best of your lord, as is the way of love for 'love believes all things' and 'does not think evil'."[33] Even should the State prove itself unkind, Luther warned, "citizens are to be diligently instructed not to be less obedient and subject toward harsh government."[34]

Third, in special view of the State that has forsaken its rightful character the prophetic Church stands against the State's unbelief and opposes its separation from the source of its authority. In this work the prophetic Church is a reconciling Church (cf. 2 Cor. 5:16-21). She does not take up the sword,[35] except "the sword of the Spirit, which is the word of God" (Eph. 6:17). As Luther put it, "the governing authority must not be resisted by force, but only by confession of the truth."[36]

The author of Hebrews exhorts believers to:

> Recall the former days when, after you were enlightened, you endured a hard struggle with sufferings, sometimes being publicly exposed to abuse and affliction, and sometimes being partners with those so treated. For you had compassion on the prisoners, and you joyfully accepted the plundering of your property, since you knew that you yourselves had a better possession and an abiding one. Therefore do not throw away your confidence, which has a great reward. For you have need of endurance, so that you may do the will of God and receive what is promised (Heb. 10:32-36).

Jesus himself said, "Do not resist one who is evil. But if any one strikes you on the right cheek, turn to him the other also" (Mt. 5:39). With this text in mind, Luther remarked, "a Christian should be so disposed that he will suffer every evil and injustice without avenging himself; neither will he seek legal redress in the courts but have utterly no need of temporal authority and law for its own sake. On behalf of others, however, he may and should seek vengeance, justice, protection, and help, and do as much as he can to achieve it."[37]

In 1 Pet. 3:14-15 believers are told, "even if you do suffer for righteousness' sake, you will be blessed. Have no fear of them, nor be troubled, but in your hearts reverence Christ as Lord." The Church can bear the injustices placed upon her, but she must endure in faith. Her testimony must be clear, her conscience clean, "so that, when you are abused, those who revile your good behavior in Christ may be put to shame" (1 Pet. 3:16). Above all, the Church must suffer, if she is to suffer, as true victims of *injustice* : "for it is better to suffer for doing right, if that should be God's will, than for doing wrong" (1 Pet. 3:17); "for one is approved if, mindful of God, he endures pain while suffering unjustly" (1 Pet. 2:19, cf. 20-21).

The Church may indeed find herself praying as the Psalmists did (e.g., Psalm 137). But she is to be ever mindful of the Apostle's admonition: "Beloved, never avenge yourselves, but leave it to the wrath of God; for it is written, 'Vengeance is mine, I will repay says the Lord'" (Rom. 12:19). The rightful resistance of the Church to the State's unbelief is the resistance of prophecy, that is, the steadfast declaration of God's truth against the State's lies. The prophetic mantle, however, involves not only word, but deed.[38]

Paul follows the teaching of Jesus in urging, "'if your enemy is hungry, feed him; if he is thirsty, give him drink; for by so doing you will heap burning coals upon his head.' Do not be overcome by evil, but overcome evil with good" (Rom. 12:20-21); "Repay no one evil for evil, but take thought for what is noble in the sight of all" (Rom. 12:17). Such conduct will recall the manner of Jesus, who suffered his trials in relative silence, with remarkable nobility (Mk. 14:61; Lk. 23:9; Mt. 27:14; cf. Isa. 53:7).[39] There is a time to match righteous deeds to godly words, and a time to let actions speak for themselves. But the Church is called to give a *Christian* testimony whether she speaks at a given moment or not.

Of course, a timely word of witness is the Church's vocation in the bad State as well as the good. Timothy is urged to "preach the word, be urgent in season and out of season" (2 Tim. 4:2). 1 Pet. 3:15 exhorts Christians to "always be prepared to make a defense to any one who calls you to account for the hope that is in you, yet do

173

it with gentleness and reverence." Jesus himself said, "you will be dragged before governors and kings for my sake, to bear testimony before them and the Gentiles. When they deliver you up, do not be anxious how you are to speak or what you are to say; for what you are to say will be given to you in that hour; for it is not you who speak, but the Spirit of your Father speaking through you" (Mt. 10:18-20). If this word is delivered in the face of injury or death, the Church is blessed still and can "rejoice and be glad, for your reward is great in heaven, for so men persecuted the prophets who were before you" (Mt. 5:12).

Fourth, the Church always vigorously upholds the reality of God's work in the history of all States, and acknowledges his dominion over all. This is true even though it is also probable that "when the Church of the New Testament spoke of the State, the emperor or king, and of his representatives, it had in mind the picture of an "angelic power" of this kind, represented by this State and active within it."[40] The State, as with every other facet of the created order, has been seriously affected by sin. The governments of mankind have come under the sway of the powers of darkness. "The kings of the earth set themselves, and the rulers take counsel together, against the Lord and his anointed" (Ps. 2:2).

But it remains a fact that God reigns over all, for in Christ, "all things were created, in heaven and on earth, visible and invisible, whether thrones or dominions or principalities or authorities — all things were created through him and for him" (Col. 1:16). Yet in this present age the Church must recognize that "we are not contending against flesh and blood, but against the principalities, against the powers, against the world rulers of this present darkness, against the spiritual hosts of wickedness in the heavenly places" (Eph. 6:12). That is why it is essential that the Church gird herself with *spiritual* armor and weaponry (Eph. 6:13-18). But the spiritual powers arrayed against the Church operate in the created order with physical force. Jesus tells his followers, "Do not fear those who kill the body but cannot kill the soul" (Mt. 10:28). Paul comforts the Church with the confidence that "neither death, nor life, nor angels, nor principalities, nor things present, nor things to come, nor powers, nor height, nor depth, nor anything else in all creation, will be able to separate us from the love of God in Christ Jesus our Lord" (Rom. 8:38-39). This is because God has "disarmed the principalities and powers and made a public example of them, triumphing over them in him" (in Christ; Col. 2:15).

Because God's reign is established over all powers,

174

but presently invisible except to the eyes of faith, two
dangers perpetually confront the Church. The first is
the temptation to take the State more seriously than is
proper. This is a temptation to unbelief. Faith affirms
"Jesus is Lord!" (1 Cor. 12:3). Christians pray in expectation, "your kingdom come, your will be done" (Mt.
6:10). Like Luther we must be ready to say:

> This is the reason it is less disastrous when the
> temporal power goes wrong than when the spiritual pow-
> er does. For the temporal power can do no real harm
> because it has nothing to do with the preaching of the
> gospel, or with faith, or with the first three command-
> ments. But the spiritual power does harm not only when
> it does wrong, but when it neglects its duty and bus-
> ies itself with something else altogether, even if
> these other works were better than the very best works
> of the temporal power. Therefore, we must resist the
> spiritual power when it does not do right, and not re-
> sist the temporal power even when it does wrong.[41]

More recently, Barth has reminded the Church that
"it is out of the Church's line to seek to improve human
society and to make plans and projects for this purpose.
The work of the Church is more modest: to call men, to
recall to them that God reigns and is present, clearly
to tell that man does not live by his own strength, but
by the grace of God."[42] It is truly a sign of unbelief
when the Church takes up a foreign vocation and seeks to
displace the State. When this happens the Church denies
that God reigns over the State as well as the Church.
Barth, who throughout the long course of his life wrestled with the proper relation of Church to State, wrote:

> In general, we cannot assert: the hand of God is
> *here* in the world. However, there is a difference be-
> tween the man who walks with the assurance that God
> reigns and the man who does not know it. God reigns
> not only in this ministerial house but also in this
> more worldly street; not only in the Church but also
> among all these people who are picking grapes and will
> drink on Sunday and will dance. God is also among our
> soldiers, among our national councillors and among all
> this nation. They are all certainly in the hands of
> God and God is ever the same. These people are differ-
> ent, and we too are different. But one thing is sure:
> whatever happens in the world, it is God who reigns in
> Jesus Christ. Often one believes it. Often also one
> is at pain to believe it. The essential thing is that
> this is true.[43]

The second danger that confronts the Church is the
temptation to not consider the State seriously enough.

This is a shallow, irrational fideism. A radical insistence on the complete separation of Church and State, where each literally ignores the other, is a dangerous misunderstanding of authority. God's authority in the world means the rightful existence of both the State and the Church. Each has its proper sphere.[44]

The Church must continually reevaluate its relation to the concrete State in which she finds herself. At this point particularly, the Reformation affords many valuable lessons. In their struggle, the Reformers were pressed to devote a great amount of time and energy to Church-State relations. Both on the Lutheran and Calvinistic sides of the Reformation a view of the complementary relation of these two institutions was carefully developed.

A. O. Hancock, writing with regard to the Lutheran view, cites Melancthon's understanding vis-à-vis Philip of Hesse, that "the role of the prince is to deal with outward and obvious wickedness and thereby keep order, making the unhindered preaching of the gospel possible."[45] Hancock observes, "the Word would then be free to take its course, and the conscience would be free to receive it. The church and the civil authority are complementary: the government teaches the outer man by coercion, and the church proclaims the Word which teaches the inner man"[46] The result of this cooperation is of mutual benefit: "it is not necessary to exercise the outer, civil task of restraint and coercion toward those hearing the Word, i.e., those truly hearing."[47]

Similarly, Georgia Harkness writes that, "it was the duty of the State, Calvin thought, to use its power — if need be, its sword-bearing arm — to enforce moral living and sound doctrine. But it was to do this always according to the direction of the Word of God, and it was the prerogative of the Church to interpret the Word and will of God."[48] Bloesch writes of Calvin's view that in it, "the church should give moral support to the state, and the state should give temporal support to the church."[49] In this interrelationship the Church and State respect one another but never become fused into one entity.

Today the Church, especially in the United States, must consider the State with seriousness but without any grimness. Certainly Christians are as free as anyone to engage in State work. But the Church must not usurp the State's place. Her role is a prophetic one. The Church's allegiance is first to the kingship of God. Those Christians who work for the State must retain the priority of the Church's claim upon their lives. The State, like the Church, can and must be reformed. But this reformation dare not attempt to be the creation of a so-called *Christian* State, where the government of Church and State are the same. The Gospel remains free from State dominion, and thereby frees the Church to be a faithful witness to the grace of God in Christ (2 Tim. 2:8,10).

Now Evangelicals have emerged as a potent political force. But this power can be all too quickly abused or dissipated. It can only be properly channeled if a new and a broad awareness of Church—State relationships is forged. But this evangelical awareness must be dictated solely by the Word of God. Accordingly, it will involve contemporaneous preaching directed to the citizens of the State, and although usually indirectly, at the State itself. Such an awareness will encourage individual participation at local, state, and national levels. This participation will be directly influenced by each individual's Christian confession. However, the evangelical Church will *not* become a constituent part of the ruling State. Both by her preaching and the personal involvement of her members she will occupy a prophetic role, serving the State by reminding it of its place and proper duties. It is the privilege of Christians in a democracy to fit this prophetic task to specific citizen responsibilities like voting and petitioning.

The evangelical community will serve the State by occupying itself with the diligent fulfillment of its own God-given work. This work is the Christian mission. This mission is not the work of government reform. Therefore the Church will not advocate State legislation, although individual believers may, as citizens, vigorously pursue such a course. But the Church does not and cannot look to the State for its salvation. Lys reminds, "Man is saved by the Lord, not by politics. We must understand that the New Testament basic confession of faith, 'Jesus is Lord' (1 Cor. 12:3) is not just a religious, innocuous formula. This is a polemic way of speaking that is opposed to the political submission of another formula: 'Caesar is Lord.'"[50] Mindful of this, the Church will faithfully advocate that all men and women, and every "power and principality," submit to the gracious rule of God, from whom all authority comes as the gift of order and freedom, given to enhance and protect life in all its dignity.

[1] Oscar Cullmann states that, "the fundamental importance which this question has retained throughout successive generations until today was present from the very beginning." The State in the New Testament (New York: Charles Scribner's Sons, 1956), p. 3.

[2] Richard J. Mouw, "Evangelicals In Search of Maturity," Theology Today, Vol. XXXV No. 1 (April, 1978), p. 46.

[3] Cf. Acts 4:13, 18-20; 23:1-5; 25—26.

[4] Indications of this are evident in Jesus' trial before the Sanhedrin (Mk. 14:53-65) and, especially, before Pilate (Jn. 18:33-37).

[5] Cullmann, in The State in the New Testament, contends that for Jesus, "1. The State is nothing final, nothing absolute. It will pass away. 2. For the duration of this present age it is not, indeed, a divine entity, but it is nevertheless willed by God as a temporary institution" (pp. 59-60).

[6] In addition to the famous Mk. 12:13-17, there is also the more important Mk. 10:35-45, Jn. 13:1-20, etc. Leadership as service becomes a principal motif not only in the Church, but as a key to the Christian understanding of the State proposed by Paul (Rom. 13:4).

[7] Cullmann, The State in the New Testament, p. 3.

[8] In the Old Testament, of course, the problem is in some respects more intense because of the *nation* Israel's relation to Israel, the *believing community*.

[9] Daniel Lys, "Who is Our President?" (from Text to Sermon on 1 Samuel 12:12), Interpretation, XXI, 4 (Oct., 1967), pp. 401-420.

[10] Ibid., p. 408.

[11] Ibid., p. 409.

[12] Ibid.

[13] Ibid., p. 410.

[14] Ibid., pp. 411-412. One can think of A. Ritschl, on the one hand, and many post-millenialists on the other, as examples of churchly sin in this area.

[15] Ibid., p. 412.

[16] Ibid., p. 413.

[17] Ibid., pp. 413-414.

[18] Ibid.

[19] Ibid., p. 415.

[20] Frank A. Spina, "Can the City be a Community?: The Interaction Between Politics and Religion," Seattle Pacific University Review, Vol. 1 No. 1., p. 11.

[21] John Leith, ed. Creeds of the Churches (Richmond: John Knox Press, 1973), p. 522.

[22] Karl Barth, Community, State, and Church, intro. W. Herberg (Gloucester: Peter Smith, 1968), pp. 184-185.

[23] Leith, Creeds of the Churches, p. 522.

[24] Barth, Community, State, and Church, p. 158.

[25] In other words, the Church preaches Christ, not politics. But The preaching of Christ is political.

[26] Alan Richardson, The Political Christ (Philadelphia: Westminster Press, 1973), p. 107.

[27] Leith, Creeds of the Churches, pp. 521-522.

[28] Martin Luther, "Church and Ministry," II, Luther's Works, Vol. 40, ed. Conrad Bergendoff (Phila: Fortress, 1958). p. 284.

[29] Cf., Ibid., pp. 281-284.

[30] Ibid., p. 284.

[31] A State which permits preaching but practices oppression is still a corrupt State and must be viewed by the Church as standing in opposition to the Gospel.

[32] See for instance, Hab. 1:3-11, or the remarkable Isa. 45:1-8, where Cyrus is designated by Yahweh as "his anointed." Consider, too, Peter's sermon in Ac. 2 (esp. v. 22-24), and Paul's relation to the State.

[33] Martin Luther, "The Christian in Society," III, Luther's Works Vol. 44, ed. J. Atkinson (Phila: Fortress Press, 1955), p. 92.

[34] Luther, Luther's Works, Vol. 40, p. 285.

[35] I recognize "sword-bearing" is a hotly disputed issue, which I cannot undertake to address here. Cf. the interesting discussion in O. Cullmann, The State in the New Testament, pp. 32-34.

[36] Martin Luther, "The Christian in Society," II, Luther's Works, Vol. 45 ed. W. I. Brandt (Phila: Muhlenberg Press, 1962), p. 124. Lys reminds, "Any citizen can tell the authorities when they go beyond the rights of constitution, but only the Christian can tell them about the limitation of their power by God" ("Who Is Our President?" p. 418).

[37] Ibid., p. 101.

[38] Students of the Old Testament prophets have indelible images fixed in mind of the unusual and symbolic acts of the prophets: Hosea taking a harlot to wife (Hos. 3:1-3), Ezekiel building a city on a brick (Ezekiel 4) and refusing to mourn or weep for his dead wife (Eze. 25: 15-24), etc. The New Testament is likewise not lacking such images (cf. Agabus' act in Ac. 21:10-11).

[39] These three references cite Jesus' silence before the Sanhedrin, Herod and Pilate. John's Gospel gives the fullest account of Jesus' verbal testimony (Jn. 18:20-23; 33-37).

[40] Barth, Community, State, and Church, p. 115.

[41] Martin Luther, "The Christian in Society," I, Luther's Works, Vol. 44, ed. J. Atkinson (Phila: Fortress Press, 1966), p. 92.

[42] Karl Barth, The Faith of the Church, trans. G. Vahanian (New York: Meridian Books, 1958), p. 146-147.

[43] Ibid., p. 143.

[44] Luther said, "The temporal government has laws which extend no further than to life and property and external affairs on earth . . . ." (Luther's Works, Vol. 45, p. 105). The Church belongs to a different order; when the government intrudes it "only misleads souls and destroys them" (ibid.). But the Church cannot usurp the State's place either.

[45] A. O. Hancock, "Philip of Hesse's View of the Relationship of Prince and Church," Church History, Vol. XXXV, No. 2 (June, 1966), p. 161.

[46] Ibid.

[47] Ibid.

[48] Georgia Harkness, <u>John Calvin: The Man and His Ethics</u> (N. Y.:
1931), pp. 21-22.

[49] Donald Bloesch, <u>Essentials of Evangelical Theology</u>, II (New
York: Harper & Row, 1979), p. 140.

[50] Lys, "Who Is Our President?", p. 417. Lys also remarks that,
"the church is not to be ruled as the nations are, and is
not to be saved and is not to survive through the political
means that the nations use for their own survival, that is
to say, through earthly alliances" (p. 415).

EIGHTEEN

MARRIAGE AND THE FAMILY

What has marriage, and the life of a family, to do with the Church's authority? This little-asked question needs to be answered in accordance with the one Word of God in its three forms. To some, the issue is *not* an issue. They may find the subject either trivial or too mundane to be considered proper for theological scrutiny. But to most people this issue is far more critical than any of the others I will examine.

There exists a genuine authority crisis between the Church and the Christian home. Which ought to have top priority? Which really has first claim on individuals' lives? Should the Church occupy a position above the family? Would this mean the destruction, or crippling, of Christian marriages and families? Does the Church suffer when the family is given a place before it? These queries must be faced with thoughtful answers.

Various individuals, like Bill Gothard through his nationwide Basic Youth Conflicts Seminars, have presented strong models of authority within the home, but they have hardly begun to address the question of the relation of Church and family. Such an address, as it begins to surface, must examine the authority of Christ in the home, the mediating authority of the Bible in the home, and the functional authority of proclamation in the home. As the Word of God increasingly undergirds and conditions the Christian home, the created institutions of marriage and the family will increasingly display the redeemed order.

Jesus, in revealing God, discloses the Father as the creator of all life, and the one "from whom every family in heaven and on earth is named" (Eph. 3:15). But Jesus is established by the Father "above every name that is named" (Eph. 1:21). At the name of Jesus, "every knee should bow . . . and every tongue confess that Jesus Christ is Lord, to the glory of God the Father" (Phil. 2:9-11;

182

cf. Rom. 14:10-12). The position and authority given to Jesus is "for the church, which is his body" (Eph. 1:22-23). Therefore, it is only natural that Paul should consider marriage and the family in view of Christ's place and power (Eph. 5:22-33). The Apostle subordinates marriage to the relation of Christ to the Church and, in fact, sees marriage as a reflection of this higher covenant (Eph. 5:32).

In Christ, the Word of God displays Lordship over the Church and thereby over every family in the Church. The redeemed order, celebrated by the Church's existence, must receive priority over marriage and family, the most fundamental institutions of the created order. But the Church may be properly called a "family" (although it is not in Scripture), because all believers have one holy Father (1 Cor. 8:6), and because Jesus is not ashamed to acknowledge them as his brethren (Heb. 2:11, 12). Believers, in turn, address one another as "brother" or, "sister" (Gal. 4:28; 1 Cor. 7:15; Jas. 2:15-16), mindful that Jesus is "the firstborn among many brethren" (Rom. 8:29). Christians are the "children" of God (Jn. 1:12; Eph. 5:1; 1 Jn. 3:1).

Likewise, marriage is an institution of the created order which affords important glimpses of the redemptive relationship between God and the world. Marriage, because it is not more important than the relation it imperfectly mirrors, occasionally is subjected to unfamiliar thoughts (Hosea 3: Eze. 24:15-24; 1 Cor. 7:29). Yet it is more than a mirror; it has genuine substance, for in marriage a man and a woman "become one flesh" (Gen. 1:24). God hates divorce (Mal. 3:16). He desires "godly offspring" (Mal. 3:15). All mixed marriages between the faithful and unbelievers are prohibited (Ezra 10:3-4; Neh. 13:23-27; cf. 1 Cor. 7:16), although if one partner *becomes* a believer while the other does not, a different set of guidelines is put into effect (1 Cor. 7:12-16).

Marriage is, as Luther noted, a "worldly" institution. Jesus taught that it is not an institution continued beyond this present age (Mt. 22:30). Yet in this time it has its place and must never be regarded in a condescending manner (1 Cor. 7:36). At the same time, marriage, as fundamental as it is, must not be regarded as a means of salvation (it is *not* a sacrament), or accorded a place of superiority over singleness (1 Cor. 7:38). In fact, following Christ may actually mean marital separation, either temporary or permanent (Mk. 10: 29, 30).

Christ's relation to the Church within the redeemed order becomes, in the created order through marriage, a preeminent example of salvation. In his relation to the Church, Christ becomes the example of properly exercised authority in the home. This authority has two poles: first, that of the husband over the wife, and second, the service of both husband and wife in mutual submission and respect. These facets, and others, are set forth in Eph. 5:21-33, a precise description of how marriage reflects the greatness of God's covenant with his people. Marriage is like a mirror, and at the heart of marriage, where "two become one," Christ and the Church are revealed. Like any well-placed mirror, marriage at its best is fixed at such an angle as to bid us come see, again and again, the face of Christ in all his love and glory.

Paul's letter to the Christians at Ephesus is designed to reflect Christ. Part of that reflection, in fact the very essence of it, is visible in marriage. The divine mystery of how a man and a woman become one in wedlock is God's own ordained way of reflecting to all men in every time the love of Christ for his body, the Church. Marriage, therefore, is holy. Not only so but it is evangelically holy because the Christian marriage reflects divine love and is, by this very fact, a most fundamental and powerful witness to the truth of God in Christ.

To unify his message on this matter, Paul chose several threads that blend with one another and lead to one another as they present a complete and radiant garb. Beginning with submission (5:21-23), Paul moves to sacrificial love (5:24-27), respect (5:28-30), and divine purpose (5:31-32). He concludes with his famous summation, "this is a great mystery" (5:32), and a reminder of the practical concreteness within this mystery (5:33). All of these strands are woven together to produce a fine fabric that reveals on its outside the relationship between husband and wife and on the inside the relationship of Jesus to his Church. Marriage, the outward and visible portion of this garment, hides an inner lining of divine mystery. This Paul discloses by 'turning the garment inside out,' or hanging it before a mirror.

An interesting aspect to Paul's discussion is his attitude, or approach to his message. He begins with the presupposition that we can see Christ's relation to the Church by unveiling the mystery of marriage. But in his actual discussion, Paul moves in the opposite direction. Looking first at Christ's relation to the Church, the Apostle explains how Christian marriage should be constructed. He looks at marriage to see Christ and to understand marriage. This demonstrates that while the mystery of "two become one" points beyond itself to God, it is God in Christ who explains the mystery.

What Christ makes visible about marriage is evident in his relation to believers. So Paul's first thought is in regard to the conduct believers maintain because of their Lord's example: "Be subject to one another out of reference for Christ" (5:21). The command is to a reciprocal submission between believers with each and every believer striving to emulate the unilateral submission Jesus displayed toward the Father. In other words, *because* of their reverence for Christ, believers take on a willingness to respect and honor others even, as Paul writes elsewhere, to the point where they "in humility count others better" than themselves (cf. Phil. 2:1-11). There is no thought here of a deference offered in the hopes of having praise returned. Rather, it is the glad yielding of simple obedience to the will of the Father. It is following the example of Jesus.

However, this general rule of conduct is particularly vital to marriage. It is this idea of submission, in fact, that renders a peculiar transformation of men and women. The command to be subject to one another becomes the convocation whereby God calls men and women together as husbands and wives. Reverence for Christ enables wives to be subject to their husbands, "as to the Lord" (5:22), even as it reminds husbands to "live considerately with your wives, bestowing honor on the woman as the weaker sex, since you are joint heirs of the grace of life, in order that your prayers may not be hindered" (1 Pet. 3:7).

When believers look at Christ they see that he is the head of his body, the Church. As a simple matter of fact, this headship of Christ is the very first facet of his relation to the Church that the world observes. This is why Christians call him "Lord." In a like manner the first facet of marriage which the world observes is that the husband is the head of the wife. Jesus, by virtue of his being Savior, has taken a place of authority over the Church. Wives, because of the authority given their husbands, must yield in reverence for Christ to complete submission. "As the Church is subject to Christ, so let wives also be subject in everything to their husbands" (5:24).

While the world looks to see who is in authority, the Church, as those who are under authority, looks first and also principally at how that authority is maintained. Paul, therefore, moves on to the responsible handling of authority. Although wives are to be subject *in everything* to their husbands, the true burden of responsibility lies not on them but upon their husbands. All the wife must do is obey her husband. The husband must love his wife, "as Christ loved the Church" (5:25). This is no easy task. Christ demonstrated his authority and administration by a sacrificial love. Now his Church is called to obey. By virtue of Christ's love, the obedience of the Church can only be thankful and glad-hearted; he has already fully shown himself responsible and able to preserve his Church. The husband who follows Christ's example frees his wife to the joyous service of trusting obedience. If he fails then she, of course, can only be submissive to the Word of God, and creatively also to her husband so that, even though *he* is not obedient to the Word, he might still "be won without a word" through her "chaste and reverent behavior," (cf. 1 Pet. 3: 1, 2). On the other hand, if the wife does not obey the Word, she proves that "a wife's quarreling is a continual dripping of rain" (Prov. 19:13).

The sacrificial love of the husband is to be based on a model of the priesthood. However, unlike the human model of the Jewish priests, his task is patterned on Christ's superior priesthood. He must die to self so that his wife is freed to live in him. It is not that he ceases to be or that his wife lives only for him, but it is that he finds himself when he gives himself for her and she likewise is most herself when living in peaceful obedience to him. Here again we clearly see Christ and his Church. In his death at Calvary Jesus died so that his Church might live. Christians now live *in* him and *for* him. They find themselves in him. By the power of his resurrection Jesus has found himself exalted, sitting at the right hand of God the Father Almighty, and head of his Church. The husband who loves his wife as Christ loved the Church is the true disciple of Jesus. He gives himself, sacrifices not only all that he *has*, but also all that he *is*, for his loved one. The husband gives every part of himself so that even his body is no longer his own (cf. 1 Cor. 7:4).

Yet, strangely enough, love left at this altar is beautiful, but ultimately without power. Submissive love creates order and develops character. Sacrificial love brings peace, security, and even a sense of identity. But without *purpose* even this fine love is finally lifeless. Christ's love is redeeming love. His sacrifice was not empty but, "that he might sanctify her i.e., the Church . . . that he might present the church to himself in splendor, without spot or wrinkle or any such thing, that she might be holy and without blemish" (5: 26, 27). This love was no pretentious show but a costly purchase. God wanted us. He acted out of his love for us so that he might have us, and have us in the only way befitting his godliness, "holy and without blemish."

The priesthood of the husband is likewise filled with purpose. If he is to love his wife *even* as Christ loved the Church, he must desire her complete sanctification. By his own sacrifice the husband hopes in God for the redemptive process to take full effect in his spouse so that she might be holy, ready for presentation before Christ. Like the priesthood of Christ, there is not only a sacrifice but also a purification.

The husband's love of his wife must follow precisely Christ's example if it is to be effectual. Christ Jesus' purpose of sanctifying the Church was made sure by his sacrifice. His self-giving love was for the benefit of the Church. This is displayed in Christ's cleansing of the Church, "by the washing of water with the word" (5:26). The imagery of Christian baptism reflects the inner cleansing from sin accomplished by Christ's sacrifice. The believer is passed through water to mark his passage from life to death and he is confirmed as one of Christ's own by the confession of faith. The believer's purification insures that he will stand holy and blameless before his Lord. The Church, composed of all persons so washed, stands as *one* body, the bride presented in her splendor to Christ.

The husband's goal is also the presentation of his wife as one made without blemish. He desires first to present her to himself in this form but, as God's good steward, to present her in splendor before Christ also. He who loves his wife as he does his own body regards the presentation of his wife to God as his spiritual worship. These words apply to him as a call to a holy priesthood: "I appeal to you therefore, brethren, by the mercies of God, to present your bodies as a living sacrifice, holy and acceptable to God, which is your spiritual worship" (Rom. 12:1).

When two become one flesh in marriage, it no longer is enough for them to care only for themselves. In the body of Christ the concerns of Christ are the substance of the Church's vocation, and the concerns of the Church are what Christ makes intercession for before the Father. In marriage the man's concerns are, "how to please his wife" (1 Cor. 7:33). In return the wife seeks to do good to her husband and so please him. The two are one, and so pleasing the other is "selflessly selfish". When the husband loves his wife as his own body and serves Christ by so doing he is, in effect, presenting his wife as the very soul and body of himself. This is why to see the husband is to see the wife and vice versa. He who sees Christ sees the Church and vice versa. The two are one, inseparable, a living sacrifice to present before God the Father.

But before the wife can be presented in her rightful splendor, holy and without any spot, she must have first been prepared by cleansing. This is the husband's task. Even as he has sacrificed himself for her sanctification, so he must cleanse her. The rite for such a cleansing is explicit: by the washing of water with the Word. This signifies two things that are, in reality, of one substance. First, the washing of water suggests baptism where there is the public avowal of loyalty to one person accompanied by the testimony of what has transpired in one's life since that special other was introduced. It is the sign of passing from the old into a newness of life.

The Christian wedding is the marriage parallel to Christian baptism. The couple pass from one way of life to another. In the exchange of vows they commit themselves to one another and testify to all who will hear that this other now standing with them is the one who has made a life-changing difference. They present themselves to one another to become one flesh presented as a living sacrifice to God. The wedding looks forward to a continuing commitment and backward at what commitment has already brought forth.

As the husband cleanses his wife by washing, he, by his love in action, vows his loyalty and testifies in her presence that she is the very one he has been called to love as Christ loved the Church. The wife commits her trust to him by submitting to the purification initiated and performed in her by the hands of her husband. She so testifies that God has called her to yield to this one man and him alone.

The second aspect of the cleansing washing is that it is with "the word." It is the word of confession, of testimony of God, that is the husband's instrument. He has received this from God. It is the truth that, as Jesus prayed, "sanctifies", or makes holy. The testimony of the Word who is himself the Living Word, and all that confesses him as Lord is the divine element into which the husband must place his wife if he hopes to present her in all her splendor. She is washed, baptized, totally immersed in Christ. She can only emerge to be presented before her Lord without blemish, wholly alive in the glory of God, and aglow with praise for her husband.

Through his priestly office in marriage, the husband presents a concrete picture of Christ. A unique aspect of that picture is the priestly function of mediation. If it is the priest who sacrifices, washes,

188

purifies, and presents offerings to God, then it is also the priest who does these for someone. The husband is the mediator before God on behalf of the marriage. He is not primarily his wife's advocate or his own defense, but the mediator of the marriage who brings from God love, authority, power, and the Word, and who returns to God a unity of two bodies made holy by God's working.

Precisely because the husband is the head of the wife he is also the leader in marriage. Where the head directs, the body moves. But contrary to any notion that the husband is only an initiator and the wife is only a responder is both the command to be subject one to another, and the model of priesthood. Although authority is vested in the role of the husband, it is characteristic that the wife sees where the responsibility needs to be exercised. Like a supplicant in the temple she often approaches the priest before he has seen any need to act. The two work together to become one with an easy adaptability and security that cannot be threatened by the misleading notion that a wife must not initiate actions in the marriage.

With the communion of husband and wife, of priest and supplicant, a liturgy is constructed. The order of worship in each family is unique, but if the husband does not serve in the mediating role of priest the liturgy is frustrated. Then, too, liturgy by its very nature means public worship. The liturgy of marriage must be made visible to the world. At its best in Christian marriage it constitutes a fundamental witness to Christ against which the world can offer nothing. It shows itself first in the wedding ceremony but more importantly in the way husbands and wives interact in public. Their conduct toward one another when others are present is worship when it is genuine and holy. This, too, is part of God's redemptive process.

The most outstanding feature of the way in which husbands are to love their wives is the hidden aspect of priestliness. A priest is unfit for service unless he has first been made right himself. He must respect his own person and treat it kindly. Remember, he too, is, as an individual, a living sacrifice to God. When he loves his wife as Christ loved the Church he loves her as he loves himself. "Even so husbands should love their wives as their own bodies. He who loves his wife loves himself" (5:28). This is the *summa cum laude* statement of coinherence, of two-become-one. It just makes good sense that husbands should give this love to their wives. The man who abuses his wife abuses himself for they are one-of-another. Rather, "no man ever hates his own flesh, but nourishes and cherishes it" (5:29). Moreover, the Christian must respect self and spouse, "as Christ does the Church, because we are members of his body" (5:29, 30). The husband's greatest joy can be to express to his wife the tenderness exhibited by Christ to the Church.

Where marriage begins in mutual submission because of reverence for Christ, it is in the exaltation of one another through respect that marriage reaches its highest point. Submission defers to another, respect exalts the other. Both belong together, and indeed are together in Christ, but it is respect that is reserved for special recognition. Respect nourishes and cherishes the other. It means love of self for a ready model to selfless love. Most of all respect means love at the heart of marriage where two really do become one. The husband can love his wife as himself because she is one with him. The husband who loves his wife in this manner points dramatically to Christ. The Lord Jesus respects his body the Church. He takes care both to nourish and to cherish it. He exalts the Church because he loves himself and his Church. This is the highest glory.

Inevitably, at the moment respect is consummated in marriage by sexual intercourse, and the two become one flesh, this moment becomes shrouded in mystery. How can two, who are really and in every sense two unique individuals, become one? A person might as quickly ask how Jesus can be both wholly God and wholly man. The fact creates, by its very existence, a hiddenness no understanding can fully divulge. This keeps the fact from becoming lost, and it also prevents its being relegated to the realm of the inconsequential. Instead, its hiddenness fascinates. Its mystery points beyond to where God is.

So Paul writes of marriage, "This is a great mystery, and I take it to mean Christ and the Church" (5:32). The truth emerges that a divine purpose has constructed marriage and is operative within it. "For this reason a man shall leave his father and mother and be joined to his wife, and the two shall become one" (5:31; cf. Gen. 2:24; 2:18-25). At last these words from the Scriptures of the Old Testament have divulged their hidden content. Not for marriage alone has God said the two shall become one. This joining is also for Christ and his Church. The New has made plain the Old. But the Old still remains intact as it stands with the New and in Christ. Marriage is now more blessed and vital than ever before for now it shows Christ in relation to his Church. Now marriage has become the bright witness of one flesh, one Lord (cf. 1 Cor. 6:17).

190

But what of a marriage where the partners are "unequally yoked," where one is a confessing believer and the other is not? Here, too, Christ serves as an example. In 1 Corinthians 7, Paul establishes several crucial insights. *First*, it is necessary that within the home the believing partner exercise an unfaltering obedience to Christ and self-control toward the spouse. The believer must seek to live peaceably with the unbeliever (7:12-13; cf. Rom. 14:19; 15:1-6). Self-control, a prominent motif in the chapter, plays a critical role as the believer tolerates, endures, and perseveres (cf. 1 Cor. 13:4-7). Beyond mere tolerance, however, Paul advised genuine concern. By this, simple endurance can be rendered loving, sacrificial patience. The possibility of the unbelieving partner converting to Christ is never so slender as to be dismissed, even if it cannot be counted upon. Paul was mindful of this when he wrote, "Think of it: as a wife you may be your husband's salvation; as a husband you may be your wife's salvation" (7:16, NEB).

Second, undergirding this hope, and contrasting the doubtful reality of the unbelieving partner repenting, is an element of comfort. God does not desert this family; he is faithful to his believing child (cf. 2 Tim. 2:11-13). Paul wrote, "the unbelieving husband is consecrated through his wife, and the unbelieving wife is consecrated through her husband. Otherwise, your children would be unclean, but as it is they are holy" (7:14). God deals mercifully with this marriage and this family. His authority is manifested in a power working in behalf of both partners for the sake of the believing partner. This is a potent example of the redeemed order breaking into the created order.

Third, fidelity to Christ is of preeminent concern because marriage is an impermanent institution. All of Paul's varied instruction in 1 Cor. 7 is "to promote good order and to secure your undivided devotion to the Lord" (7:35). Marriage and family concerns can intrude and threaten the proper order in human existence, making a lie of professed faith, and producing an unhappy anxiety (cf. 7:32-35). The hope of the family is Christ. He is the Eternal One, while marriage belongs to this impermanent world. Anxiety is only set aside by trust (Mt. 6:25-34) and "undivided devotion." The authority of Christ must reign: "unless the Lord builds the house, those who build it labor in vain" (Ps. 127:1).

Fourth, even in the mixed home Christ's relation to his Church must be manifest. This means an unfaltering willingness to reside with the unbelieving partner (7:12-13). It means also the giving of oneself (7:3-4).

191

There should be a reflection of the peace God has effected (7:15). Contentment, or at least steadfastness, is part of God's calling (7:17-24). Above all these should reside a steady hope and eager expectation that Christ will soon return (7:26-31). These marks are signs that can be present whether only one member or the whole family are part of the Church.

Obviously, the authority of Christ over the Church, manifested as it is, becomes an important model for the Christian marriage. Likewise, marriage and the family can be ideal, concrete reflections of this higher relation. All this is made known to the Church by the Bible. But the second form of the Word of God represents, in itself, other important considerations bearing on marriage and the family. These spring from the nature of Scripture as a mediating authority in the home.

Holy Scripture is a mediating authority between the Church and the Christian family. The Bible, as Canon, has authority *over* both as well. By the Scripture the Christian home can understand itself both in itself and in its many relations. Confessing believers in a Christian family characterize that home as part of the confessing Church. The home, like the Church, is fundamentally established upon the confession of Christ (Mt. 16: 13-20; 1 Pet. 2:4-10). Without this confession it cannot be a *Christian* home. Accordingly, the role of instruction in this confession which the Bible occupies is of critical importance. The Bible mediates God's guidance and comfort, and the pursuit of Bible study and prayer in the home become indispensable. Yet these are more than the exercises of a pietistic imagination. By such study and prayer the objective authority of the Bible is made immediate and personal. The biblical confession of Christ's lordship becomes the substance of the home as a godly institution into which redemption is continually set forth for display.

The mediating authority of Scripture unites Church and home while retaining their distinctions. Both Church and home are under the authority of the Word of God. In both Christ is central. Each is called to an obedience to one confession. The same Bible instructs both. The family is actually included in the Church. But the distinct identity of each is retained. The Bible does not address both equally. The home (as marriage and family) is subordinate to the Church. Therefore the Bible also represents a restriction and a liberation for the Christian home's identity and vocation. This liberation and this restriction exist simultaneously.

The restriction introduced by the authority of the

Scripture relates to the identity of the godly home. The Bible develops this identity by setting the home's limits and illustrating its character. At the same time, there is a liberation to a true identity for the godly home in that this home is now freed from its illusions. It is now capable of seeing itself for what it is, that is, a worldly institution that is part of the created order given by God to manifest, as an imperfect mirror, the redeemed order.

At the same time, the Bible both restricts and liberates the home in its vocation. The idea that a Christian household has a vocation *as a household* has not been called attention to very often. Yet, it is important to understand that the household does have a calling from God in that it is called to manifest the Church. It manifests the Church in its peculiar responsibilities of exercising a mission of hospitality and a willingness to suffer the loss of its possessions to uphold the Christian confession (Heb. 10:32-39; 1 Pet. 4:9). The Bible can free the Christian home from trying to be all that a particular culture might demand of it. It can free the home from trying to be more than what it ought to be. It does this precisely in its restricting the home to its particular and unique, peculiar vocation. That vocation is one that belongs to the Christian household as such, and to it alone.

The Bible's mediation between Church and home means also the Church's use of the Bible to assist the home. As the Church facilitates the unity of the home, the home reciprocates by fuller participation in the Church. This may or may not mean greater involvement in programs. The Church helps the home not by fragmenting it into a multitude of programmed diversions, but by freeing it for service and action as a corporate unity that is also a glad part of the greater corporate body of the Church. The home freed to be itself will freely serve the Church.

The Church, in its relative authority over the home, only serves that authority correctly when the home is carefully preserved in its distinctive reality. Where the Church subsumes the family so that the family identity is submerged or lost, then the Church has seriously abused her relation to the family. The Christian home should trustingly commit itself to the Church, not fearful for its identity. In the Church the family retains its distinctive identity even while gladly listing itself as a vital constituent part of the community of saints.

Finally, a note must be made at this point concerning the concept of households and Christian community. Such a concept has received relatively little attention.

At no point in the Church's tradition has the concept of households and Christian community been assigned, in a practical expression, any real prominence. Yet, while it is uncertain as to what the exact living conditions were of the early believers, it seems clear that from the beginning Christian households did exist. These were structures wherein more than one family, or a family plus independent members existed. The concept of Christian community is, at any rate, certainly not precluded by good Christian theology, which stresses that the Church ought to be regarded as a body, and as a household (cf. Eph. 2:19-22).

We are now brought to the third form of the Word of God, which is the functional authority of Church proclamation in the home. In this regard, there are two important functions that must be acknowledged and respected. The *first* of these is that the home is ruled as the Church is. This means that the Christian home must be governed by the preaching of the Gospel, by the confession of Christ, and by a steadfast witness to the Word of God. In so doing, there is a maintenance at all times of the real possibility of a reconciled life-style, since Christ, the Reconciler, is thereby permitted a consciously active role in the home. Again, the facilitation of this is brought about by conscientious prayer and study of the Scripture.

At the same time, allowing the proclamation of the Gospel to rule the home solidifies the foundation of justification by faith; it promotes an awareness of continuing sin in the home, but the simultaneous forgiveness and declaration of righteousness in Christ is also promoted. This can breed, and will breed within the home, a tolerance and patience among the members, and cultivate both forgiveness and peace.

Preaching the Gospel, maintaining the confession of Christ, and a witness to the Word, presents a unity of purpose to the home and gives to it a fixed center. The purpose of the home must be to confess Christ, and this confession will come in the particularly concrete expressions of the word of forgiveness and in acts of neighborly love. The center is fixed in Christ so that all in the home must relate to him, and in their relating to him, thereby relate to one another.

The *second* main expression of the functional authority of proclamation is in the home's work in translating the Word of God to its members. This work is done in the Church primarily through the sermon. In the home, this is done through the concrete application of the Word to individual and recurring situations. Such work presents the home in its submission to Christ, to the Church, and cultivates an individual submission of one to another. At the same time, this work of application brings about the character of a servant so that those in the house serve one another. This means both the service of the home, and service in the home.

Inevitably, there is a suffering of the home in the world. This suffering must be anticipated. Rather than attempt to avoid it, households must learn to cope with it in as positive and constructive a manner as possible. Whenever suffering occurs, there is a temptation to feel shame, and succumb to the danger of the sin of conformity. Such suffering can produce a deprivation of honor. It may come as a cultural attack on the home, loss of possessions, castigation of character, or ridicule. Yet it is through its conduct in the midst of suffering that the Christian household commends itself as a witnessing institution in the world.

Finally, we must consider the relation of the home to the world. In this light, we need mention three important facts. First, the home belongs to the created order, although redemption breaks into it. This means that the home always remains a worldly institution. It is not, therefore, to be assigned a spiritual significance greater than that belonging to the Church. Second, the home is impermanent, fallible, and dependent upon God for survival. In its quest to survive, and to be maintained as a Christian home, God has provided the Church as both a shelter and a continuing community support to upgird the home and continue it. Finally, third, there is a necessity of Christian authority in the home. This Christian authority should drive the home to the Church, and in this movement toward the Church, should demand the reform of the Church even before the home's own reform. It should be noted at this point that Church preaching focused on the home in inadequate, and ill-conceived. Rather, Church preaching should direct its attention to Church reform as the best remedy for the reform and renewal of the Christian home. The Church, particularly the evangelical church, will continue to weaken the home until it strengthens its ecclesiology.

NINETEEN

INERRANCY

In view of today's furor in evangelicalism over biblical inerrancy, how can a discussion of authority in the
Church avoid addressing a few brief remarks to the debate? Since I have already addressed the topic of biblical authority by proposing five theses, my purpose here
is of a different nature. I wish, instead of repeating
my discussion with regard to biblical authority, to particularly examine the subject of inerrancy, and its place
and practice inside today's conservative church community.

Bloesch has correctly advised that, "as we seek to
affirm biblical authority . . . there is a need to reinterpret this authority, particularly in light of the
present-day impasse in evangelicalism on this question."[1]
Nowhere is dogmatics more critically necessary today than
in this sphere. As Richard Coleman has observed, "the
whole question of biblical inerrancy does not want to
die."[2] But all too many discussions of this issue have
been polemical rather than irenic. I concur with the
urging by Coleman that "the time has come for us to recognize that not all Christians fit into either-or molds."[3]
We need a greater measure of charity in our disputation
and allowance for some middle ground.

As far as the authority of the Word of God is concerned, at least as delineated in preceding chapters, the
inerrancy issue must be subsumed under thesis two, that
is, the mediating authority of Holy Scripture. We are
not concerned here with the inerrancy of Church proclamation, as in the issue of papal infallibility or, perhaps, pentecostal prophetic utterances. It is the inerrancy of the biblical text that is at the heart of the
present concern. I have not addressed this issue earlier
because inerrancy is not a *necessary* corollary from my
proposition on biblical authority.

Obviously, if inerrancy is upheld, it must be fitted

196

into a wider framework of authority. But is that possible? In light of our own theory of authority, it seems highly unlikely that inerrancy can ever assume a place of prominence akin to that which it now enjoys in some of the narrower circles of evangelicalism. That is not to say, however, that our theory of authority must preclude inerrancy. It does, however, restrict it.

But it is important to recognize the main options of opinion being exercised inside today's evangelicalism. Clark Pinnock believes it possible to distinguish "at least three positions being taken at present *within* the evangelical coalition."[4] He identifies these as:

> *First*, there are the militant advocates of unqualified biblical inerrancy who continue in the tradition of Warfield and the fundamentalists.
> *Second*, there are advocates of a modified definition of biblical inerrancy.
> *Third*, there are the evangelical opponents of biblical inerrancy.[5]

The first of these positions is often associated with the names of Harold Lindsell, whose book, The Battle for the Bible, sparked widespread attention to the inerrancy controversy, and Francis Schaeffer. This position frequently equates infallibility with inerrancy.[6] Inerrancy is "unqualified," meaning it extends beyond doctrine to encompass also matters of science and history.[7] Inerrancy is regarded as the *sine qua non* of biblical authority. In fact, Lindsell suspected that "embracing a doctrine of an errant Scripture will lead to disaster."[8] Such a move, he wrote, "will result in the loss of missionary outreach; it will quench missionary passion; it will lull congregations to sleep and undermine their belief in the full-orbed truth of the Bible; it will produce spiritual sloth and decay; and it will finally lead to apostasy."[9] At best, Lindsell said, evangelicals no longer holding to inerrancy can only be regarded as "relatively evangelical," and he insisted: "I do not for one moment concede . . . that in a technical sense anyone can claim the evangelical badge once he has abandoned inerrancy."[10]

Many supporters of unqualified inerrancy have not followed Lindsell in all of his particular conclusions. Today there is a greater willingness to discourse with other confessed evangelicals in a persuasive fashion and without condemnation. But the position itself is still as strongly assertive as Lindsell was in upholding the necessity of inerrancy to an adequate doctrine of biblical authority. They still look to A. A. Hodge and B. B. Warfield as the principal architects of the correct

understanding of inspiration and inerrancy.[11] This position still identifies itself as the "orthodox" one.

The advocates of a modified definition have grown
in number in recent years. Pinnock himself has moved
toward finding a less volatile term. G. C. Berkouwer has
long preferred the term "infallibility."[12] When the term
inerrancy is used in this position it is carefully qualified. Inerrancy refers to matters bearing on "faith and
practice" only. Proponents generally seek to avoid dis-
putes over possible "errors" in other matters. They also
uphold a "high" view of biblical inspiration and authority. This position attracts moderates who desire to stay
clear of the entanglements of a stricter view and still
retain the desirable features of many inerrantist arguments.

Evangelical opponents of the inerrancy positions
often feel, as Pinnock states it, that "biblical inspiration is a much less formal and more practical affair.
It relates to the sufficiency of Scripture through the
Spirit of God to nourish and instruct the church for its
faith and life and not to an abstract perfection."[13] As
Carl Henry has observed, even despite many inerrantists'
arguments, "scores of young evangelicals emphasize that
scholars uncommitted to inerrancy are producing substantial evangelical works. They repudiate the 'domino theory' that a rejection of inerrancy involves giving up
'one evangelical doctrine after another.'"[14] Those within this position are dissatisfied with the rigidity of a
view they argue is not truly a Reformation product but
an unfortunate reaction by Protestant scholasticism to
the Catholic counter-Reformation.

Personally, I am more comfortable avoiding the use
of inerrancy for two reasons. First, it inevitably demands tedious explanation and initiates unnecessary debate. The atmosphere surrounding the word is so murky
as to render its practicality very questionable. Second,
inerrancy is an inferior theological term to infallibility. I think infallibility better expresses the genuine
thrust of the biblical self-understanding of authority,
namely, the absolute dependability (trustworthiness) of
Scripture to witness to Christ. I heartily agree with
Bloesch's statement that, "the Bible's authority is functional in that it is a signpost to Jesus Christ. But it
is not simply functional . . . . It not only conveys the
truth of Christ but also embodies this truth."[15]

However, it would not be desirable to completely
disdain the use of inerrancy to designate certain legitimate ideas. In other words, good dogmatics ought to be
able to reclaim, in time, a cautious, sensible meaning

for inerrancy that will clarify certain issues and not muddle them instead. But before this task can be accomplished, it is necessary to honestly confront the principal problems associated with the use of this term. It may very well prove to be the case that a mild moratorium on the use of inerrancy will be necessary to adequately rescue the term from its current scandal.

There are several very acute problems with regard to inerrancy that have been, if anything, overexamined. It is not my purpose to catalog or delineate fully the problems of inerrancy as a position. At this stage in the debate such an action would probably be futile, in that most of those who are already persuaded of the position would simply bypass this, while those already in agreement would simply use these arguments to reinforce their own. I shall content myself to merely outline some principal difficulties.

The essential problem of inerrancy is, as I see it, in giving a place of preeminence to apologetics over the proclamation of the Church. That is, a doctrine of inerrancy, in at least the way it has been practiced and developed in today's climate, tends very obviously to promote apologetic endeavors and defenses of the Scripture over the living, dynamic proclamation of the Gospel by the Church. It is interesting to note that where inerrancy has garnered more and more attention, true Gospel proclamation has received correspondingly less attention.

Six other problems must be noted. *First,* inerrancy tends to follow from either a misapprehension of biblical inspiration or superficial deduction. The desirability of inerrancy has rested in its apparent inescapable logic and self-evident reasonableness. Pinnock is aware that the question is frequently asked, "if the Bible is God-breathed it must logically be free from every error; how could it be anything other than inerrantly flawless?"[16] He responds:

> Although this position may seem reasonable at first sight, it is difficult to see how human beings would be capable of drawing such inferences from the fact of inspiration. God uses fallible spokesmen all the time to deliver his word, and it does not follow that the Bible *must* be otherwise. We are simply not in a position by sheer logic to judge how God ought to have given his Word. The logic of the case for inerrancy has been confused by a mistaken piety and the errorlessness of the Bible defended, not so much out of the conviction that it *is* inerrant as from the belief that it *must* be.[17]

Donald Dayton, evangelical historian, observes of the tradition in which inerrancy gained firm sway that:

The determinative feature of the view of Scripture
conveyed in this tradition is found in a seldom articulated "suppressed premise" grounded not so much in
exegesis as in the rationalist and scholastic tendencies
of post-Reformation orthodoxy. The syllogism goes some
thing like this: God is perfect; the Bible is the Word
of God; therefore the Bible is perfect (inerrant). The
"suppressed premise" here is actually the focusing of a
whole metaphysic emphasizing the "perfection" and "im-
mutability" of God and a highly deterministic view of
God's working in the world more obviously at home in
the "high Calvinism" of the old Princeton theology.[18]

Obviously, this calls for a more widespread reexam-
ination of the doctrine of inspiration. Even Hodge and
Warfield are very commonly misunderstood at this point.[19]
But biblical exegesis must dictate theological propositions. Evangelicals must avoid an undue overappreciation
of inspiration (which is, as Alan Richardson once wrote,
"hardly a biblical term"), as much as they do unbiblical
depreciation. Certainly inspiration does mean important
ideas like God's active authorship and a definitive continuing importance for the Bible. Equally certain is the
unavoidable impression that in some quarters of the evangelical camp the term has been grossly over-extended.
Whatever relation exists between inspiration and inerrancy must be subjected to careful, restricted description.

Second, the notion of "limited inerrancy," that is,
biblical inerrancy confined to just doctrinal and ethical
matters, has obvious theological inadequacies. Primary
among these, of course, is deciding where the line is
drawn separating biblical materials safeguarded by inerrancy and those not so protected. In general, the inherent ambiguities of the position have qualified it as
an excellent tool in ecclesiastical compromises but have
relegated it as relatively useless in theological discussions of any sophistication at all. Whatever minor
benefits accrue to the position are still offset, at the
present, by its many liabilities.

Those who desire to maintain this position must also
refine it. Some have attempted this and discovered it is
no easy task. It may be that the position can only retain some measure of credibility by refusing to become
more than what it essentially is: a confession of the
authority and the trustworthiness of Scripture for the
Church's thinking and acting. If this is the case, then
refinement will consist in clearly stating the purpose,
nature, and limitations of the position.

Third, verification of inerrancy, especially for

200

those asserting a position of "unqualified inerrancy," is plagued by a multitude of difficulties. Chief among these remains the still unresolved question of what constitutes an "error."[20] But beyond this, appeals to unobtainable original autographs neatly cuts short many queries with the perfect "unanswerable answer." Among the more sophisticated, special tactics borrowed from Hodge and Warfield are used. These consist of conditions to test supposed errors in Scripture. These are:

    1. The error must be shown to have existed in the original autographs.

    2. The error must be demonstrated to be the professed intent of the biblical author.

    3. The error cannot be attributed to a difference in form as long as the same basic truth is conveyed.

    4. The error must be proved incapable of being harmonized with other biblical statements.

    5. The error must be indisputable, not a difficulty open to future resolution.[21]

Quite evidently, these conditions are empirically unassailable. Yet, trying to leave the Bible susceptible to empirical testing has not really done anything more than encourage vigorous interpretive debates over various data and drive the Church to even greater apologetic efforts.

Unfortunately, the verification issue is probably inescapable as long as inerrancy is maintained. Most inerrantists are also apologists who eschew anything even faintly resembling fideism. Hence, inerrancy is continually being supported by new "proofs". What is needed, though, is some freshness in the endeavor. This can come by focusing less strictly on inerrancy and instead tracing its connections to other facets of biblical authority (besides simply inspiration).

Fourth, inerrancy seems to promote scholasticism. Without trying to be too harsh it must be honestly noted that where a strong attachment to inerrancy exists, so too does a more static theology, generally regressive dogmatics, and a denegration of the biblical role of the Holy Spirit. Inerrancy tends to overemphasize and exaggerate certain theological points at the expense of other points. The principal problem with scholasticism is its distance from Christian life. In it, the confession of the Church is so *exactly* preserved from one generation to the next that it is threatened by eventual meaninglessness. Inerrancy belongs to scholasticism and it has come down to many as a fundamental premise that must be preserved even if it is not understood.

Somehow inerrancy must become more contemporaneous

and more generally accessible and meaningful. It needs to become associated with more vital movements in the Church. Its *positive* bearing on Christian life must be substantiated more clearly. If inerrancy is to be an integral part of the evangelical future it must cease to be isolated and join the mainstream of evangelical doctrine. In particular, inerrancy must be articulated in closer connection with the ministry of the Holy Spirit and the proclamation of the Church.

Fifth, inerrancy tends to obscure the purpose of Scripture rather than to protect it as it was originally anticipated. Inerrancy draws attention always back to the *centrality* of the Bible. But the Scriptures themselves desire to bear witness to Christ (Jn. 5:39; Lk. 24:27; Ac. 8:35; Gal. 3:8). It is in their testimony to Jesus that they fulfil their purpose. Whenever inerrancy degenerates biblical theology into exercises of asserting textual accuracy it betrays its genuine worth. Biblical theology should, of course, indicate the accuracy of the Scriptures. But its higher task is to proclaim the Gospel. The "power of God for salvation" (Rom. 1:16-17), will vindicate itself. Infallibility, referring to the Scripture's purpose in unfailingly testifying to Christ, is therefore a better term than inerrancy. But certainly a movement to put these terms in a union without fusion, distinction without separation, is highly desirable.

A better fitting of inerrancy to the avowed purpose of the Bible must be forthcoming. This will necessitate a clear articulation vis-á-vis infallibility. Equating inerrancy and infallibility only confuses the theological issues at stake. Inerrancy must be subordinated to infallibility and redefined to reflect this subordinate position. Perhaps Hans Küng's suggestion of "indefectability" should be utilized alongside inerrancy, although not precisely as he uses it.[22] However it is accomplished, inerrancy must begin to clarify the Bible's purpose instead of continuing to obscure it.

Sixth, oftentimes the worst problem with inerrancy is the inerrantists. Pinnock, and others, warned after the appearance of The Battle for the Bible, "It threatens to create a new wave of bitterness and controversy on account of its militant tone and sweeping attacks."[23] The theological disputation has occasionally bordered on slander. Personal attacks have sometimes replaced sensible discussion. This is inexcusable no matter which side it issues from. No cause is so noble that Christian charity should be set aside (cf. 2 Tim. 2:24-26).

Only repentance and discipline can suffice here. Yet, perhaps certain other steps will assist. Notably, as non-inerrantists display a persistent tolerance and openness, the lines of communication will open to more fruitful dialog. The reverse, I am sure, is likewise true. None of us can afford too much pride, nor are many of us in danger from too much humility. Peace in the evangelical camp is dependent on each of us (Rom. 14:17—19), and is available for *all* of us under our *one* Lord (Eph. 2:14-22).

What, then, do I hope for? I hope that inerrancy will be subjected to wide review with a positive purpose fixed in mind. The term must be retained, sharpened, and given new relevance. Inerrancy should be subsumed under infallibility and advanced cautiously with *a posteriori* reasoning. This demands that, in one respect, inerrancy only be upheld on preliminary grounds. I hope that movement in this direction will combat pride, promote tolerance, and avoid making inerrancy the test of orthodox belief.[24]

The new inerrancy advanced must be assigned a proper place in relation to the whole of theology. At the same time, it must be positive in orientation. This means that inerrancy positions must avoid the fundamentalistic mistake of maintaining, as E. J. Carnell expressed it, a "status by negation."[25] Those who advocate inerrancy must become more theologically responsible, so that their position, and they themselves will carry a glad servant character and not appear (as they so often do now), as harsh taskmasters in the field of dogmatic orthodoxy.

This means a renewed bearing of responsibility by inerrantists. This responsibility must be first to dialog with those who do not espouse their own particular position on biblical authority. It means, too, a true willingness to be reformed, corrected, and renewed. This does not mean that those who dialog with them should refuse themselves to be corrected. Indeed, a properly held inerrancy can only serve to sharpen, stimulate, and correct the whole of Christian theology. Inerrantists must begin to produce truly theological, responsible work of a decidedly non-reactionary quality and character. Then, finally, inerrantists must consciously utilize inerrancy in the service of the Church's mission to testify to the righteousness of God in Christ rather than as an apologetic prop for biblical authority. I believe that the possibility exists that these things can be done. Inerrancy as a positive tool can still be appropriated to the benefit of the Christian mission.

[1] Donald Bloesch, "Theological Table-Talk: Crisis in Biblical Authority," Theology Today, Vol. XXXV, No. 4 (Jan, 1979), p. 455. Cf. Bloesch, Essentials of Evangelical Theology, I (New York: Harper & Row, 1978), ch. 4.

[2] Richard J. Coleman, "Biblical Inerrancy: Are We Going Anywhere?" Theology Today, Vol. XXXI, No. 4 (Jan., 1975), p. 295.

[3] Ibid., p. 301.

[4] Clark H. Pinnock, "Theological Table-Talk: Evangelicals and Inerrancy: The Current Debate," Theology Today, Vol. XXXV, No. 1 (Apr., 1978), p. 66.

[5] Ibid., pp. 66-67.

[6] See, Harold Lindsell, The Battle for the Bible (Grand Rapids: Zondervan, 1976), p. 23.

[7] Ibid., p. 107.

[8] Ibid., p. 25.

[9] Ibid.

[10] Ibid., p. 210.

[11] Hodge and Warfield, colleages at Princeton, wrote a highly influential article entitled "Inspiration," in the Presbyterian Review (1881). This, and other writings by the two, became the arguments undergirding the strong fundamentalist adherence to inerrancy. The writings of earlier Protestant scholastics also contributed to this position.

[12] G. C. Berkouwer's Holy Scripture, trans. Jack Rogers (Grand Rapids: Wm. B. Eerdmans, 1975), published as Vol. 13 of his Studies in Dogmatics is a major work of great importance to this issue and warrants a thorough reading.

[13] Pinnock, "Theological Table-Talk," p. 67.

[14] Carl F. H. Henry, Evangelicals In Search of Identity (Waco: Word, 1976), pp. 50-51.

[15] Bloesch, "Theological Table-Talk," p. 459.

[16] Clark H. Pinnock, "Three Views of the Bible in Contemporary

Theology," Biblical Authority, ed. Jack Rogers (Waco: Word, 1977), p. 64.

[17]Ibid., p. 25.

[18]Donald W. Dayton, "'The Battle for the Bible': Renewing the Inerrancy Debate," The Christian Century, Vol. XCIII (10 Nov., 1976), p. 977. This "old Princeton theology," of course, refers to Hodge and Warfield.

[19]See Bernard Ramm's comment on their 1881 "Inspiration" article in his essay, "Is 'Scripture Alone' the Essence of Christianity?" in Biblical Authority, ed. J. Rogers (1977), p. 111. Cf. C. F. H. Henry's comment, Evangelicals In Search of Identity, pp. 53-54. Note especially, Jack B. Rogers and Donald K. McKim, The Authority and Interpretation of the Bible (New York: Harper & Row, 1979), pp. 335-348.

[20]Although this question has received some attention, I think the most stimulating discussions of it are still to be found in Berkouwer, Holy Scripture, pp. 180-182, and K. Barth, Church Dogmatics, I/2, trans. G. T. Thomson and H. Knight, Edinburgh: T. & T. Clark, 1956), ch. 3 (and, especially, pp. 506-507; 512-514). With reference to Barth see K. Runia, Karl Barth's Doctrine of Holy Scripture (Grand Rapids: Eerdmans, 1962), pp. 65-73. See also, Bloesch, Essentials of Evangelical Theology, I, pp. 66-68.

[21]Cited by Coleman, "Biblical Inerrancy: Are We Going Anywhere?" p. 300.

[22]See Hans Küng, Infallible? An Inquiry, trans. F. Quinn (New York: Doubleday, 1971), pp. 139-141 and 181-183. Küng's discussion has first reference to the authority of the Church. See Bloesch's comment on this term in Essentials of Evangelical Theology, I, pp. 68, 84.

[23]Clark H. Pinnock, "The Inerrancy Debate Among the Evangelicals," Theology News and Notes (Special Issue, 1976), p. 11.

[24]C. F. H. Henry observes of Hodge and Warfield that "they did not make inerrancy a theological weapon with which to drive those evangelicals not adhering to the doctrine into a non-evangelical camp" (Evangelicals In Search of Identity, pp. 53-54).

[25]E. J. Carnell, "Fundamentalism," A Dictionary of Christian Theology (Cleveland: Meridian Books, 1958), pp. 142-143.

CONCLUSION

HEARING AND OBEYING

Jesus Christ is the one Word of God whom we are to hear and obey. But to hear him and to obey him demands of us a submission to Holy Scripture, and to biblical Church proclamation as true forms of the one Word of God. Explicating the Word of God with reference to authority and the Church is a dogmatic task to be undertaken in every generation. My attempt to frame a theological understanding of authority, and to apply it to issues of our time, is admittedly preliminary in that it belongs to "a theology along the way," that is, a theology that must be scrutinized, criticized, reformed, and renewed if it is to genuinely serve the Church.

I have no illusions about having surfaced the final answers on the matters which have been discussed. But I firmly believe I have indicated correctly the direction from which final answers are summoned: the Word of God. My understanding has value only when submitted to the service of God's people. This I now do, but with the exhortation that I be permitted to serve, even as I am corrected. We all must hear and obey our one Lord. This alone will reveal the right and glad nature of authority, be it in the Church, the State, or the home.

Finally, I am keenly mindful of Paul's prophetic word in Rom. 14:10-12, "*We shall all stand before the judgment seat of God; for it is written, 'As I live, says the Lord, every knee shall bow to me, and every tongue shall give praise to God.' So each of us shall give account of himself to God.*"

INDEXES

I. SCRIPTURE REFERENCES

211

NAMES

Alexander, Judy, 150, 158
Allen, Diogenes, 9, 52
Anderson, Beverly J. 147
Augustine, 71
Barr, James, 72
Bartchy, Scott, 149f., 153
Barth, Karl, 15f., 17f., 19,
    28, 34, 86, 139, 170, 175,
    205
Baum, Gregory, 72
Bavinck, Herman, 71
Berkouwer, G. C., 72, 198, 204,
    205
Beza, Theodore, 66
Bloesch, Donald, 71f., 127,
    135, 176, 196, 198, 205
Bonhoeffer, Dietrich, 19, 34,
    51, 52, 86f., 91, 102, 144
Bromiley, G. W., 28, 72
Brown, Raymond E., 153
Büchsel, Friedrich, 132, 142
Bultmann, Rudolph, 72
Calvin, John, 20, 65, 66, 71,
    137-138, 145, 176
Camus, Albert, 5
Carnell, E. J., 203
Chatfield, Joan, 148-151, 154
Clark, Gordon, 72
Coleman, Richard, 11, 196
Coenan, Lothar, 134
Cullmann, Oscar, 166, 178, 180
Cyprian, 134
Davids, Peter, 150, 154, 161
Dayton, Donald, 199f.
Dederen, Raoul, 3
Drummond, Richard, 11, 28, 35f.
Edwards, Jonathan, 71
Elert, Werner, 21
Esser, Hans-Helmut, 127, 141
Eusebius, 80, 84
Flacius, 71
Forstman, H. J., 73
P. T. Forsyth, 11-12, 28, 43,
    53, 71, 106-108
Fosdick, H. E., 72
Francke, August Hermann, 71

Gerhard, Johann, 71
Gilkey, Langdon, 72
Gothard, Bill, 182
Hancock, A. O., 176
Harkness, Georgia, 176
Henry, Carl F. H., 72, 198, 205
Hermann, Wilhelm, 72
Hippolytus, 135
Hitler, Adolph, 33-34
Hodge, A. A., 197, 200, 201,
    204, 205
Holbrook, Clyde, 2
Huss, John, 19
John Paul I, 3
John Paul II, 3
Johnson, Robert C., 10
Kittel, Gerhard, 132
Knox, John, 125-128, 133, 143
Kraft, Marguerite G.,148
Küng, Hans, 135, 202, 205
Kuyper, Abraham, 72
Leith, John, 34, 36
Lindsell, Harold, 197
Luther, Martin, 1, 12, 19f., 36,
    42, 43, 54, 65, 66, 71, 73,
    81, 82, 88, 94, 97, 103-106,
    114, 136-137, 138, 171, 172,
    175, 180, 183
Lys, Daniel, 167-169, 177, 181
McKim, Donald K., 205
Melancthon, Philip, 19, 21, 66,
    176
Meland, Bernard, 72
Mollenkott, Virginia R., 148f.
Montgomery, J. W., 72
Mortenson, Patricia J., 150-151
Mouw, Richard, 4, 12, 164
Muller, Ludwig, 34
Nida, Eugene, 92f.
Niemöller, Martin, 34
Noth, Martin, 167
Ogden, Schubert, 8-9, 72
Pascal, Blaise, 71
Paul VI, 3
Philip of Hesse, 176
Pinnock, Clark, 197, 198, 199,

212

Evangelicalism (cont.)
  theological maturity of
    (cont.), 164
Exegesis, 92, 93-98, 99-100,
  148, 154, 162
  defined, 94, 96
  presuppositions of, 95-96
  steps in, 97-98
Faith, 2, 11, 12, 21, 34, 35,
  36, 45, 66, 72, 76, 87-88,
  91, 96, 98, 104, 116, 131,
  133, 149, 167-168, 173,
  175, 177, 187
Fall, 50-51, 57, 60, 87
Family, 111, 182-183, 191-192
Fideism, 176, 201
French Confession, 20
Gifts (see, Spiritual Gifts)
God, 28, 56, 87, 91, 102, 168,
  200
  freedom of, 44, 51-54, 57,
    60
  hiddeness of, 41, 44, 48-49
  revelation of, 8, 32, 39,
    43-45, 48, 51, 54, 65,
    71, 82, 159
  Servanthood of, 52
  Triunity of, 15, 26, 36,
    45, 48, 50, 54, 118,
    153, 165
Gospel, 8, 16, 21, 43-44, 74,
  76, 85-88, 96, 103, 107,
  122, 127, 129, 138, 139,
  142, 151, 156-159, 166,
  170-172, 176, 179, 194,
  199, 202
Gospel and Law, 81
Hermeneutics, 71, 85, 92, 94,
  98
Holy/Holiness, 1, 43, 48, 76,
  184, 187-189, 191
Holy Scripture, 16, 33
  application of (see, Ap-
    plication)
  authority of, 12, 26, 36,
    65, 69f., 72-76, 81, 139
  divine election of, 70-71,
    82
  errors in (see, Errors)
  exegesis of (see, Exegesis)

Holy Scripture (cont.)
  inerrancy of (see, Inerran-
    cy)
  infallibility of (see, In-
    fallibility)
  inspiration of (see, Inspir-
    ation)
  interpretation of (see, Exe-
    gesis, Hermeneutics,
    Translation)
  mediating authority of, 36,
    62, 78-83, 102, 154, 165-
    166, 182, 192-193, 196
  purpose of, 70f., 76, 81f.,
    202
  revelation and, 44, 71
  sacramental character of, 44,
    71, 73
  state and, 164-177
  theses about, 62, 73-76
  translation of (see, Transla-
    tion)
  Witness of Spirit and, 62,
    65-66, 69, 75-76
  Word of God and, 12, 28, 69-
    71, 120
Holy Spirit, 5, 21, 32, 36, 44-
  45, 49, 62, 69, 79, 87, 95,
  105, 115, 118, 125-126, 143,
  174, 198, 202
  Christ and, 39f., 41-42, 48,
    115
  Witness of, 36, 62-67, 69,
    75-76, 95, 103, 166
Husbands (see, Marriage)
Identity, 99, 186, 192-193
Indefectability, 202
Inerrancy, 29, 65, 67, 69, 111,
  196-203
Infallibility, 65, 70, 94, 197,
  202-203
Inspiration, 25, 26, 27, 29, 67,
  69, 73-74, 79-80, 198, 200-
  201, 204
Interpretation (see, Exegesis,
  Hermeneutics, Translation)
Jesus (see, Christ Jesus)
Judgment, 1, 39, 59, 61, 63, 99,
  120, 206
Justification, 15, 42

216

217

About the Author

Gregory G. Bolich is an administrator and theologian-in-residence at the Christian Studies Institute, Spokane/Cheney, Washington. He holds three Masters degrees including the M. Div. from Western Evangelical Seminary. Currently he is pursuing a doctoral degree at Gonzaga University. He is also the author of Karl Barth and Evangelicalism (IVP, 1980).

About Christian Studies Institute

Incorporated in 1979 as a non-profit institution, CSI exists to serve the Christian churches of the Inland Empire region (Eastern Washington, Northern Idaho and Western Montana). The Institute's purpose is expressed by its motto, "Developing a Christian Perspective through Theological Excellence for Service in the Local Church," and in its operations designed to further the comprehensive educational ministries of churches throughout the area.

Gregory G. Bolich
c/o
 Christian Studies Institute
 Rt. 2 Box 74
 Cheney, WA 99004